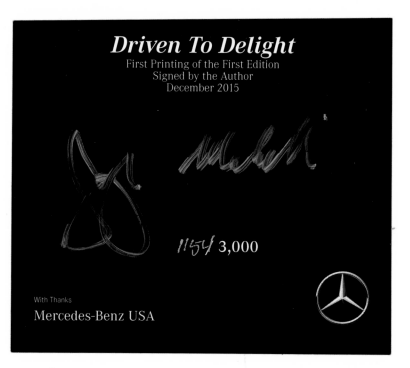

Driven To Delight

First Printing of the First Edition
Signed by the Author
December 2015

1154 / 3,000

With Thanks

Mercedes-Benz USA

Praise for *Driven to Delight*

Once again Joseph Michelli gives us a glimpse into one of the world's great brands and customer experiences. Joseph helps us understand how Mercedes-Benz USA leadership transformed and elevated sales and service experiences. Additionally, he takes the readers on a journey to examine their own organizations and determine how to apply these principles and lessons in their own businesses. This is an important read for leaders who want to grow their businesses by improving customers' lives.

> —Jeanne Bliss, President, CustomerBliss, and
> bestselling author of *Chief Customer Officer 2.0* and
> *I Love You More Than My Dog*

Mercedes-Benz USA's story demonstrates the leadership and commitment that's required to transform customer experience within a large organization. The book does a great job of capturing how the company engaged all of its employees and partners on a journey to deliver upon its brand promise, which required much more than just designing great cars.

> —Bruce Temkin, CCXP, Customer
> Experience Transformist & Managing
> Partner, Temkin Group

Most business leaders will tell you how important it is to delight their customers—who wouldn't? But most don't. This is the story of Steve Cannon's journey to take Mercedes-Benz USA from "good to best"—the diagnosis, the plan, the process design, the management and measurement, but most importantly, the leadership that is making 31,600 people, 99.5 percent of whom don't work for him, WANT to deliver it.

> —Andrew Robertson, President and CEO,
> BBDO Worldwide, Inc.

A powerful and inspiring look "inside the tent" of Mercedes-Benz USA that will help you learn how large companies make big changes in short time spans.

—Guy Kawasaki, Chief Evangelist of Canva and
author of *The Art of the Start 2.0*

I can't remember having read a more compelling example of how great luxury brands aren't just made but are nurtured. *Driven to Delight* offers essential lessons on the direct and undeniable relationship between how much you value and respect your customers and how they reward you for that consideration.

—Mike Jackson, Chairman, CEO,
and President, AutoNation, Inc.

Joseph Michelli's latest book is a masterful road map for transforming the relationship between leaders, employees, and the customers they serve. —Tom Rath, author of *StrengthsFinder 2.0*
and *Are You Fully Charged?*

The revolution in customer care that Mercedes-Benz USA is currently undertaking is rivaled only by the revolution that Mercedes-Benz began with the invention of the automobile. Dr. Michelli's book provides the most comprehensive look at how MBUSA is undertaking and succeeding at this transformative initiative.

—Alex Gellert, CEO, Merkley & Partners

Kudos to Steve Cannon and Joseph Michelli. Steve is the rare CEO who is brutally honest—in a public forum—about his own iconic organization's growing pains. Joseph's ability to present a compelling case study is unparalleled. If *Driven to Delight* can't convince you of the bottom line benefits of balancing service and technology to differentiate from your competition, your days are numbered. —Doug Lipp, international business consultant
and bestselling author of *Disney U*

Driven to Delight

Driven to Delight

Delivering World-Class
Customer Experience
the Mercedes-Benz Way

Joseph A. Michelli

#1 *New York Times* bestselling author

NEW YORK   CHICAGO   SAN FRANCISCO   ATHENS

LONDON   MADRID   MEXICO CITY   MILAN

NEW DELHI   SINGAPORE   SYDNEY   TORONTO

1 2 3 4 5 6 7 8 9 0   DOC/DOC   1 2 1 0 9 8 7 6 5

ISBN   978-0-07-180630-5
MHID   0-07-180630-X

e-ISBN   978-0-07-181227-6
e-MHID   0-07-181227-X

Design by Lee Fukui and Mauna Eichner

Library of Congress Cataloging-in-Publication Data

Michelli, Joseph A., - author.
  Driven to delight : delivering world-class customer experience the Mercedes-Benz way / Joseph Michelli.
      pages cm
  ISBN 978-0-07-180630-5 (alk. paper) — ISBN 0-07-180630-X (alk. paper)
  1. DaimlerChrysler. 2. Mercedes automobiles. 3. Automobile industry and trade—Germany—Management. 4. Automobile industry and trade—Customer services—Germany. I. Title.
  HD9710.G44D3845 2016
  658—dc23
                                                              2015029398

This book was prepared with the assistance of Mercedes-Benz USA, LLC. The titles of Mercedes-Benz USA employees and other Mercedes-Benz USA facts were accurate at the time the book went to print. The author is not employed by or affiliated with Mercedes-Benz USA.

All Internet addresses provided in the book were accurate at the time the book went to print.

Joseph "Andrew" and Leah,
may you enjoy a lifetime of love and laughter

Contents

Foreword

The book you are holding tells a story of transformation and determination.

Driven to Delight offers an in-depth and behind-the-scenes look at a dramatic journey undertaken by one of the world's most iconic brands, Mercedes-Benz. It chronicles the hard work of a talented group of people with a laser focus on a singular goal: to make the Mercedes-Benz customer experience THE BEST in the world!

To some people, that may sound like pure fantasy. A car company aspiring to create THE BEST customer experience in the world? But the Mercedes-Benz brand promise is "The Best or Nothing," and our beliefs are grounded in the proud 129-year history of the company that literally invented the car and thus revolutionized the world. So in our minds, it is our reality. It is our intrinsic duty to our customers to honor our commitment and deliver on that promise. We will never give up on our pledge to delight all our customers!

However, we recognize that the experience we offered our customers may not always have lived up to those expectations or to the other great experiences that our customers immerse themselves in every day. Our extraordinary vehicles have always stood on their own and represented THE BEST, but the human touch of the car buying, servicing, and ownership experience simply had not kept pace.

That is where our Driven to Delight journey begins. Where it ends—well, it will never really end, as our focus on the customer experience has no final destination, but rather represents a relent-less effort to make tomorrow's experience even better than today's. So take a look, read on about our story, and find out for yourself all that we've done thus far. I can assure you that we are well on our way and that we are creating real change every day that you can lit-erally feel. That feeling . . . well, it's something special!

I am honored to serve as the president and CEO of Mercedes-Benz USA and proud to have witnessed this transformation in ac-tion. The progress we've made has been fueled by a dedicated and unrelenting investment in people, process innovation, and the in-tegration of technologies that connect us with our customers and make their lives easier. I'm awestruck by the commitment of our dealerships and all the team members who bring the experience to life each time, every time, no exceptions! We have become "cus-tomer obsessed," and people are noticing.

One person who took note early on was Joseph Michelli, who approached me about capturing our quest to put our customers first in all that we do. We had enlisted him to help us benchmark "best of the best" customer experience providers, and he believed that learning about our journey could help other business leaders who wanted to move their product-centric brands in the direction of customer-centric experiences. Joseph has a strong track record when it comes to helping brands and leaders discover how to de-liver and make sense of the challenges those leaders face when they aspire to deliver exceptional customer experiences. I hope you will find something of value in our journey to date as you look to de-liver the best possible experiences for those you serve every day.

I am appreciative that Joseph, someone who has shared in-sights on other world-class customer experience brands like The Ritz-Carlton Hotel Company, Starbucks, and Zappos, has aptly chronicled our journey. Most important, I am humbled to be a part of this great and noble adventure.

On behalf of everyone at Mercedes-Benz USA and our dealer partners, I wish you happy reading. I trust you will find that we are putting action behind our brand promise to be the best or nothing. Moreover, I hope you will see that everyone at Mercedes-Benz, like me, is *Driven to Delight*.

Steve Cannon, President & CEO
Mercedes-Benz USA

Acknowledgments

Pulitzer Prize–winning author Thornton Wilder once observed, "We can only be said to be alive in those moments when our hearts are conscious of our treasures." After completing a book, I am given a few paragraphs to appreciate my treasures.

I love the word *treasure*! It reflects something more than high tangible value. Treasure implies an emotional assessment that something is special and endearing. So let's start with one of my most important treasures: *you*!

Your willingness to pick up, talk about, and encourage others to read my books has been life-changing. I live my calling when readers like you find ways to use my ideas for the betterment of your business and your life.

As you may have noticed, I get to work with some extraordinary leaders. They are visionaries and architects of the world's greatest "people-centered" businesses. In the pages ahead, you will learn from Mercedes-Benz USA's president and CEO, Steve Cannon. Steve is among the most visionary, disciplined, and empowering leaders you could ever encounter. I am grateful for having had the opportunity to work with Steve and his entire leadership team and to be entrusted with presenting their story. I am particularly appreciative of Harry Hynekamp, general manager of the Mercedes-Benz USA Customer Experience team. As a consultant and author, I have *never* encountered the level of attentiveness and customer passion that I have seen while working with Harry. He and his entire team have been strong advocates of the customer experience at Mercedes-Benz USA and of this book. Particular thanks go to Kelly Tanis, Jenni Harmon, and Maura Wilson on Harry's team, who were instrumental in bringing this book to life.

Many of my treasured relationships (ones that have inspired me to write books) are actually with leaders of companies that I have yet to write about. In order to remedy that to a small degree, I will share a sampling of the names and some of the qualities of those whom I value most:

Scott Burger. President, Pandora Jewelry Americas; humility, kindness, and transparency.

Bob Yarmuth: CEO, Sonny's BBQ; intellect, commitment to community, and abiding faith.

John Gainor: CEO, International Dairy Queen; approachability, steady execution, and insight.

Ben Salzmann. President and CEO, Acuity; authenticity, energy, and playfulness.

William Yarmuth: CEO, Almost Family; commitment to doing the right thing, warmth, and thoughtfulness.

The last three categories of treasure through which my life work is enriched are colleagues, friends, and family. The only person who fits in all three of those categories is Lynn Stenftenagel. Lynn and I have worked together for well over a decade. She is the grit, fiber, and organizer of every book we write. She has grown our business to levels I would have never imagined. Lynn has been a source of support through the death of my wife, and she has believed in me in ways I will never understand. I can only wish that everyone could have a Lynn tucked among their most prized treasures.

While Donya Dickerson is an executive editor at McGraw-Hill, I will always view her as "my editor." She has journeyed with Lynn and me on six books with McGraw-Hill. Over that decade of collaboration, I have never heard Donya say a negative word to or about anyone. Donya inspires me by her steady enthusiasm and resourcefulness. She is the kind of person you want to have walk into a room with you and the kind that I always want on my team. Thanks to all my other team members who make unique and critical contributions, not least of whom are Kelly Merkel and Lloyd Rich.

Like most people, I have a rich cache of acquaintances, for which I am grateful, but there are a few people who have loved me, encouraged me, and helped me find my way after deep personal loss. I will never know how to fully express my appreciation to this group for reengaging me in a truly happy and contented life. Thank you, Patti, Rob, Judy, Bob, Paul, William, and Susan.

The last two names I will mention before I close are unequivocally my most sacred treasures. I have always known that my children, Andrew and Fiona, are special blessings. I delighted in them when they were little, but now I savor the gift of being able to watch them grow and develop as young adults. I learn so much from Fiona's compassionate and giving nature and from Andrew's loving spirit and hunger for knowledge.

While I have only scratched the surface of my treasure chest, it's time to say thank you again for inviting me onto your Kindle, desk, nightstand, or bookshelf. I sincerely hope that *Driven to Delight* will make a small contribution to your efforts to be an even more treasured resource to your company, your teammates, your customers, and all those you treasure in your life.

A customer is the most important visitor on our premises.

He is not dependent on us. We are dependent on him. He

is not an interruption in our work. He is the purpose of

it. He is not an outsider in our business. He is part of it.

We are not doing him a favor by serving him. He is doing

us a favor by giving us an opportunity to do so.

—Mahatma Gandhi

Introduction

◇◇◇

C ustomers crave consistently outstanding experiences and expect businesses to deliver them. When companies provide
exceptional experiences, customers become loyal advocates for
their brands.

This is the story of leaders at a legendary company who realized that the sales and service interactions their customers were
having weren't in keeping with the quality that was engineered into
the company's products. It is a story of transformation and what it
takes to move a legacy brand in the direction of true customer obsession. It is the story of an audacious vision, a seismic culture shift,

sustained sales growth, and measurable/award-winning customer experience improvements. Most important, this is your guide to help you drive delight throughout your organization and to your customers.

Gottlieb Daimler and Karl Benz were founders of the company we know today as Daimler AG. Daimler is one of the largest producers of premium cars and is the global leader in commercial vehicle production. Its divisions include Mercedes-Benz Cars, Daimler Trucks, Mercedes-Benz Vans, Daimler Buses, and Daimler Financial Services. From his company's inception in 1886, cofounder Gottlieb Daimler promised that the company's vehicles would be "the best or nothing."

For well over a century, Daimler products have lived up to Gottlieb's preeminent quality promise. This has been accomplished largely through an unyielding commitment to engineering excellence along with a passion for safety and innovation. In fact, Karl Benz invented the automobile itself (Benz "Patent Motorwagen") and invented the first commercial vehicle. Since then, Daimler vehicles have contributed to breakthroughs well beyond the internal combustion engine. A few of the areas in which Daimler has either introduced or advanced technological innovation include the development of the first drop chassis, building the first diesel-powered passenger car, the creation of direct fuel injection, the introduction of the first generation of the antilock braking system, the development of air bags, the creation of an electronic stability program, Active Lane Keeping Assist enhancements, and most recently, autonomous driving. In fact, in 2015, Daimler's Mercedes-Benz brand was named the most innovative premium brand of the last decade after a comprehensive review by the Center of Automotive Management and PricewaterhouseCoopers. Accolades for Mercedes-Benz products extend to the brand's commercial line as well, with the Mercedes-Benz Sprinter earning three consecutive Vincentric Best Fleet Value in America awards and the 2015 Mercedes-Benz Sprinter receiving ALG's Best Residual Value recognition.

But in 2011, despite the company's innovative engineering, the organization was facing a challenge in the United States. Customer studies conducted by outside research firms validated what leaders inside the company were already recognizing: the dealership experience of Mercedes-Benz customers was falling far short of being "the best."

As the problems with the customer experience were becoming more apparent, the senior leadership at Mercedes-Benz USA (MBUSA) was also changing. On January 1, 2012, Stephen Cannon moved from vice president marketing for Mercedes-Benz USA to president and CEO. From the onset, Steve gave priority to the Mercedes-Benz sales and service experience. As he explains, "In the first 60 days, I sat down with people in every department to identify our strengths, weaknesses, opportunities, and threats. What crystallized to me from those conversations was that we had an extraordinary opportunity to improve the experience customers encountered when they purchased or received service on their vehicles. As a leadership team, we believed that an investment in this area would result in a disproportionate return."

In order to generate that level of return on investment, leaders at Mercedes-Benz USA had to overcome two rather large obstacles: (1) an existing and dominant product-centric culture and (2) limited ability to exert control over the experiences delivered by their more than 370 independently owned and operated dealer partners.

It has been said that a company's greatest strengths are often its greatest weaknesses. From the perspective of Daimler, engineering excellence, safety, and innovation were the foundation that had led to a very product-focused mindset. Many Mercedes-Benz dealers in the United States (many of whom had been in business for decades) relied heavily on product quality to build customer loyalty and hadn't addressed the overall experience of customers in their dealerships. Because Mercedes-Benz had such a strong product focus, new competitors entering the marketplace added value to their products by creating a better dealership experience.

Peter Collins, retired area manager for MBUSA and current general manager of the Mercedes-Benz dealership in Alexandria, Virginia, puts it this way, "When I started with the brand in 1984, there was no Lexus. There was no Infiniti. There was no Acura. Heck, there wasn't even the Internet. Truthfully, whatever Daimler sent us, we sold. That was the luxury market. That clearly was an era where you were privileged to get a Mercedes-Benz. However, as the age of consumerism, competition, and technology advanced at warp speed, we became vulnerable if all we offered was a great product."

Mercedes-Benz of Virginia Beach service manager Pat Evans highlights changing consumer attitudes as a risk factor encountered by the Mercedes-Benz brand over the last several years. "I've been with Mercedes for 30 years. In the 1980s and early 1990s, we were selling 50,000 to 60,000 cars a year, and our customers were so in love with our product, it didn't matter what happened to it. Just fix it and get me my car back. Now we're selling 400,000. There's a clientele buying our product who simply don't want the cars any longer if there is even the slightest problem, and that includes a simple rattle or squeak. Mercedes-Benz leadership is faced with positioning the brand in a changing consumer marketplace. Newer customers—especially those who haven't been committed to the product for 5 to 10 years—not only want the best cars in the world, but they also want the best reliability and the best consumer experience in the world, too."

When Lexus entered the luxury automotive marketplace in the United States in the late 1980s, the Lexus USA newsroom website signaled how that brand was going to differentiate itself based on the desired experience of customers: "A single consumer complaint launches a special service campaign, earning the brand recognition as the new standard in personalized service." The site added that in 1990, "Out of thousands of parties interested in a Lexus franchise, only 121 top-notch dealers are selected for Lexus' first year of business." Those dealers were required, among other things, to agree not only to comply with strict and enriched dealership design guidelines but to behave in accordance with a "covenant" that includes the statement "Lexus will treat each customer as we would a guest in our home."

Rather than designing an optimal customer experience from the outset and selecting distribution partners who were contractually obligated to deliver that experience (the foundation of the Lexus brand), Mercedes-Benz USA, under Steve Cannon's new leadership, faced the challenge of transforming the mindset and behavior of longstanding dealers beyond an established product-centric perspective entrenched through generations of dealer ownership.

Exemplifying the types of negative experiences occurring in U.S. Mercedes-Benz dealerships, one customer shared, "I used to get the impression that I should feel grateful that I was allowed to purchase their product." By contrast, the best Mercedes-Benz dealerships were producing extraordinary and memorable customer experiences commensurate with the quality of the vehicles sold. Therein lay the problem. The Mercedes-Benz retail/dealership experience was uneven and lacked a well-defined objective with attendant accountability. A customer could go into one dealership and have an unsatisfactory experience, then drive a short distance and be treated in an extremely positive and memorable way. Fran O'Hagan, CEO of Pied Piper Management, also characterized the overall Mercedes-Benz experience as detached and lacking warmth: "In 2007, visiting a Mercedes dealership was like visiting a museum. Salespeople were friendly and answered questions, but they did not take the next step of actually selling the car. They stopped short of saying, 'I know you want to buy a car, and I want to work with you on figuring out how to make that happen.'"

Mixed results from independent consumer satisfaction research also highlighted the disengagement and variability of the Mercedes-Benz dealership experience. For example, the research group Pied Piper (which utilizes a mystery shopper strategy) placed Mercedes-Benz at the top of the luxury automobile category for the experiences it provided in 2010 and 2011, while J.D. Power (which measures the satisfaction of customers with the sales and service functions at dealerships) placed Mercedes-Benz in the middle to lower segment of luxury automakers.

Against this backdrop of increasing customer expectations, variable consumer experiences, and competitors that provided high-quality customer sales and service interactions, the leaders at Mercedes-Benz USA set out to foster new systemwide competencies to look at the entire business from the customer's perspective. Their goal became to map the customer journey, solicit customer feedback, rapidly resolve customer issues, and deliver emotionally engaging experiences "Driven to Delight" customers.

To make their challenge more complex, leaders at Mercedes-Benz USA knew that they would have to not only change the attitudes and behaviors of their own employees but also affect similar changes across the more than 370 authorized Mercedes-Benz dealerships nationwide. Additionally, to ensure a seamless and integrated experience though the financing and payment stage of a vehicle lease or purchase, MBUSA would also need to work in collaboration with its sister company, Mercedes-Benz Financial Services (MBFS). While approximately 1,700 corporate staff members receive their paychecks from Mercedes-Benz USA, the employees of dealerships (small, medium, and large independent enterprises) and Mercedes-Benz Financial Services staff total more than 29,000 (1,100 at MBFS and 28,000+ at dealerships). In essence, if the customer experience at Mercedes-Benz was going to be transformed perceptibly, the leaders at Mercedes-Benz USA would have to both collaborate with Mercedes-Benz Financial Services and *influence* the way the owners and managers of dealerships ultimately leveraged people, processes, and technology to fully satisfy and engage Mercedes-Benz sales prospects, buyers, and owners.

As if shifting from a product-dominant to a customer-obsessed strategy (dependent largely on employees who do not report to you) wasn't a sufficient stretch goal, president and CEO Steve Cannon and his team at Mercedes-Benz USA decided to set the bar even higher. Rather than defining "best" to mean becoming the premier customer experience provider in the luxury automotive category or even becoming the best customer experience provider across all car manufacturers (luxury and mass market), Steve notes, "Our priority was to become the global leader across all brands in customer service and in customer experience." In essence, Steve and his leadership team set out to rival other businesses about which I have had the good fortune of writing—companies like The Ritz-Carlton Hotel Company, Zappos, and Starbucks. In contrast to Mercedes-Benz, The Ritz-Carlton Hotel Company is perennially known not only for its product excellence (outstanding hotels, spas, resorts, and residential living facilities) but also for the consistently elevated customer experiences that it provides.

Driven to Delight was written to address how Mercedes-Benz leaders sought to make the company an experience provider that was on a par with—if not better than—other iconic service brands. To that end, this book has two principal objectives. The first is to give you an exclusive view inside the strategic vision, tactical planning, victories, and setbacks along a multiyear journey at Mercedes-Benz USA. In addition, this book offers a road map that you can use to steer your team and your business toward a customer-obsessed culture and a provider of innovative customer experiences.

Before we analyze how Mercedes-Benz USA's leaders went about addressing the primary focus of Steve Cannon's visionary customer experience objective and before I offer tools for you to use to elevate your customer experience, let's first take a look at the foundation of excellence that served to underpin Mercedes-Benz USA's customer experience journey.

A World-Class Product and a Legendary Marketing Brand

World-class products produce throngs of raving fans! Along my journey with Mercedes-Benz, I have encountered countless zealots who talk about the brand image, safety, and product quality. Here are but a few of their voices:

> Mercedes-Benz owner Lawrence Jakobi notes, "I fell in love with the car. It was an emotional buy. I made the mistake of test driving it. I had to have it. I was told when I was test driving, I had a smile on my face."

> Mike Figliuolo, managing director of THOUGHTleaders, LLC, shares, "I've owned my car since 2005. I'm sitting here looking at it sitting outside my window. I repainted [it] this past year, and I still love it, even with 170,000 miles on it."

> Mercedes-Benz owner Steve H. states, "I have a 2009 C300. It's my first real luxury car. When I think of Mercedes, I think of luxury comfort. Just driving a Mercedes feels like an accomplishment and makes me feel more confident. When I first got the car, it was one of the more exciting moments of my life."

> Susan Jennings notes, "I wanted a vehicle that was safe for my family. Mercedes-Benz provides me with peace of mind,

roominess, and the extremes of comfort. I took a lot of time to research the car that would best meet our needs, and our ML350 has exceeded every expectation."

Mercedes-Benz owner John R. Modric, a professional pianist, states, "Driving a Mercedes is like playing Mozart with the sophistication of Bach."

Not only by the accounts of owners but by virtually every U.S.-based and global metric, Mercedes-Benz is recognized as one of the most powerful companies in the world when it comes to brand awareness, marketing, and product quality. For example, in 2014, Interbrand (the world's largest brand consultancy group) placed Mercedes-Benz tenth among the top 100 of "the world's most valuable brands" based on the company's longstanding excellence in performance, styling, and engineering. Interbrand has also noted that Mercedes-Benz has achieved the number one luxury manufacturer position in the United States and Germany as well as cultivating strong popularity in Russia and China through a balance of traditional and forward-looking styling. Interbrand suggests that the future brand strength of Mercedes-Benz hinges on "its 2020 growth initiative focused on building the best customer experience," along with a new product lineup geared toward future generations of Mercedes-Benz buyers. Similarly, Harris's 2014 EquiTrend Automotive Scorecard of consumer sentiment placed Mercedes-Benz as the lead luxury auto brand. Reflecting on the EquiTrend Scorecard, Nielsen's automotive solutions consultant Mike Chadsey suggests that in the "brutal" competition of the sector, "As the luxury category reaches feature, performance, and style parity, brands that fail to create connections and affinity with target customers will be left behind."

Mercedes-Benz's appeal transcends the European and North American markets, representing a truly global phenomenon. In

2013, the editors of *Forbes* magazine ranked Mercedes-Benz as the World's 16th Most Powerful Brand. In a 2013 study conducted by research firms Brand Equity and Nielsen, Mercedes-Benz was viewed as India's ninth "most exciting brand" across all industries and the number one automotive brand in India. In November 2013, the Mercedes-Benz S-Class was named the car of the year in China. Additionally, Russian prime minister Dmitry Medvedev gave Mercedes-Benz vehicles to each of his country's Olympic medalists during the 2014 games.

While the Mercedes-Benz brand is powerful around the globe, its leaders in each region of the world face different challenges. For example, in 2015, Daimler CEO Dieter Zetsche told the *Wall Street Journal* that in China, sales growth was a primary focus, "The more we catch up in China, the faster we will be No. 1 [globally]." To that end, Zetsche notes that in China, "We have increased our dealer body. We've added 100 dealer[s . . .] last year."

For the purpose of this book, the challenges addressed by Mercedes-Benz will be limited to the customer experience and culture decisions made by leaders in the United States. However, while the content of the book focuses on actions designed to affect U.S. customers, clearly this transformational process has an impact and relevance globally. As you will see later in the book, progress made on customer-centricity in the U.S. market is contributing to customer-centric improvements at Mercedes-Benz worldwide. Conversely, global advances in customer experience at other Mercedes-Benz locations have reciprocal benefits in the U.S. market.

Prior to Steve Cannon's ascent to president and CEO at Mercedes-Benz USA, the brand's accolades and written recognition centered on marketing, engineering, and innovation. *Driven to Delight* is the first book to suggest that any of the Mercedes-Benz regional leadership teams should be held out as worthy of emulation in the area of design and execution of the customer experience.

Mercedes-Benz USA—Seizing a Window of Opportunity for Customer Experience Excellence

The strength of the global Mercedes-Benz brand, coupled with a variety of favorable economic and situational factors, has allowed Steve Cannon and his leadership team to actively pursue their desired customer experience transformation goals. As Steve puts it, "Our leadership team benefited greatly from a number of quality, environmental design, and employee engagement strategies deployed prior to my positioning as CEO."

In 1998, Mercedes-Benz's parent company, Daimler-Benz AG, merged with the Chrysler Corporation. In an article for *CNN Money* around the time of the merger, Jürgen Schrempp, then chairman of Daimler-Benz, noted, "Today we are creating the world's leading automotive company for the 21st century. We are combining the two most innovative car companies in the world." Despite these aspirations, the merger of Daimler and Chrysler was dissolved nine years later. In a 2008 *Automotive News* article, Dieter Zetsche, the Daimler-Benz CEO who replaced Jürgen Schrempp, noted, "We couldn't actually achieve global integration because it was at odds with the image of our brands, the preferences of our customers, and many other success factors—all of which were far more diverse and fragmented."

After the failed merger, in 2005–2006, Mercedes-Benz leaders worldwide were given the task of addressing a series of product quality issues. Coming off of those quality challenges, leaders at Mercedes-Benz USA identified workplace morale as a significant business need and set out to elevate the engagement level of employees at the corporate office. As Hendrik "Harry" Hynekamp, general manager customer experience at Mercedes-Benz USA, notes, "After 2005, leaders championed the importance of all

Mercedes-Benz managers driving employee engagement in their departments. It was through those efforts that Mercedes-Benz USA was the first and only automaker to make *Fortune* magazine's *100 Best Companies to Work For* list in 2010 at position #49. This emphasis on employee engagement continues at Mercedes-Benz USA, and the brand has made the *Fortune* list regularly since 2010, ranking as high as the 12th position. In addition, we are consistently the only original equipment manufacturer (OEM) on the list." These accomplishments suggest a sustained emphasis on the importance of providing a dynamic and purposeful experience for MBUSA employees. The same steadfast leadership that resulted in these enviable employee-centered recognitions served as the foundation for achieving the lofty customer experience goals outlined in this book. Leaders at Mercedes-Benz USA are committed to providing a work environment for their people that allows them to serve the dealership community so that those dealers can, in turn, serve Mercedes-Benz customers and prospective customers.

In addition to a highly engaged MBUSA workforce, Steve and his leadership team inherited a network of more than 370 dealers, who recently invested in a substantial upgrade to the look and feel of their dealerships. In 2010, the leaders at Mercedes-Benz USA began construction of a 333,000-square-foot flagship dealership on Eleventh Avenue in Manhattan. The design of that facility, referred to as "Autohaus," became the style standard for all other Mercedes-Benz dealerships throughout the United States. Writing in 2011 for the *Los Angeles Daily Journal*, Jonathan Michaels, a lawyer who specializes in the automotive industry, explains the rationale and substantial investment involved in transforming Mercedes-Benz dealerships in the United States to the new Autohaus standard: "The point of all of this is to create a uniform look among a sprawling dealer base and give their product brand identity. In years past, manufacturers only required dealers to use conforming trademarks and proper signage, but those days are long gone. Automakers now have complete design plans, and regulate which architects and vendors must be used and what type of furniture may be bought." According to Jonathan, "The cost of construction is borne almost entirely by the dealers and the costs are staggering. . . . To be fair, manufacturers do contribute to the cost of construction by providing incentives to dealers who participate in the programs. Mercedes pays its Autohaus dealers $400 per car sold over a three year period." To affect this enhanced consistency in brand presentation across the physical environment of Mercedes-Benz dealerships, Mercedes-Benz USA invested approximately $230 million in partnership with the $1.4 billion investment of its dealers.

The Autohaus transformation of U.S. dealerships was well under way by the time Steve Cannon took the reins at Mercedes-Benz USA. This consistent facility design allowed Steve and his leadership team to focus on the service experiences inside those dealerships. The focus of those experiences needed to be worthy of Mercedes-Benz automobiles and the environments in which they were sold and serviced.

An additional foundational component that enabled Steve and other leaders at MBUSA to set a bold customer experience agenda was strong overall new car sales. As Steve assumed responsibility for the company, year-end new car sales for Mercedes-Benz USA were up 13 percent from the prior year, with sales of 245,231 units. Since dealerships were thriving, the leaders at MBUSA could challenge the dealer network to co-create a differentiated, exemplary branded sales and service experience that would set the standard within the automotive sector and beyond.

Finally, Steve and his team had the benefit of a fresh customer service training program that had been rolled out in the dealer community the September before Steve made the transition from vice president of marketing to president and CEO. That program, titled Driven to LEAD (LEAD is an acronym for Listen, Empathize, Add value, and Delight), emerged from three MBUSA general managers—Frank Diertl, Harry Hynekamp, and Niles Barlow, colloquially referred to as the "three amigos." Frank had seen Lior Arussy, president of Strativity, speak at an outside function on the topic of creating customer-centric cultures. Subsequently, Frank, Harry, and Niles met with Lior to explore the possibility of developing a training program on customer experience at Mercedes-Benz USA. Lior recounts, "Frank was basically raising the case that Mercedes-Benz vehicles are excellent, but the customer experience was not. In Frank's words, 'We're not as great as we think we are.' Frank shared with me some of their efforts to improve customer satisfaction in the past. From that discussion, it was clear that Mercedes-Benz USA needed a different approach in order to build an awareness of the customer experience problem and create a sustainable solution through culture. Frank, Harry, and Niles managed to forge a budget for the training, and literally we charted the first full day of the Driven to LEAD program on the back of a cocktail napkin." Driven to LEAD (which will be discussed in more detail in Chapter 2) was launched in September 2011 and was Mercedes-Benz USA's first intense foray into raising awareness of the need for change in customer service delivery and identifying quick-fix opportunities to improve the dealership experience.

The chapters that follow track the evolution of Mercedes-Benz USA's strategic and tactical approaches to customer experience excellence. They examine the creation of a mission statement declaring that Mercedes-Benz USA aspires to be the "premier customer care brand in the world." The title of this book is based on the internal vision statement through which corporate employees and dealership staff are encouraged to lead all those they serve to be "Driven to Delight"—suppliers, team members, and customers.

Shortly you will encounter the early visioning process for this ambitious "Driven to Delight" culture shift and learn how

Mercedes-Benz USA benchmarked the brands that provided the best global customer experience. You will understand the key strategic targets identified by the leadership team and how the team measured the voice of the customer, both internally and through outside sources. You will read about a wide range of operational and cultural initiatives that were undertaken and promulgated within the dealer network. You will also see the measurable successes and challenges that occurred, as the transformation had to be achieved by influencing the staff at MBUSA, Mercedes-Benz Financial Services, vendors, and the leadership and frontline staff at dealerships.

Before you launch into your journey with Mercedes-Benz USA and gain lessons for your customer experience elevation journey, let's hear how a commitment to customer obsession affects Mercedes-Benz prospects and owners. Beyond the slogan, the vision, and the strategies that follow, *Driven to Delight* becomes real in the lives and stories of customers like these:

> Cheryl Birnbaum: "I am a social worker by trade, and what I do for my job is take care of people. It is really important when you find someone who takes really good care of you to pass that along. Tom is the salesperson from White Plains Mercedes that I lease my car from, and it was not six weeks later—I didn't have a thousand miles on the car— that I picked up the phone in my car and I said, 'You won't believe this. I just had a horrible accident, and I don't know what to do.' Tom said, 'I am going to take good care of you; don't worry about it.' He walked me through calling the insurance company. He walked me through every step of what I needed to do and really made me feel taken care of. It was outstanding."

> John L. Alper: "It was November of 2011. I got diagnosed with lymphoma (B cell non-Hodgkin's lymphoma). We go

into the dealership and people start coming up to me. They gave me this card that is signed by everybody in the dealership: 'We are with you.' 'We support you.' 'God bless you.' We did not know what to think. It was unbelievable. These guys are for real. It is not just about fixing your car. They are interested in you."

A customer whose Mercedes-Benz limousine sustained substantial damage in 2012 from Hurricane Sandy: "For two months we had very hard days. For two months I didn't smile because I needed to work. I needed my car to work. Mercedes got us back on our feet, as we were really experiencing a hardship. Thank God for my Mercedes-Benz dealership! You helped me. You brought me back to my life. You helped me start back to work to support my family."

To see these customers share their stories, please visit www.driventodelight.com/customerstories.

Most of us aren't content with our customers being simply satisfied. We want to hear our customers sharing stories like the ones given here. We know that those stories are the foundation of customer loyalty and referrals. Given the importance of having "delighted" and emotionally engaged customers, let's accelerate into an exploration of what Mercedes-Benz USA has done to consistently transform the way each person representing the brand is Driven to Delight.

If you want to build a ship, don't drum up

people to collect wood and don't assign them

tasks and work, but rather teach them to long

for the endless immensity of the sea.

—Antoine de Saint-Exupery

2

Building the Map

How do you want customers to feel when they are being served at your business? What is your aspiration for the customer experiences that your company delivers? Do you want to be the best provider in your neighborhood, your region, or your industry? Because the leaders at Mercedes-Benz USA took the time to answer these types of questions, the desired vision for the MBUSA journey was both clear and challenging. Steve Cannon encouraged his leadership team to help lift the brand to be "the undisputed best provider of overall customer experience." He knew that Mercedes-Benz customers were receiving extraordinary service experiences from a wide swath of luxury providers, and he envisioned their Mercedes-Benz sales and service relationships consistently eclipsing what they were encountering elsewhere.

Within his first 60 days as CEO, Steve sought to align his team members with his vision and to inspire them to begin laying out the road map that would help them delight their customers on a consistent "world-class" basis. To that end, Steve had an offsite retreat in February 2012 and included leaders not only from his organization but from Mercedes-Benz Financial Services as well. As a strong signal that Mercedes-Benz would have to learn from other providers of legendary experiences, a former executive from Disney was brought in to help participants focus on the importance of driving a customer-centric culture. During the early phase of the offsite, the presenter shared the trials and tribulations that the Disney leaders encountered as they sought to flawlessly create "magic" in the lives of their guests. A compelling part of the Disney presentation was the link that was made between a culture of guest experience excellence and Disney's overall business performance. In essence, Disney guests who are delighted by their experience produce meaningful profits, which, in turn, delight shareholders.

With strong messages about Disney's selection, training, and empowerment of employees (referred to as cast members) and an emphasis on the importance of crafting a clear customer experience value proposition, leaders at Mercedes-Benz USA were benefiting from an outside resource, benchmarking a world-class customer experience provider, and articulating the benefits and challenges of executing the type of customer-obsessed, Driven to Delight approach that was being considered at MBUSA. Participants at the offsite heard real-world examples culled from outside the automotive industry. These stories included situations at Disney theme parks, where Disney cast members are empowered to delight guests. In one such example, a cast member observed a child crying over spilled popcorn and not only replaced it but did so while saying, "Mickey saw what happened and asked me to deliver this." Armed with these types of examples, leaders at Mercedes-Benz USA could appreciate the elevated nature of experiences that people have with customer-focused brands.

Harald Henn, MBUSA's vice president finance & controlling, shares the benefits of looking at global brands outside of one's own industry: "We would have limited ourselves if we had only looked to the best practices of other car companies. That's what we did in the past. But to achieve a true transformation, we needed to look beyond automotive and even beyond product-focused businesses. By looking at service and experience-creating businesses, we set an even higher bar. Having worked in Japan for three years, I have seen very advanced approaches to service delivery. We wanted to learn from world champions, not just the best providers in the United States." Armed with examples from "world champion" experience providers like Disney, leaders were primed to assess the current state of their Mercedes-Benz USA and Mercedes-Benz Financial Services customer experiences and set clear aspirational goals for the journey ahead.

Several key leadership lessons emerged from even this most rudimentary step in the Mercedes-Benz USA transformational journey. Beyond active listening and a SWOT (strengths, weaknesses, opportunities, and threats) analysis, Steve Cannon began his tenure by:

1. Seeking alignment at the top leadership level for aspirational, inspiring, enterprisewide change initiatives

2. Providing leaders an opportunity to remove themselves from their day-to-day work demands and envision the optimal customer experience they wish to deliver

3. Offering examples of customer experience greatness and having those examples presented by recognized leaders outside of their traditional competitive landscape

Visual Wayfinding

So where should you start your journey to an improved customer experience? The obvious and accurate answer is that you should start where you are. Map makers, website developers, and customer experience designers like myself will tell you that orientation is the first step in wayfinding. In other words, before you set off on any journey, it is important for you to know your exact location. Think of the "you are here" indicators that are typically prominent on mall directories. Based on their renewed appreciation for service excellence and inspired by stories from benchmarked companies like Disney, the leaders at Mercedes-Benz USA set off on their customer experience journey by asking questions that are relevant to every change leader, namely: Where are we now with regard to our customer experience? What will success look like as we approach our destination? How do we get from where we are to where we want to be?

As the leadership team at Mercedes-Benz USA wrestled with these questions, the fruits of their discussions were captured in both words and hand-drawn pictures. Whereas many leaders return from offsite planning meetings with lengthy Word documents and photos of scribbles on flipcharts, Mercedes-Benz leaders understood the wisdom behind the adage "a picture is worth a thousand words." Therefore, a detailed visual map was created. The complete depiction will be shown at the end of this chapter (see Figure 2.4) and also can be found at www.driventodelight .com/map, but for now let's look at this visual map in terms of three component parts: current state, future state, and action plan.

Current State

Figure 2.1 MBUSA Vision Map: Current State

The artist's rendering of the beginning state of the Mercedes-Benz USA customer experience (see Figure 2.1) reflects many of the observations I shared in Chapter 1. Specifically, the new leadership team viewed the brand as being strong and relevant in the consumer's mind. They noted that the company had award-winning products and the efforts and strengths associated with being recognized as one of America's best places to work. They evaluated the existing and upcoming product offerings as being attractive to Mercedes-Benz buyers. The leaders also valued strong sales numbers and an aesthetically pleasing and well-designed "Autohaus" dealership environment. What was lacking in the current state was a consistent set of customer experiences that would differentiate the brand into the future.

Future State

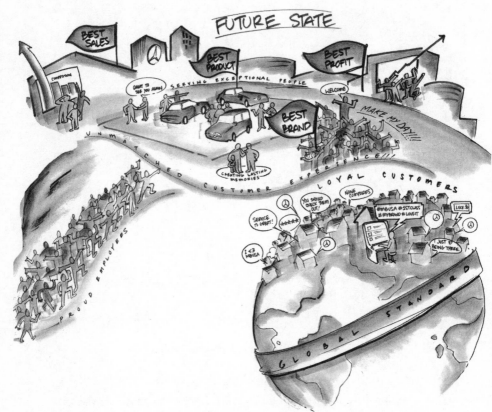

Figure 2.2 MBUSA Vision Map: Future State

From an aspirational perspective, the artist depicted how the leaders at Mercedes-Benz USA sought a new global standard for customer experience excellence (see Figure 2.2). They identified success on their transformational journey as being measured by a high volume of customer conversations about their extraordinary experiences, many of which would be shared on social media and customer discussion sites. When they achieved their objective of setting a new global standard for customer experience excellence, these leaders expected even greater employee pride, record car sales with attendant profitability, enviable customer loyalty, and enhanced brand strength. They asserted that when MBUSA became the new global standard in customer experience delivery, it would enjoy a cascade of benefits that would fuel success in all key aspects of the business. But how would Mercedes-Benz USA (or your business, for that matter) go from its current customer experience state to that of a customer experience leader?

Action Plan

Figure 2.3 MBUSA Vision Map: Action Plan

From the outset of their customer experience transformation discussions, senior leaders at Mercedes-Benz USA perceived that there was a sizable chasm between their current customer experience state and their aspirational state. As depicted in the "Action Plan" drawing (see Figure 2.3), they knew that they had to bridge that chasm with a multiphase, multiyear approach. These executives understood the need to commit resources to a long-term change process. A short-term customer experience improvement would not produce the sustained long-term benefits that they envisioned.

In the current "we want everything now," "instant gratification," and "focus on quarterly profits" business world in which we live, many leaders do not have the patience to bring about methodical and sustainable change. In fact, many well-intentioned executives have asked me to provide short-term consulting solutions to support a customer service "initiative" or to bolster the "year of the customer." In such cases, I have often wondered, if this is the "year of the customer," what was last year and what will next year be?

In the case of Steve and his leadership team at Mercedes-Benz USA, "Driven to Delight" was *not* an initiative. It was a long-term strategic journey—one that would require many years of investment, oversight, and stewardship. To emphasize this point, the leadership team crafted a mantra, which they have creatively placed across MBUSA (to see examples of the visual presentation of the mantra, please go to www.driventodelight.com/mantra). The mantra reads as follows:

driven to de(;ght

driven to delight. it is not just a phrase. it is a path, a promise, a belief. it is a commitment to creating positive relationships. to making people smile and to leaving them with a sense of complete trust. driven to delight means exceptional personal treatment. it is a reminder that the journey is never done. that there is always a more thoughtful way. and throughout each interaction we must remember that *the best or nothing* cannot just be a description of our vehicles but it must also represent the people behind them.

Steve publicly and repeatedly declared the significance and importance of living the mantra and pursuing a customer-centric path. For example, in an interview with Diane Kurylko for *Automotive News*, he suggested that in the future, luxury manufacturers will battle over customer experience delivery. Steve went on to add, "That is going to be my legacy. I am taking on what seems to be our biggest challenge and finding a way to collaborate with our dealers and leverage our resources to propel this brand where it belongs—to create a customer experience that fits with our tagline 'The Best or Nothing.'"

In the same article, Steve emphasized that MBUSA would need time to change the Mercedes-Benz culture in a way that would place the brand in the upper tier of experience providers. In follow-up conversations with me, Steve added that prudent change had to occur without an influx of dollars into departmental budgets at Mercedes-Benz USA. The customer experience transformation needed to be achieved through efficiencies and a willingness to reprioritize resources.

As illustrated by construction cranes in the artist's rendering, Mercedes-Benz USA leaders knew that there would have to be a number of customer experience construction projects going on simultaneously over a transformation timeline of 2012–2017. While the finer details of the map will be explored in more depth as we dive into the tactics that MBUSA leaders have used since their visioning session, projects that were already under way at the time of the map's development (such as launching the Driven to

LEAD training) are depicted on the solid ground to the left of the chasm (near the "current state" portion of the map).

John Kotter, a thought leader and author on organizational change, characterizes the early phases of a successful change initiative as stages such as establishing a sense of urgency, creating the guiding coalition, developing a change vision, and communicating the vision for buy-in. In essence, this early leadership retreat created a sense of urgency for customer-obsessed change at MBUSA. It resulted in a clear vision and aligned the senior leaders in pursuit of an ambitious customer experience goal. In fact, leaders within Mercedes-Benz USA and Mercedes-Benz Financial Services objectively compared their company to its competition and to the broader world of luxury customer experience delivery. They explored "what might happen" if they did not take action to elevate customer experiences across Mercedes-Benz dealerships. They further explored the likely business benefits of igniting a spirit of customer obsession in all interactions with consumers. This exploration led to a sense of urgency and a desire to create a differentiated experience that exceeded the expectations of the brand's changing customer base. The leaders also acknowledged that success on this journey of cultural change required impassioned and accountable efforts from every leader and could not be achieved through the solitary efforts of a single department or job category. Therefore, the senior leaders who were present at this offsite knew that they would have to live the vision of the future and enthusiastically share it throughout the organization in a way that would inspire others and explain why immediate action was needed.

More important, they could not confuse their communication of the vision with buy-in. Sharing an idea and having others join you in pursuit of that idea are quite different things. To be truly successful, this group of leaders would have to articulate the importance of customer experience excellence; they would have to *listen* to their teams to hear whether that vision resonated with those who would have the challenge of executing the transformation. These leaders also needed to listen to stakeholder groups (dealer principals, other MBUSA and MBFS leaders, frontline staff members, and employees throughout the nationwide dealership community) to understand how this change agenda would be likely to affect them. For example, with regard to dealers, MBUSA leaders would need to engage a very diverse and savvy group of business owners in the transformational journey. Dealer principals (those individuals who own Mercedes-Benz dealerships) can own a single location or lead a publicly traded dealer group such as AutoNation. (AutoNation is the largest auto retailer in the United States, with roughly 300 dealerships.) If the experience of customers at Mercedes-Benz dealerships was going to be a priority, Mercedes-Benz USA would have to invest considerable energy in securing the buy-in and focus of all dealer principals.

Efforts to engage stakeholders began with a round of all-employee meetings within Steve Cannon's first couple of months as CEO. Shortly thereafter, in April 2012, Steve reached out to the dealer network at the National Dealer Meeting in Chicago. After initial comments about victories that the brand had enjoyed the previous year and positive signs of a postrecession recovery, Steve set the stage for his leadership focus at Mercedes-Benz USA: "So, 90 days behind me, this is what I know. We have great products with quality that is at the top of the industry. We have a great team and a great partnership. And now we have the best facilities in the business. Our next big challenge is delivering to our customers a 'best or nothing' customer experience every time. I think, by comparison, this challenge that involves people and process and culture and passion will be much harder than building an Autohaus facility."

Steve commended the dealers for their participation in the recently initiated Driven to LEAD training program, noting that it was an important starting point for the brand's journey ahead. Prior to that dealer meeting, a large number of the dealership employees had participated in the daylong Driven to LEAD training course, and the dealers had made a sizable financial investment in that training (although the bulk of the costs was shouldered by MBUSA). In addition to dealership staff participation, there was widespread attendance at the Driven to LEAD event by MBUSA's corporate staff and by employees of Mercedes-Benz Financial Services.

While developing the curriculum for Driven to LEAD, Lior Arussy and his team at Strativity interviewed 10 percent of the Mercedes-Benz dealer principals in the United States and sent surveys to 3,000 of their employees to gather their insights and perceptions about the quality of the customer experiences that the dealerships were delivering. The employee survey feedback was the foundation for the training curriculum. Beyond the interviews and surveys, many individuals from Mercedes-Benz and the Strativity group worked together to design and deliver the training. This team created content, conducted a pilot phase, trained trainers, and delivered Driven to LEAD over 83 training dates in a 23-city tour. In total, 15 people were involved in the development of Driven to LEAD, and 20 additional trainers participated in breakout sessions.

Steve Cannon and other leaders at Mercedes-Benz were not only heartened by the level of participation and engagement in Driven to LEAD but also encouraged by the reports of how participants were experiencing a shift in their perspective and behavior after attending the sessions. For example, it was common to hear stories like the following shared by an employee at Fletcher Jones Motorcars, a Mercedes-Benz dealership in Newport Beach, California:

> A salesman called from New Jersey because one of his clients will be coming to California for vacation. They are

shipping their car here to drive. I have agreed to accept the car and pick them up at the airport when they arrive. I will then take them to the airport when they leave and then process the shipping of their car. All of these actions are due to what I learned at our Driven to LEAD/ CustomerOne training. It's my job to exceed the expectations of a Mercedes-Benz owner!

From a content perspective, Driven to LEAD training amplified the challenges and opportunities that Mercedes-Benz faced in the luxury customer experience arena and was founded on three pillars:

1. *Awareness.* We have to realize that what a service professional thinks is good enough may not be memorable to the customer.

2. *Perspective.* Every day, 365 days per year, customers are having great experiences with one brand or another. Does the experience that is being delivered to the customers at Mercedes-Benz dealerships measure up to the best of the best?

3. *Personal, team, and leader commitments.* The keys to providing the best customer experiences can be found in the acronym LEAD, which stands for Listen, Empathize, Add value, and Delight.

As an example of the awareness and perspective-building components, Lior Arussy, who led the majority of the Driven to LEAD meetings throughout the United States, asked participants to imagine a customer coming into a Nordstrom store and declaring that he or she had $75,000 to spend. Lior went on to ask, "What do you think the staff and leadership at Nordstrom would do in that situation?" Lior continued, "Your customers are coming in the same way. Do your experiences match the effort and execution you would see at Nordstrom?" While this example was posed to the dealership staff members in the context of a car-buying experience, it is equally applicable across all industries. How enriched an experience would the "best of the best" customer-centric businesses offer to a customer who was eager to buy their products? I suspect that if a similarly significant purchase were at stake, a Nordstrom employee would be willing to visit a customer's home, look at that person's wardrobe, and offer style consultation as a personal shopper. How far are your people willing to go to celebrate the presence of a customer who is interested in making a similar purchase?

The Driven to LEAD training offered by Mercedes-Benz USA challenged participants to look beyond the automotive industry for benchmarking, and structured cross-functional dealership teams to identify quick customer wins while also honestly looking for the factors that limited customer-centric execution. In addition to the daylong offsite training, the impact of the educational events was extended through a dealer-facing Driven to LEAD website, supporting videos, and a customer delight story contest at the dealership level. One example of a winning customer delight story involved a family who was in the service drive of a Mercedes-Benz dealership with a flat tire early on a Sunday morning. The service department was closed, but a couple of staff members of the dealership happened to be in the building; one of those individuals shares:

> The [customer] looked up as I approached and said, "Do you work here? Can I get some help?" I said, "Sure," and was about to make a phone call on the client's behalf to Roadside Assistance when my colleague approached and asked if they had to be anywhere right away . . . , and if they had another car at home, could he offer them a ride and pick up some breakfast on the way. They gratefully accepted [the] offer. [My colleague] solicited the

services of our Roadside tech within 10 minutes and drove the clients to their home.

In this example, the dealership staff member not only listened to the presenting problem (the need to have a flat tire fixed on a day when the dealership was closed) but also actively listened for unstated needs (like hunger and a need to have transportation elsewhere). The staff member empathized with the plight of a family who had ventured into the dealership on a flattened tire, only to find that the service department was closed. This staff member also added value and delighted the customer and his family by not only dispatching a roadside assist for the flat tire but purchasing food for them and delivering them back to their home.

As part of the Driven to LEAD training, participants were asked to sign a written commitment card pledging to Listen, Empathize, Add value, and Delight those they serve. This step of formalizing the training commitment should not be overlooked. There have been widespread research studies dating back to the 1950s looking at the power of "commitment contracts." While results vary from study to study, the act of formalizing a commitment in writing has consistently been shown to have a substantial (that is, 30 percent) likelihood of increased follow-through with a pledge. Since people seek to be internally consistent, the act of formalizing and publishing a commitment increases the likelihood that they will do what they have publicly said they would. If our public commitments are refreshed on a regular basis, our compliance tends to increase further.

So what do these findings about commitment contracts have to do with us as leaders? In a nutshell, we should offer our teams a clear vision for elevating the customer experience and publicly pledge (both orally and in writing) to lead our organization in pursuit of that objective. We should offer training to our staff members to heighten their awareness of our vision. Additionally, we should listen for their reactions to the proposed challenges ahead, offer them tools to achieve the transformation, and then seek a commitment contract from them. Once leaders and frontline workers make those written and oral commitments, leaders should routinely recommit to the contract both in writing and orally. Similarly, we should seek recommitments from our people, so that all of us have a greater likelihood of acting in accordance with the pledges we have made.

In addition to securing written commitment cards, participants in the Driven to LEAD program also completed a "What's Holding You Back (WHYB)" form, which allowed them to actively challenge both personal and organizational barriers to delivering consistent customer delight. Participants were asked to look at the conversations that were occurring inside their own heads, particularly those which could get in the way of making progress on cultural transformation and customer delight. These conversations often sound like: "We have tried this before," "This will never work," or "This is going to inconvenience me." Participants were also asked to identify other factors across Mercedes-Benz that might derail customer-centric change. These issues might include "too much change occurring too quickly," "ineffective change leadership," "poor communication systems," or "low team morale."

Information collected on the WHYB form was used to create action plans, and thousands of feedback points were captured from dealer attendees. A Mercedes-Benz USA project manager categorized and tracked every action plan that was generated. Those action plans were shared with people in the dealer network so that they could measure their progress. When participants suggested that the actions of Mercedes-Benz were limiting their ability to serve customers, that feedback was pushed out to senior leaders across MBUSA/MBFS, and the results were shared with the dealers. Participants left the Driven to LEAD sessions with Dealer Ideas/Action Plans, Commitment Posters, and their own personal

What's Holding You Back forms so that they could take future actions with their teams.

Jump-start kits and additional video tools were provided for use at the dealership and to offer those who did not attend the conference an orientation to the concepts and expectations of service delivery at Mercedes-Benz dealerships. Additionally, a Driven to LEAD e-learning curriculum was made available. MBUSA, MBFS, and dealership staff members were required to attend the live training or complete the e-learning curriculum by the end of 2012. New hires at MBUSA and Mercedes-Benz dealerships were exposed to the Driven to LEAD e-learning curriculum during orientation and onboarding. All of this served to create an enterprisewide understanding concerning the "why, what, and how" involved in delivering delight.

At the National Dealer Meeting in April of 2012, Steve Cannon described Driven to LEAD as an initial "culture shift that says for our customers—satisfied is not enough. We need to surprise, to delight . . . to transform the ordinary into the extraordinary!" Building on the momentum coming from Driven to LEAD, Steve reinforced the importance of delighting both employees (as evidenced by Mercedes-Benz USA being recognized as a "Best Place to Work") and customers. Moreover, he shared his sense of urgency concerning the ability of Mercedes-Benz dealers to lay claim to being the best in customer experience by reporting, "According to the industry standard J.D. Power Customer Satisfaction Index . . . we aren't even close. We've made some great strides, moving from a humiliating 22nd place to the middle of the pack. . . . [But] that is not an acceptable place for our brand. We might be getting better, but so is everybody else. . . . By 2020, we will sell more cars and make more money than all of our luxury competitors. I want to be very clear. Customer experience will be the number one priority for this company for as long as I am the President and CEO. This is my Autohaus, folks, and I am convinced that with the strength

Figure 2.4 MBUSA Vision Map

of our product and brand, if we truly lead in customer experience, we will be unbeatable!" For a brand claiming to be the "best or nothing," rankings of 22nd or even "middle of the pack" on customer experience metrics were clearly the urgent "call to arms" that prompted dealers to action. As you will see in Chapter 11, those actions (which serve as the foundation of this book) resulted in a prized accomplishment for Mercedes-Benz USA—a number one finish on an important J.D. Power and Associates metric, the Sales Satisfaction Index (SSI), as well as noteworthy progress on the Customer Service Index (CSI).

Using one of Mercedes-Benz USA's core competencies, the ability to produce compelling marketing messages, and leaning on his own recent background as vice president marketing, Steve Cannon drew a line in the sand for his leadership agenda in the context of an internal marketing video titled "The Standard," which he presented at the close of his remarks to dealer principals at his first

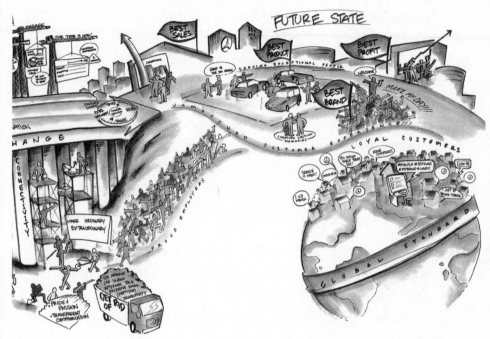

dealer meeting. That video can be seen at www.driventodelight .com/standard. The language for "The Standard" took shape at Steve's first offsite with his team and leaders from Mercedes-Benz Financial Services. The video ultimately offered a mix of powerful automobile images, the faces of Mercedes-Benz USA staff members, and the following narrative:

> The Mercedes-Benz automobile brings with it the expectation that every encounter with the brand will be as extraordinary as the machine itself—as thoughtful, innovative, and breathtaking, as confidence-inspiring and worthy of trust. When our customers enter our dealerships, their standards are predetermined. They rightfully anticipate and deserve the best or nothing. They will not be disappointed. 2012 will see the introduction of the most comprehensive pledge to an extraordinary

customer experience in the history of Mercedes-Benz. Every department will be mobilized. Every touchpoint in the brand will be examined and refined. Every employee at every dealership will be trained and equipped. We will begin immediately, and we will not rest until we are regarded as the global benchmark—until expectations are exceeded with such frequency that the Mercedes-Benz name will be as famous for our total customer experience as it is for our legendary engineering. Mercedes-Benz. The best or nothing.

Coming out of Steve's first National Dealer Meeting, Mercedes-Benz leaders made good on the promises stated in "The Standard" as they related to every department being mobilized, every touchpoint in the brand being examined and refined, and every employee at every dealership being trained and equipped. Buckle up! We're about to dive into Chapter 3, which looks at how Mercedes-Benz leadership fulfilled its promises. Hopefully, it will inspire you to make and fulfill your own.

KEYS TO DRIVING DELIGHT

➤ Take a strong stand for a purposeful customer experience vision.

➤ Honestly assess your current state relative to what you envision.

➤ Explore a detailed and granular picture of your desired future destination and build a multiyear, multiphase action plan.

➤ Chronicle your assessment of the present state, vision for the future, and action steps that will guide future action.

➤ Create a guiding coalition of change agents who are committed to lead in the direction of your vision.

➤ Make a case for urgent action. What is the business reason for the change? What will happen if the change is not made? Why should someone follow you immediately on your desired course of action?

➤ Pledge (orally and in writing) to lead your organization in pursuit of your desired customer experience change. Seek commitment contracts from your team members and routinely recommit, both in writing and orally. Similarly, seek recommitments from your people individually.

➤ Take a moment to look at personal and organizational factors that are likely to get in the way of change. Engage team processes to plan ways to overcome barriers to change.

➤ Internally market your transformational message through face-to-face meetings with stakeholders, and leverage assets like videos to inspire and engage change.

➤ Commit to a clear course of action through a tool like "The Standard," and live up to your commitments.

icles but it must also represent the people behind t
ven to **delight**. it is not just a phrase. it is a path, a pron
elief. it is a **commitment** to creating positive relationsh
making people smile and to leaving them with a sens
mplete **trust**. driven to **delight** means **exceptional** pers
atment. it is a reminder that the journey is never done.
re is always a more **thoughtful** way. and throughout

Losers make promises they often break.

Winners make commitments they

always keep.

—Denis Waitley

ven to **delight** means **exceptional** personal treatment.
minder that the journey is never done. that there is alw
re **thoughtful** way. and throughout each interaction we

cies but it must also represent the po   d the
en to **delight**. it is not just a phrase. it is   promi
lief. it is a **commitment** to creating po   onshi
aking people smile and to leaving th   sense
plete **trust**. driven to **delight** means e   perso
ment. it is a reminder that the journey   ne. t
e is always a more **thoughtful** way. a   ut ea

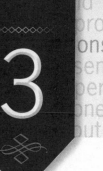

From Promises to Committed Action

◇◇◇

Trust is at the heart of every successful endeavor, be that a personal relationship or a grand-scale business objective like the transformational customer experience journey undertaken at Mercedes-Benz USA. To earn trust in business, leaders need to communicate their intentions, demonstrate that those intentions serve the interests of all stakeholders, and make commitments to translate those intentions into action.

In the case of MBUSA, Steve Cannon and his leadership team fostered trust by articulating an inspiring goal of creating a world-class customer service experience that would be consistent

n to **delight** means **exceptional** personal treatment. it is
nder that the journey is never done. that the   s always
thoughtful way. and throughout each interaction we m
mber that the best or nothing cannot just be a description

with the needs of Mercedes-Benz staff members, dealers, and the customers they served. At the same time, Steve and other senior leaders declared three foundational commitments to their shareholders. In essence, "The Standard" promised that:

- Every department would be mobilized.

- Every touchpoint in the brand would be examined and refined.

- Every employee at every dealership would be trained and equipped.

This chapter looks at the actions that the leaders took to fulfill the first of these three promises, with subsequent chapters examining the process of mapping the customer journey and strategic alignment deployed at Mercedes-Benz USA, as well as the metrics, tools, and incentives created for dealerships.

Mobilization—Aim Before You Fire

One of the biggest challenges for any customer experience initiative—or, for that matter, any cultural change that is systemwide in scope—is determining how to mobilize the diverse parts of an organization. Since most departmental leaders have incentives aimed at driving performance in their specific area, it is often difficult to get vice presidents or managers to think about, let alone improve, the customer's journey across other areas of the business.

In an effort to address this organizational linkage challenge at Mercedes-Benz USA, senior leaders studied how other companies set up departments or teams dedicated to improving enterprise-wide customer-centricity. Steve Cannon looked to three senior leaders, Frank Diertl, Niles Barlow, and Harry Hynekamp (the "three amigos" who demonstrated a strong dedication to the cause of improving the customer experience), to provide recommendations concerning the structure of a customer experience department at Mercedes-Benz USA. This carefully chosen group of senior leaders first turned to Forrester Research, a global advisory company that focuses on leadership guidance in areas such as business technology marketing and strategy, to identify the best placement for a soon-to-be-developed customer experience team.

Three models were explored. The first was a department, with the customer experience team being a division under the vice president of marketing. Marketing leaders are typically the "keeper of the brand" and are adept at communicating the brand pillars and brand promise. With this placement, the customer experience department could also leverage consumer data and activate the communication assets that typically exist within the marketing branch. A marketing-based customer experience department would also have the core competencies to paint a picture of the desired brand experience for staff members throughout Mercedes-Benz.

The second option was a freestanding division under a newly created executive officer, a position that many companies often refer to as a chief customer officer (CCO). Starting around 2005, CCO-type organizational structures have gained increased popularity across industries. By creating a C-level officer, many brands have put in position an individual who is analyzing the company's strategy and operations from the customer's perspective. This type of senior officer is given a mandate to create, execute, and improve the customer experience for every customer across all contact points with the brand. Curtis Bingham, founder and executive director of the Chief Customer Officer Council, defines the role of the CCO as "an executive that provides the comprehensive and authoritative view of the customer and creates corporate and customer strategy at the highest levels of the company to maximize customer acquisition, retention, and profitability."

While both the CMO and CCO models have their benefits, Mercedes-Benz USA was looking for a customer experience department structure that was consistent with its company size, the talents and engagement of senior leaders, and the developmental stage at which MBUSA found itself on its customer experience elevation journey. Given these factors, the recommendation that ultimately gained approval involved the creation of a relatively small area (approximately 14 individuals at MBUSA and an additional 5 individuals from Mercedes-Benz Financial Services) that would not be combined with any other MBUSA group. This new area would also have powerful linkage to senior leadership. In the final Mercedes-Benz USA model, the general manager who would oversee the group, referred to simply as the Customer Experience team, would report directly to the man who had staked his legacy on improving the customer experience at MBUSA: President and CEO Steve Cannon.

If you are the owner of a small business, a team of 14 might seem large, but in the context of a company the size of Mercedes-Benz USA, it is an extremely lean department. When you are considering how to staff and where to place your core customer experience team, a number of lessons emerge from the process and outcome at Mercedes-Benz. Those lessons include the need to:

1. Evaluate the structures of other successful customer-focused businesses.

2. Decide on an organizational leadership approach that best fits your developmental needs and talents.

3. Be careful not to make the department so large that it is viewed as being "responsible for" as opposed to "a catalyst for" customer experience elevation. Stay lean, but be sure to staff the group adequately.

4. View customer experience delivery as an enterprisewide competency that needs to be attended to and tracked by the leadership to ensure that customer experience creation is not the responsibility of a single department.

Defining the Core Team and Its Purpose

Harry Hynekamp, one of the three amigos, was chosen in April 2012 to lead the Customer Experience team. In addition to an MBA and a history of demonstrated leadership in customer care, Harry possessed a deep and diverse understanding of the operational aspects of Mercedes-Benz USA. He had joined MBUSA 12 years earlier and had worked in auditing, accounting, business development, and the companywide project management office. Immediately prior to his appointment as general manager of the Customer Experience team, Harry had served as the general manager of MBUSA learning and performance (training). Most important, Harry melded enterprisewide knowledge of Mercedes-Benz USA with a demonstrated passion for service, championing the Driven to LEAD program discussed in Chapter 2 and constantly advocating for ways to deliver better customer experiences.

Harry describes the original thought behind the development of the Customer Experience team at MBUSA by noting, "We didn't need a huge team, but we needed a team big enough to accomplish our mission, which is to assist the rest of the organization in strategizing, connecting to the customer journey, and planning how to utilize their resources now and going forward. We also had to be able to shape our overall business strategy by bringing the voice of the customer into that discussion and into the journey with each business area, across not only Mercedes-Benz USA but also the financing arm—Mercedes-Benz Financial Services." In order to accomplish this mission—leveraging the voice of the customer strategically and connecting the entire organization and dealership body to the customer journey—the team was bifurcated into a Strategy and Planning group and a Metrics and Insights/Voice of the Customer group.

The Metrics and Insights/Voice of the Customer subteam was, from the onset, designed to qualitatively and quantitatively listen to the voice of the customer. Harry notes, "We wanted one place to go to find out what our customer experience journey looks like and how we are doing from our customer's perspective. We also needed that team to quickly access hard numbers and offer an insightful qualitative view across every facet of the customer journey."

The manager of the Strategy and Planning group was charged with taking the analytics collected by the Metrics and Insights/Voice of the Customer group and developing a comprehensive understanding of that customer journey. That team was then responsible for working with every vice president, general manager, and department manager to assist them in understanding the Mercedes-Benz USA customer journey and identify how each of these leaders could address needs in areas that his department affects.

Metrics and Insights

The Metrics and Insights component of the Customer Experience team has consistently been composed of a handful of employees with very specific functions. For example, one individual is a subject-matter expert on all research in which Mercedes-Benz is compared with competitors like BMW and Lexus on metrics such as customer satisfaction and loyalty. This data expert is also tracking high-profile research such as J.D. Power and Associates satisfaction surveys, Strategic Vision studies, Polk measurements, Forrester

customer experience analyses, and the American Customer Satisfaction Index. Additionally, this team member monitors the pulse
of all other research that may provide useful insights concerning the
wants, needs, satisfaction, or emotional engagement of Mercedes-
Benz USA customers.

By contrast, another individual in the Metrics and Insights
group is responsible for maintaining Mercedes-Benz USA online
customer communities. This person not only oversees the thousands of customers enrolled in these communities, but also seeks
to grow their membership. Functionally, these communities often
serve as online focus groups and as such are also engaged in conversations involving products, auto shows, and events. The groups
are made up of existing customers and prospective Mercedes-
Benz owners. The Metrics and Insights team member engages the
community members in conversations about a variety of topics,
ranging from existing products and soon-to-be-launched services
to the price of accessories and what these owners and prospective
owners value most. The conversations also explore out-of-sector
brand comparisons, such as: "What do you think of the Mercedes-
Benz brand compared to the Louis Vuitton, Ritz-Carlton, or
Tiffany brands?"

But these Mercedes-Benz communities go well beyond online product focus groups. In fact, members of the communities
are frequently invited to participate in unique and exclusive opportunities, such as a visit to Mercedes-Benz headquarters for a
prelaunch peek at the new S-Class Coupe. David Thorne shares
his connection to the Mercedes-Benz online community: "I will
make a confession right up front. I have a disorder. It's some sort
of addiction to the brand, and I can't really explain it. I've driven
lots of different cars; I've experienced lots of different brands. My
background is in marketing, and I understand branding. I understand the consumer perception of a brand, and I can't rational-
ize my addiction to this brand through any of that. The fact that

Karl Benz received the first patent for an automobile speaks to me. I appreciate the attention to detail. My first Mercedes was a 1988 190E. It was like the baby Benz. I marveled that they paid as much attention to their most inexpensive vehicle as they did to everything else across the line. I also have this strong desire to help them, even though they don't need my help. And that's why I jumped at the chance to become part of the MB Advisors Community and provide input."

Mercedes-Benz communities enable leaders across Mercedes-Benz USA to speak to and hear from the people they are charged with serving. Harry Hynekamp notes, "We are fortunate to have active, impassioned community members who openly share their thoughts, opinions, and ideas in ways that help all of our leaders at MBUSA improve their experience. Before the Customer Experience team was created, those communities were usually polled only by the marketing team. Today every department of the organization seems to be gaining insights from them." The engagement of Mercedes-Benz customers and brand fans through online communities reminds us all of the valuable input we can receive when we simply ask for insights and feedback.

Other members of the Metrics and Insights team were responsible for launching, and are now charged with managing, a very specific and powerful tool—the Customer Experience Program, or CEP—that Mercedes-Benz USA developed to gain "real-time" insights into customers' sales and service experiences. Since I address the effective use of customer feedback in Chapters 5 and 6, I will save a more detailed overview of the Metrics and Insights team member functions until then.

Strategy and Planning

Like the Metrics and Insights group, the Strategy and Planning team consists of six individuals. These Mercedes-Benz USA employees were responsible for mapping the customer journey (see Chapter 4) and subsequently helping every leader at Mercedes-Benz USA understand how to maximize the positive impact his team has on the portion of the customer journey that his team influences. Even more important, the Strategy and Planning group highlights the different handoffs that are going on between what these leaders see as "their areas." This thorough understanding of a customer's movement from purchase intent through completed service interactions helps ease the transition points along the customer's brand journey. The Strategy and Planning group also works with leaders in specific business areas to explore the current allocations of resources and how those allocations align with what customers actually want and need.

In essence, the Strategy and Planning group is a guidance resource that helps all the leaders at Mercedes-Benz USA align their actions around the company's mission and the leadership's goal of being "Driven to Delight." As such, this group starts its process by focusing leaders throughout the organization on five key performance indicators (KPIs) that will mark MBUSA's overall strategic success. The five objectives, which reflect measurable aspirations of MBUSA's senior leaders, include:

1. To Be the Most Admired Automotive Brand

2. To Maximize Customer Loyalty

3. To Be the Leading Premium Brand in New Vehicle Sales

4. To Be the Most Profitable Market Performance Center Among the Daimler Market Performance Centers

5. As a Leading U.S. Employer, to Enhance Employee Engagement Each Year

The Mercedes-Benz Strategy and Planning team guides leaders across MBUSA through multiple-day meetings looking at specific components of the customer journey (for example, the arrival experience of a customer who brings his Mercedes-Benz in for service).

According to Lourence du Preez, then department manager of the Strategy and Planning group, "This was new territory for our brand. We methodically put ourselves in the place of our prospects and customers and analyzed the customer journey completely from their frame of reference. We initiated that exploration by starting with what we knew and had learned that our customers wanted and needed." Once the leaders gained a full understanding of customers' typical wants, needs, and desires during that phase of the journey, they identified the resources that they were currently deploying to serve customers during those interactions. The leaders were also guided to look at any and all projects, special initiatives, and expenditures involved in addressing the needs of customers during that customer touchpoint.

After the customer journey was defined and departmental resources were explored in the context of that segment of the customer journey, the Strategy and Planning group shared information from the Metrics and Insights team to help the leaders hear what customers were sharing about their biggest pain points during that portion of the Mercedes-Benz USA journey. Harry Hynekamp, general manager of the Customer Experience team, describes this process as helping leaders "look at pain points from a customer's perspective, not from ours at MBUSA. By walking leaders through the steps of this process, they quickly get a glimpse into resource misalignments or well-intentioned efforts that do not hit the mark or aren't valued by the customer. Leaders also gain insights into how a staff member might be handling an initiative that would best be handled by an individual in another area. As we moved leaders through this process, we heard everything from, 'Wow, I didn't know we were doing that' to 'This is the first time we made strategy and resource decisions from the perspective of what customers experience and what they say they need throughout their journey.'" Imagine such a process at your business, where leaders conduct their departmental planning sessions informed by the voice of the customer and with an eye to deploying resources to address customer needs. How might some of your departmental plans change?

Gareth Joyce, MBUSA's vice president customer services, was one of the first senior leaders to take his department through customer-centric leadership strategy and planning meetings. Gareth was a relative newcomer to the MBUSA senior leadership team, having been appointed in February 2012 (approximately a month after Steve Cannon assumed the role of CEO). While he was new at Mercedes-Benz USA, Gareth brought a wealth of international experience, including roles as vice president after-sales for Mercedes-Benz Netherlands and vice president after-sales for Mercedes-Benz South Africa. Most important, Gareth brought an enthusiasm for customer experience delivery to a position in which he had to develop strategy and oversee all engineering services and customer service operations, as well as direct after-sales marketing, the Mercedes-Benz Customer Assistance Center, and parts logistics.

Gareth views customer-centric strategic planning as a breakthrough for Mercedes-Benz USA leadership: "The quality of answers you get is always dependent on the quality of questions you ask. When I first came to this job, I had a slate of projects that had been identified for my department, all which were well designed and well engineered. But they were so numerous, and they did not connect purposefully in the hearts of those who needed to execute them. The power of our customer experience objective is that it resonated with everyone on my team. By going through a process of looking at everything we do from the perspective of a customer, we have to challenge many of our assumptions and closely scrutinize preexisting resource allocations."

One powerful example of how leaders like Gareth used customer-centric planning sessions to make bold moves in resource allocation can be seen in the area of the Mercedes-Benz Roadside Assistance program. Historically, Mercedes-Benz was the only automobile manufacturer to offer proprietary roadside assistance to all customers for as long as they owned their vehicle, with very few limitations. This service amenity had a long history and was seemingly an untouchable perquisite of Mercedes-Benz ownership. But MBUSA had begun the process of analyzing the overall benefits and liabilities of the program in relation to customer retention in 2011, when it made the bold move of linking MBUSA-provided roadside assistance to service loyalty.

As the corporate focus on the customer experience grew within the organization, Gareth realized that he already had sufficient assets at his disposal. He recognized that improved customer experiences were not going to be achieved by seeking more human or financial resources, so he set out to see how he could streamline every program and asset in his area to maximize both customer and business benefit.

For our purposes in exploring how to steward resources in customer-centric ways, I will spare you the details and finer points of the Roadside Assistance program. In essence, as long as your vehicle had been serviced at an authorized dealership within 18 months of your roadside assistance request, you retained complimentary MBUSA-provided "Sign and Drive" roadside assistance. A Mercedes-Benz technician would provide fuel should your vehicle run out; your tire would be replaced with a spare if it was flat; if your battery was dead, someone would jump it; and if your vehicle required service, the roadside technician would provide complimentary towing.

As part of that effort, Gareth and his team examined the way the Roadside Assistance program was being delivered. They concluded that the program needed to be further modified, and that the financial benefits of that modification needed to be directed to other high-value customer experience needs. So they narrowed the program and stratified the level of complimentary services by offering the "Sign and Drive" roadside benefits listed previously only to those customers who were covered by a factory warranty and "grandfathered" customers who had purchased their vehicles prior to January 4, 2011.

Some of the millions of dollars saved by this modification were initially repurposed into a cutting-edge customer experience enhancement to support the 2013 launch of the Mercedes-Benz CLA and the new S-Class through a program called MB SELECT. (Since so much can be learned from the MB SELECT program, through which Mercedes-Benz USA provided "no-strings-attached" money to dealerships to "delight" CLA and S-Class customers when it mattered most, it will receive a detailed explanation in Chapter 10.) Suffice it to say that the funding for a progressive customer experience program like MB SELECT could have been procured only by reallocating resources based on listening to and understanding what customers said they wanted and needed most.

While you would think that a change such as this—from a ubiquitous roadside assistance program to one that was offered only to loyal service customers to one that was offered only to customers under warranty—would happen fairly seamlessly, Gareth had to work with dealers who knew that every customer with whom they reconnected as the result of a roadside assistance call was a potential source of parts, service, and sales revenue. Since dealers were also Gareth's customers, he suggested an additional modification consistent with dealer feedback, and that was Mercedes-Benz USA would reimburse dealers for a portion of the towing and technician charges as long as the customer agreed to be towed to an authorized Mercedes-Benz dealership to resolve her immediate need (the tow was free to the customer). Furthermore, the roadside towing benefit was expanded to provide all owners (both in and out of warranty, for the life of their vehicle) with complimentary "anytime, anywhere" towing, as long as the vehicle was towed back to an authorized Mercedes-Benz dealership service department—something that no other automobile company offers. Customers who wished to be towed to a repair shop outside of the dealer network would be charged accordingly.

These thoughtful and challenging stewardship decisions often result in customer-centered outcomes that are not about doing more with less but rather about doing what is most right with less. Looking at your business from the vantage point of your customer, where are your resources misallocated? Where might you be able to save money in areas that are not producing significant value for you and your customers and, in turn, reapply those resources to address more salient consumer needs?

Champions—Igniting Everyone at MBUSA to Be Driven to Delight

It is essential that you get all levels of formal leadership involved in elevating the customer experience through strategy and planning. Additionally, to achieve the needed tipping point on a cultural initiative as grand as MBUSA's Driven to Delight, it takes more than leaders and managers to drive change. One member of the Customer Experience Strategy and Planning group was, and continues to be, responsible for aligning and transforming a culture of experience excellence at Mercedes-Benz USA by activating staff members to make change happen throughout the organization. This is done through the Mercedes-Benz Customer Experience Champions program.

In the early phase of the customer-focused journey, MBUSA general managers and dealers were asked to nominate team members for the champions program who were known catalysts for change and who had a strong customer focus. To be considered for selection as an MBUSA Customer Experience Champion, the nominee could be anyone in the organization, as long as that individual could spark change and see a project through to completion. Participating as a Customer Experience Champion would allow those who were selected to be part of a high-priority, enterprisewide, action-oriented community. Further, their participation was designed to enable them to network with others like themselves and to afford them the opportunity to participate in and benefit from training events about the science and art of customer experience creation. In the first year of the program's launch, for example, participants learned about the process of journey mapping and explored how that process was related to the journeys of those they were serving. More specifically, Customer Experience Champions connected their departments to MBUSA's overall business objectives and explored how their efforts impacted the lives of those who drive Mercedes-Benz cars, their colleagues in the next office or another MBUSA department, and vendors.

With the support of the Mercedes-Benz USA Customer Experience team, Customer Experience Champions have met on a monthly basis; made excursions to Mercedes-Benz USA's only owned and operated dealership, located in Manhattan; visited the Disney Institute; and gained exposure to customer experience industry leaders such as Chris Zane, founder and president of Zane's Cycles, and Jill Nelson, CEO of Ruby Receptionists. They have also heard speakers from Hertz, The Ritz-Carlton, and 11 Madison and conducted an offsite at Tiffany & Co. in Manhattan. All of these activities have served to enhance their knowledge of what cutting-edge organizations do to innovate customer solutions and move the entire enterprise in the direction of dealing with customer needs.

In addition to gaining and sharing knowledge about best practices in customer experience delivery, MBUSA Customer Experience Champions have been given the task of developing customer experience initiatives for their respective departments. These change leaders serve as sounding boards for one another and help to plan and execute projects that enhance the service delivered by MBUSA headquarters personnel. Champions serve for a one-year term and receive coaching from the MBUSA Customer Experience team. Since its inception, the program has evolved to include 45- and 90-day project challenges, the creation of KPIs that measure each champion's effectiveness, and the delineation of 12 core standards for the Customer Experience Champion role. Additionally, a book of successes achieved by participants has been created, not only as a keepsake for past champions but also as a template for those who have been newly selected. This book demonstrates the behaviors required to lead transformational customer experience change. The following are a few of the varied service accomplishments generated by these champions and change leaders:

- Streamlined the dealer financial statement submission process.

- Created the owner picture program, which offers digital pictures of the owner with her vehicle of choice to create a lasting memory.

- Introduced "Operation Hang Tag," in which dealers were sent hang tags to display on vehicles after service, alerting customers that their vehicle had been washed and vacuumed.

- Simplified direct deposit for new hires.

Customer Experience Champion Jennifer Perez stated, "My awareness has changed since becoming a Champion. I evaluate how I am treated as a customer in my personal and professional life, and I am more aware of how I treat others." Champion Stephen Quinones added, "My overall perception of our company's culture is what has changed the most. The ability to collaborate across the company with others who share a positive attitude and a desire to impact our culture in some way really opened up my eyes to the strides we are making as an organization." In the champions' success book, CEO Steve Cannon shared his view of Mercedes-Benz Customer Experience Champions by noting, "Our Champions are change agents. Building our culture. Recognizing delightful behavior. Reminding us of whom we serve. Welcoming new employees. Leading cross-functional teams. Helping us integrate the voice of the customer. Initiating change and action to better serve our customers. Listening. Leading. Communicating."

The leadership team at Mercedes-Benz USA made the commitment to all stakeholders that it would mobilize every department in the company. By creating a small but empowered Customer Experience team, the company leveraged customer knowledge to change the way its leaders strategize, plan, and deploy resources to meet customer needs. Additionally, that same team supports change agents throughout the organization by sharing customer experience knowledge, completing projects that improve service delivery, and better supporting associates at the dealership level. How does your business compare? Is your organization broadly mobilized to translate customer information into intelligent business decisions? Does your understanding of your customer guide strategic planning and deployment issues? How has your senior leadership's vision been embraced through the tactics and implantation of middle management and frontline change agents?

I think you would agree that the leaders at Mercedes-Benz USA have made good on the "every department will be mobilized" pledge shared at Steve Cannon's first National Dealer Meeting just months after he took over as CEO. That said, the journey to true culture change at Mercedes-Benz USA continued to evolve. For the transformation to be maximally effective, the actions of every individual representing the Mercedes-Benz brand had to be guided by a full understanding of the customer experience at every touchpoint with the brand. Further, every individual needed to leverage his understanding of the customer journey to deliver experiences that not only satisfied those customers but delighted them consistently.

In the next chapter you will see how the leaders at Mercedes-Benz USA made a sizable investment in defining customer "moments of truth." You will watch the evolution of the company to understand the customer journey and, in turn, make the journey understandable to everyone who provides leadership, service, or support at Mercedes-Benz USA, its dealerships, and its partners at Mercedes-Benz Financial Services. In essence, you will appreciate the challenging yet rewarding work involved in fulfilling the second promise in "The Standard," namely, "Every touchpoint in the brand will be examined and refined."

Let's explore mapping the customer journey the Mercedes-Benz USA way.

➤ Make clear, concise promises about your customer experience transformation.

➤ Create a team of people who are responsible for driving customer-centric change throughout your organization.

➤ Assemble as much disparate customer information as possible into a centralized, accessible, and usable location. Develop subject-matter experts who can provide consultation regarding your customers' wants, needs, and desires.

➤ Use your customer experience team to help all leaders throughout the organization align their strategy, develop projects, and deploy resources to address customer pain points and respond to what your customers tell you about their needs.

➤ Select frontline change agents in every department to champion the cause of the customer.

➤ Provide tools to educate and enrich your change agents as they seek to improve the service delivery in their departments.

➤ Challenge your change agents to accomplish customer-centric initiatives that move key performance indicators.

➤ Chronicle the successes and stumbles encountered by those effecting customer-focused solutions. Utilize those resources to assist and inspire other change agents who seek to do the same.

➤ Appreciate that shifting from a product- or service-based business to one that is truly focused on the customer experience is a slow and methodical (albeit rewarding) process.

cies but it must also represent the people behind th
en to **delight**. it is not just a phrase. it is a path, a prom
elief. it is a **commitment** to creating positive **relationsh**
naking people smile and to leaving them with a sens
nplete **trust**. driven to **delight** means **exceptional** pers
tment. it is a reminder that the journey is never done.
re is always a more **thoughtful** way. and throughout e

If there is any one secret of success, it lies in the

ability to get the other person's point of view and

see things from his angle as well as your own.

—Henry Ford

ven to delight means exceptional personal treatment. it
ninder that the journey is never done. that there is alwa
re thoughtful way. and throughout each interaction we
nember that *the best or nothing* cannot just be a descripti

4

Examining and Refining Every Touchpoint

W hen Steve Cannon shared "The Standard" with the dealer network early in his time as president and CEO, he offered a promise that would fundamentally change the way everyone at Mercedes-Benz USA understood the customer experience. His promise was, "Every touchpoint in the brand will be examined and refined." While this is simply stated, the process of examining, let alone refining, customer touchpoints was anything but easy.

Before we explore the process that Mercedes-Benz USA leaders put in place to secure a usable view of customer touchpoints, it seems worthwhile to understand the thinking behind the mapping

en to delight means exceptional personal treatment. it nder that the journey is never done. that the s alway e thoughtful way. and throughout each interaction we m mber that the best or nothing cannot just be a descriptio

61

of the customer journey. As a customer experience designer, I often assume that the world knows about and understands the process involved in defining customer touchpoints (so much so that I have not dedicated any time to the topic in any of my previous books). While such mapping efforts are at the core of what I do from a consulting perspective, a customer journey map is a tool that is often overlooked or underutilized by many leaders and business owners.

In the mid-1980s, G. Lynn Shostack, then a senior vice president in charge of the Private Clients Group at Bankers Trust Company, was among the first to champion the concept of touchpoint assessment. In a 1984 article in the *Harvard Business Review* titled "Designing Services That Deliver," Lynn referred to the mapping process as a service blueprint in which processes, fail points, time frames, and profitability are all outlined in a single document. In her argument for the importance of dedicating time and resources to developing a "blueprint" for the customer journey, Lynn noted that such a process "helps cut down the time and inefficiency of random service development and gives a higher level view of service management prerogatives. The alternative—leaving services to individual talent and managing the pieces rather than the whole—makes a company more vulnerable and creates a service that reacts slowly to market needs and opportunities." Journey blueprints have gained considerable traction since Lynn wrote this because most companies (probably including yours) typically aspire to offer well-designed and seamless customer journeys, while quickly adapting to the changing wants, needs, and desires of their customers.

Since the mid-1980s, these customer experience blueprints have evolved to typically include:

- A systematic view of the actions that customers take as they move through their brand experience

- The goals and needs that customers experience throughout their journey

- The identification of the high-value touchpoints (often referred to as moments of truth) on which customers place great importance

- The gaps, pain points, or service challenges faced by the customer

- The level of customer satisfaction and the emotions that customers experience

- The processes, departments, and systems of the business that interface with customers at each touchpoint

- The identification of opportunities to enhance the current customer journey

If you don't have a map of your customer experience journey, the process taken by Mercedes-Benz USA has great relevance for you (whether you are a small, medium-sized, or large business), as it demonstrates the challenges that companies face and strategies for overcoming them. If you have created a map, the work at MBUSA reveals best practices for embedding that depiction of the customer journey deeply into the culture and operation of your business.

The Mercedes-Benz Customer Journey Mapping Team

Fueled by the desire to fulfill Steve Cannon's promise to craft a blueprint of Mercedes-Benz USA customer touchpoints and armed only with the information obtained from reading about touchpoint or customer journey mapping, the Customer Experience

Strategy and Planning group and several other individuals began sketching out the customer journey on a pad of paper. From that austere beginning, it quickly became apparent that a diverse and extremely energetic team would be needed to take on this high-priority project. While many of the best and brightest from within the Mercedes-Benz USA corporate office were assembled for the task, both internal and external staffing selections were made based on the qualities needed for success, not necessarily for the specific skills involved in creating customer maps. According to Harry Hynekamp, general manager of the Customer Experience team, "As we filled positions on our newly forming team, I was conscious of 'selecting'—not 'hiring'—each individual for a reason. For example, to head the team, we chose a young man who represents Gen Y and who enriches the diversity and energy of our department. He had helped a Mercedes-Benz dealer with social and Internet reputation management and was comfortable dealing with the digital as well as the real-world experiences of our customers, dealers, and field teams. We didn't need a subject-matter expert in customer journey mapping. Instead, we were looking for someone who was creative, who was comfortable with the unknown, and who demonstrated perseverance and resilience. We knew what needed to be done and selected the person to get it done."

Tylden Dowell, the person who was ultimately responsible for customer journey mapping at Mercedes-Benz USA, reflects on his selection and the magnitude of the task that he faced, "I came into this new department as a relatively unknown quantity—one of the very few hired from the outside. I immediately sensed the importance and urgency of formulating the customer journey map as the backbone underpinning the overall customer experience strategy. I wanted to help make this map a true-to-life representation of what our customers go through when they buy and service their vehicles. To get started, I relied on the wealth of knowledge from across the organization, as well as on my recent experience working for a large dealership group. Ensuing revisions to the map helped develop a rough sketch into a living, working business resource that shapes strategy decisions on a daily basis." While Mercedes-Benz USA leaders could easily have hired people based solely on their demonstrated "mapping" skill, they instead built their team around the skills and leadership qualities needed to achieve the mission, knowing that experience-mapping experts could be consulted as resources when needed. An important lesson to be considered: understand the characteristics needed to be successful in completing a project, and select accordingly. Technical skill alone does not guarantee success.

Often the art of leadership requires a willingness to take action in the absence of expertise or the "perfect" in-house subject-matter expert. As you will see from the mapping efforts at Mercedes-Benz USA, solid leadership also requires the wisdom to know when to bring in resources to expedite and advance the cause.

Turning the Wheel

Upon being assembled, the mapping team faced a challenge that is fairly common among established businesses: charting a new course. While start-ups and entrepreneurial businesses like the on-line retailer Zappos (the focus of my book *The Zappos Experience: 5 Principles to Inspire, Engage, and WOW*) have the benefit of mapping the customer journey before they open their doors to customers, a mature business like Mercedes-Benz USA has to correct its course in order to create a consolidated view of the customer journey through all aspects of the customer life cycle (presales through sales and on to after-sales functions). Previous efforts to document the customer journey at Mercedes-Benz USA had been fairly siloed: sales leaders crafted solutions based on their perceptions of what customers wanted in the sales experience, and after-sales leaders took care of what they felt customers needed when they sought service for their vehicle. To start forging an optimal, consolidated view, the Metrics and Insights team began running customer focus groups and brought owners into dealerships to walk through their journeys with them.

Later, members of the Customer Experience team merged the knowledge and feedback gleaned from diverse customer data sets such as surveys, focus groups, and side-by-side customer journey walk-throughs as the team sprawled out in a conference room referred to as the "customer experience war room." The walls of the "war room" were plastered with a large sticky roll of brown paper, upon which the team and other MBUSA staff members began affixing Post-it notes. The process was methodical. Leaders from departments as diverse as marketing, sales, after-sales, and logistics were brought in over a several-month time frame to help the team list the customer's thoughts and needs at the top of the paper. Once the customer's needs were identified, participants listed the phases through which customers would travel in order to get those needs met. At a deeper level of detail, participants stepped into the customer's perspective and identified very specific contact points and interactions that the customer would encounter within each phase. Staying with the customer's vantage point, participants sought to refine the touchpoints by identifying ways in which the customer's needs could be better met (for example, removing unnecessary steps and streamlining processes) and approaches for helping customers experience delight (having their needs anticipated and exceeded as well as feeling appreciated and valued).

Essentially, the members of the mapping team were given the task of putting themselves in the position of a customer who was just beginning to consider buying an automobile and empathetically mapping that customer's journey all the way through the purchase and into aftercare. In the six-month presale portion of the journey, the mapping team explored the customer's evolving responses to the question: "What car should I buy?" Team members and participants from departments like marketing then populated the map with discrete customer stages involved in answering that question. These stages included an initial period during which the customer was exposed to a vast array of automobile and brand options. Customers then generated a list of viable candidates, after which they narrowed that list down and ultimately decided on the car that they wished to buy. During the presale period, the mapping process uncovered a large number of customer touchpoints involved in moving from brand awareness to product choice. These included possible exposure to a wide range of advertising, considerable editorial content, and varied written information, as well as numerous marketing events. Also during the awareness phase, customers might seek or receive input from friends or family members, initiate online searches, and begin to visit the websites of automobile manufacturers. As customers moved from awareness to consideration, they might begin looking at third-party research websites and start venturing into dealership sites to take a peek at the inventory. As the customer started to form a purchase intent, she would probably start considering and researching finance options and identifying dealerships in her area. Some might seek an online or telephone quote.

After evaluating the customer journey to the point at which a purchase was imminent, the mapping team looked at the sales process as addressing the customer question "How do I get the car I want?" The mappers concluded that there were three discrete phases within this fairly compressed (approximately one week) portion of the customer journey: (1) deciding from whom to buy the car, (2) figuring out how to pay for it, and (3) purchasing the vehicle.

The much longer after-sales cycle (which covers the average lease term of approximately 36 months) served to answer two discrete customer questions, "How do I get the most out of the vehicle

I acquired?" and "Will I buy a Mercedes-Benz again?" During the postsale segment, customers moved through phases of getting to know the product, maintaining the vehicle, having the car serviced, and reflecting on their ownership experience.

As was true for the presale phase of the customer journey, the sales and after-sales map was enriched by a listing of all contact points, identification of moments of truth and places where the customer experienced pain, a review of all business processes and departments responsible for addressing customer needs at each contact point, and a thorough identification of customer thoughts, emotions, and priorities during each step of the journey.

With all that foundational work done, leaders on the Customer Experience team brought in Razorfish, a global brand marketing/digital performance media company, to help refine the map and produce a digital version of the brown-paper document that had enveloped the customer experience war room. The digital map could be easily distributed and would allow the viewer to see the entire presale-to-postsale customer journey laid out on the width of a computer screen. Do you have a similar tool at your disposal that allows you to see your customer's entire journey on a single piece of paper or a single computer page view?

Simplification and Clarity

The digital map had been built, but could Mercedes-Benz use it effectively? Unlike the memorable line from the movie *Field of Dreams*, "If you build it, they will come," the senior leaders didn't assume that a detailed customer experience map sent out via e-mail or posted on the company's intranet would magically lead to improvements in the customer experience or a cultural shift toward greater customer-centricity. In fact, the creation of the digital map was only an early step in fulfilling the promise to "define" every brand touchpoint. The map first had to be understandable and understood!

Leaders at Mercedes-Benz USA had spent months painstakingly putting themselves in the position of the customer, and the detailed nature of the resulting customer journey map was both its strength and its weakness. Harry Hynekamp, general manager of the Customer Experience team, notes, "Don't get me wrong; the map was great. But it didn't take long for us to realize we wouldn't be able to use it internally. We had a map that would delight a Ph.D.-level customer experience designer, but how could Mercedes-Benz Financial Services, the parts logistics team, the field people, and our dealers actually make sense of all the information depicted? The map was spot on and rich in detail, but it was overwhelming. In military terms, we were outrunning our supply lines. We had to decomplexify the map if we were going to get the entire organization to wrap their hearts and minds around the customer's perspective." Unlike many leaders, who create elegant flowcharts, maps, and other tools that both bedazzle and befuddle their followers, the leaders at MBUSA saw the people who needed to use the touchpoint tools as their customers and, as a result, sought to simplify the presentation so that people could both understand and improve the customer experience.

While senior leaders still refer to the detailed customer journey map for strategic purposes, by the end of 2012, the Customer Experience team needed a way to cull the essence of the journey so that every individual in the organization would have a working knowledge of the customer's perspective. To help translate the map into usable language, the Customer Experience team turned to a leader who had piloted much of the customer strategic planning processes outlined in Chapter 3: Gareth Joyce, vice president customer services for Mercedes-Benz USA.

As they met in late 2012, the partnership between Gareth's division and the mapping team had an added sense of urgency, as a

National Parts & Service Managers Meeting was scheduled to be held at the Mercedes-Benz Superdome in New Orleans in March 2013. That event, which is held in alternate years, would bring together approximately 1,000 leaders and vendors responsible for parts and service at MBUSA and across the dealership network. The theme of the 2013 meeting was the Mercedes-Benz customer experience. A usable customer journey map was essential for the event's success.

While the team was looking for ways to simplify the digital journey map, Gareth went to a whiteboard and drew a circle. With the complex journey map as context, he depicted four quadrants of the circle as reflecting the customer's after-sales journey. Gareth notes, "As I was standing at that board, I thought about the phases our customers move through when they need our services. I started with customers sorting through options to determine with whom they will do business. Then I moved to a phase where the customer presents to a dealership, hoping they made the right choice. From there, customers want to be taken care of flawlessly, and they ultimately hope to drive away from their time at our dealerships feeling not only that their car was taken care of but that they were taken care of in a memorable and positive way." From Gareth's creative spark, a simplified customer experience wheel was fine-tuned (see Figure 4.1). That tuning involved taking the four quadrants that Gareth had initially suggested, finding the essence of the customer's need in each area of the interaction, and selecting words that would best describe those four overarching areas of the after-sales customer journey.

In its finalized form, the service wheel was color-coded to show a customer journey going through four stages, starting with "Win the Business" (red) and progressing through "Start on the Right Foot" (blue), "Keep Your Promises" (green), and "Create Lasting Memories" (yellow). (Please go to www.driventodelight.com /journeywheels to view the color-coded versions of the customer

Figure 4.1 Service Experience

journey wheels.) The wheel also included key touchpoints for each stage of the service journey described later in this chapter.

The customer service wheel visually depicts the journey from the customer's perspective. Additionally, the wheel uses approachable language that is easy to relate to so that individuals at Mercedes-Benz USA and Mercedes-Benz dealerships can quickly understand the behaviors and processes needed if they are to succeed during the four important phases of the service journey. In essence, the wheels help individuals throughout Mercedes-Benz USA and Mercedes-Benz dealerships truly understand what it takes to help a customer get "started on the right foot." For example, each individual representing Mercedes-Benz can understand how customers want to be greeted as they drive into the service lane, have their needs assessed quickly and thoroughly, receive an accurate and understandable estimate, and be efficiently returned to other aspects of their busy lives (whether that means using Wi-Fi in the service lounge, having a loaner vehicle ready for them, or securing a complimentary ride to their desired location).

The utility and clarity of the service wheel was reviewed widely at Mercedes-Benz USA headquarters, and was validated by its smashing success at the National Parts & Service Managers Meeting in March 2013. In fact, the entire event was organized around the customer service experience, oriented by the four colored sectors of the journey wheel. According to Cai-Marc Ramhorst, department manager product management parts at MBUSA, "We basically built the wheel on the floor of the exposition hall in the Mercedes-Benz Superdome, and all of our meetings used the customer journey as our communication platform. Unlike a typical meeting of this nature, which often focuses on business updates and strategic objectives, that National Parts & Service Managers Meeting represented a fundamental shift in understanding our business and in seeing how our customer encounters us. From the onset, that meeting immersed participants in the customer journey and linked the customer journey to the key performance indicators that drive after-sales revenue in the dealership. The event received rave reviews and has had a huge impact on participants. The wheel was the linchpin."

That wheel was the linchpin for far more than the success of the National Parts & Service Managers Meeting. From the perspective of senior leaders like Gareth Joyce, the wheel also represented a critical "aha" moment concerning the importance of taking a "user-centric" approach to communication and tool development. When it came to aligning, rallying, planning, and implementing actions across all Mercedes-Benz USA stakeholders, communications and tools had to be elegantly simple. They had to demonstrate a sincere desire to inspire and enable action by those for whom the tools were designed.

Given the success of the after-sales wheel, detailed presales and sales journey maps were also translated into a wheel format. For example, the original presales map had customer thoughts, stages, an interconnected set of business touchpoints, arrows, and depic-

Figure 4.2 Presales Experience

tions of circular processes, along with a list of defined business opportunities. In contrast, the presales wheel defined the three stages of the buyer's presale journey as "Awareness" (red), "Consideration" (blue), and "Intent" (yellow). The wheel then depicted the important touchpoints for each stage.

The Presales and Sales Journey

The presales wheel (see Figure 4.2) clearly and efficiently depicts the customer's movement from exploration to the formation of purchase intent and allows marketers to concentrate their efforts to satisfy prospective buyers' wants and needs during the key phases of that movement. Mark Aikman, former department manager digital marketing & CRM, notes, "The presales wheel helped us articulate how the marketing department brings a customer into the sales process or the dealership. The wheel also gives us the opportunity to take something like word-of-mouth marketing and determine whether we are doing enough to deliver a Mercedes-Benz experience."

Mark notes that the automobile industry, like so many other sectors, needs to appreciate how customers are changing and redesign its prepurchase tools in the context of those changes: "We're seeing two major shifts inside the auto purchasing process. The first is the role of the digital platform in the shopping process. In 2006, the average car shopper went to 4.3 dealerships. In 2010, that number was down to 1.3 dealerships. If you look at it from the customers' perspective, they are not walking into a showroom to kick the tires or be handed a brochure by a salesperson, then go home, sit at their kitchen table, and try to figure out which car is right for them. Instead, the customers are going online, doing their research, and essentially walking into a dealership ready to buy. In addition, a lot of that shopping experience is actually happening more on our customers' mobile devices than on their desktop. For us, being in a high-consideration category with a lot of information and technology features inside of our vehicles, we needed to look at the phases of the wheel associated with online and mobile to ensure that we provided an optimal mobile and digital shopping experience."

When customers do enter dealerships to engage that part of the sales journey, the original, detailed customer journey map had identified 23 separate segments with feedback loops to the presales phase. The sales wheel (see Figure 4.3), in contrast, streamlined the customer's journey through the sales process into four phases: "Create a Memorable First Impression" (red), "Champion Customer Needs" (blue), "Create Peace of Mind" (green), and "Create Lasting Memories" (yellow). Each of those four phases included two or three important touchpoints.

With the finalization of the three wheels, the Customer Experience team had truly fulfilled the promise of defining every

Figure 4.3 Sales Experience

touchpoint in the customer journey. In addition to demonstrating that promises matter to the Mercedes-Benz leaders (and, in so doing, building trust throughout the organization), completion of the wheels and the customer journey map enabled everyone to see the entire end-to-end customer journey from the customer's perspective. Additionally, leaders began introducing the wheels to all stakeholder groups. With these tools in hand, the organization was ready to elevate touchpoints across the customer journey and look for opportunities to delight Mercedes-Benz customers in ways they had never been delighted before.

Whether it is a rudimentary paper-and-pencil effort, a vendor-guided digital version, or a simplified customer experience wheel, you can look at and visually present the customer journey in a way that makes the customer's perspective accessible to your team members. In so doing, you demonstrate to them that the specific services they are delivering are part of a larger set of interactions for the customer. Depiction of the customer journey can also serve as a series of thought starters for ideas that will not only improve transactional service but streamline your overall customer journey. Most important, the map lays the foundation for developing new processes and routines when caring for your customers.

For the customer wheels at Mercedes-Benz USA to fully offer the enterprisewide return anticipated based on the sizable amount of time investment dedicated to their creation, training based on the wheels would also have to enhance the entire organization's empathy for customers' needs. In addition, the wheels would have to offer insights into when and how to ask customers about the experiences that they received, and the feedback that was obtained would have to be able to be translated into meaningful customer-centric action. For example, is Mercedes-Benz getting started on the right foot with service customers? How are dealerships doing at greeting customers upon arrival in the service lane? How accurately and effectively are needs being identified upon a customer's arrival?

As you will see in the upcoming chapter, building the right "voice-of-the customer" listening tool at MBUSA required a learning curve through which leaders had to strengthen the organization's competency at collecting and quickly acting upon customer experience feedback. In addition, the success of the measurement tool that MBUSA sought to develop would depend upon the full commitment of the leaders at Mercedes-Benz dealerships. In essence, those dealers would have to be willing to be measured, in large part, by the feedback provided through the customer listening tool. The journey to create important tools in the dealership's customer experience tool kit—the Mercedes-Benz Customer Experience Program and the Customer Experience Indexes—awaits you in Chapter 5.

KEYS TO DRIVING DELIGHT

➤ Invest the time and effort to blueprint or map your customer's journey. In the words of G. Lynn Shostack, this will help "cut down the time and inefficiency of random service development."

➤ Start from the customer's perspective and analyze your brand throughout the customer's journey. What question, problem, or need is the customer attempting to have resolved at each step in the journey?

➤ Dive into details concerning what your customers are thinking, feeling, and doing throughout their journey with you. Define the high-value moments, the pain points in the journey, and your opportunities to delight your customers.

➤ Be willing to "decomplexify" the details of your customer journey map. Craft a conceptual and visual model of the customer journey that is easily understood and embraced by every individual in your organization.

➤ Don't be content to have a picture of the customer experience. See the objective of mapping the customer journey as driving a cultural shift in customer empathy, offering a framework to understand customer needs, and providing a tool to look for opportunities to refine and elevate the experience that you deliver to every customer, every time.

➤ View the customer journey map as a way to position important questions to your customer about the quality of the experience you are providing. Ask your customers to provide input on their experience based on the key phases and touchpoints identified during the mapping process.

➤ The customer journey map should not be used for "one and done" training. Repeated conversations about service and experience delivery should be framed within the conceptual framework of the customer journey.

Measure what is measurable, and make

measurable what is not so.

—Galileo Galilei

cies but it must also represent the po ... d the
en to **delight**. it is not just a phrase. it is ... prom
lief. it is a **commitment** to creating po ... onshi
iaking people smile and to leaving th ... ense
plete **trust**. driven to **delight** means e ... perso
ment. it is a reminder that the journey ... one. t
e is always a more **thoughtful** wav. ar ... ut ea

5

Measuring Customer Experience: The Voice of the Customer as a Tool for Change

I n order to deliver the complete tool kit necessary to fulfill the final promise of "The Standard"—to train and equip every employee at every dealership—the MBUSA leaders needed to create an effective and consistent way to capture customer feed-back. With the right customer listening tool in place, leaders at a Mercedes-Benz dealership could evaluate how effectively they

en to **delight** means **exceptional** personal treatment. it i
nder that the journey is never done. that the ... s alway
e **thoughtful** way. and throughout each interaction we

79

were meeting customers' needs and make targeted changes to address those needs even more effectively.

Leveraging the voice of your customer is difficult. Most businesses don't ask their customers for enough information or ask at poorly timed intervals. Other companies ask too frequently and annoy their customers with constant in-depth surveys. In either case, it is often unclear how the customer feedback is used (if it is used at all) on behalf of the customer who provided the information. Successful listening to customers often starts with the type of customer journey mapping used by Mercedes-Benz USA and described in Chapter 4. The next step, which is described in this chapter, involves the creation of assessment and feedback instruments that are sensitive to positive and negative changes in your customers' perceptions. Such tools allow your business to not only respond to an individual respondent's needs but also make effective improvements in your customer experience.

While a subgroup of the MBUSA Customer Experience team was hunkered down in the customer experience war room, surrounded by various versions of the customer experience map and/or customer journey wheels, another group was addressing the question of how to measure the voice of the Mercedes-Benz USA customer. As with many other product-focused brands, listening to customers had *not* been a core competency at Mercedes-Benz USA. Before the MBUSA leadership set its course toward delivering a world-class customer experience, dealers were required to send out a customer satisfaction program (CSP) survey two days after a sales or service event. The items on the questionnaire were diagnostic in nature and were designed to help the dealer resolve any lingering customer issues. Customers who responded to the CSP received a brief follow-up survey approximately three weeks later, referred to as the Mercedes-Benz Loyalty Index (MBLI). The MBLI quickly assessed whether the customers were satisfied with their sales or service experience, and whether they were likely to return to and refer others in the direction of that Mercedes-Benz dealer. If the customer did not respond to the initial brief survey, instead of receiving the follow-up loyalty index, he would receive a more lengthy survey instrument. That questionnaire would essentially mimic the J.D. Power survey. In all cases, the results of these different measurement tools were difficult to compare with one another, track, or leverage to elevate customers' experience.

Similarly, information gained from customer satisfaction research conducted by independent third-party studies such as Pied Piper, American Customer Satisfaction Index, and J.D. Power and Associates is useful at a brand level but offers limited utility when it comes to crafting or improving the overall customer experience at individual Mercedes-Benz dealerships. Typically these studies produce divergent results and represent lagging indicators of a company's overall customer experience.

From the standpoint of conflicting results for Mercedes-Benz, in the 2012 time frame during which the Customer Experience team was mapping the customer journey, Pied Piper ranked Mercedes-Benz number one on its Prospect Satisfaction Index (PSI). The PSI links mystery shopping data to metrics of sales success. On another national measure of customer experience, the American Customer Satisfaction Index, which is also the only study that standardizes methods and assesses satisfaction across industries, Mercedes-Benz ranked seventh in the automobile category. When compared to other luxury manufacturers on the well-known J.D. Power surveys, Mercedes-Benz ranked seventh in service and sixth in sales experience. Each of these metrics provided a moment-in-time snapshot of customer satisfaction—albeit a somewhat confusing one—and did little to help an individual dealership deliver an outstanding experience for the next customer who was about to walk through the doors.

For example, one survey conducted by J.D. Power focuses on sales satisfaction (referred to as the Sales Satisfaction Index, or SSI) and the other on customer service satisfaction (titled the Customer Service Index, or CSI). The J.D. Power Sales Satisfaction Index Study was designed to offer a thorough view of customers' perceptions of the new vehicle purchase process. It is intended to show how dealerships execute all aspects of the sale, and it measures satisfaction among both new-vehicle buyers (buyer score) and those who shop a dealership or brand and purchase elsewhere (rejector score). Combining the buyer and rejector scores and weighting them equally produces an overall SSI score. Useful information can be derived from the SSI as it relates to:

- Why customers visit and purchase from a given dealer

- Factors that drive the purchase of a specific model

- Reasons why customers fail to purchase from a dealership

- The time customers spend at different points in the sales process

- The effectiveness of the salesperson and other dealership staff

- How well a vehicle is presented at delivery

- The likelihood that a customer will repurchase from and advocate for a specific dealer

Similarly, the J.D. Power Customer Service Index Study assesses the satisfaction of vehicle owners who bring their vehicles into a dealer's service department for maintenance or repair during the first three years of ownership. The overall CSI score is based on aggregate measures of the service experience, including:

- Service initiation (including timeliness at vehicle drop-off, ease of service appointment scheduling, and flexibility of scheduling)

- Service advisor (courteousness, explanation thoroughness, and responsiveness)

- Service facility (waiting area comfort, parking convenience, ease of entrance and exit, amenities, cleanliness)

- Vehicle pickup (speed of retrieval, helpfulness during pickup, and fairness of charges)

- Quality of service (completeness of work, service time, condition upon return)

While a great deal can be learned from the CSI and SSI surveys, most of their benefit comes from benchmarking manufacturers against their competitors through numerical (although not necessarily statistically significant) rankings in either the luxury or the mass automotive segment. In addition to the industry rankings, J.D. Power awards are given to the brands that deliver the highest-rated sales and service experiences. Those awards are prominent customer-facing recognitions that afford bragging rights and fodder for marketing messages to prospective consumers. As such, J.D. Power awards and rankings matter to leaders and customers in every sector in which they are granted, including the automotive sector. J.D. Power awards essentially validate customer experience excellence.

The J.D. Power surveys offer important data within the industry; however, they, like the other third-party surveys and rankings mentioned, must be viewed as describing a moment in time in the dynamic experience of customers. For example, the CSI survey results are gleaned from the responses of approximately 3,700 Mercedes-Benz owners, who are sent surveys in the months of October through December regarding service carried out during the previous 12 months. Similarly, the SSI surveys mailed in the months of April and May represent a minuscule percentage of the sales visitors to a given dealership. In fact, small Mercedes-Benz dealerships may have responses from only a handful of customers, while larger dealerships may see 15 to 20 customer responses. To put this sample size into perspective, a large Mercedes-Benz dealership may sell upwards of 5,000 new vehicles in a year. Additionally, since manufacturers and dealerships are aware of the timing of the surveys (and know the possible competitive impact of the rankings), the manufacturer can give its dealerships incentives to alter their processes in an attempt to drive performance during the survey period. Additionally, the manufacturer can adjust equipment packages and pricing during these periods. These alterations essentially can create an atypical sales or service offering during the J.D. Power survey windows.

In addition, the lengthy nature of the paper-and-pencil survey that J.D. Power has traditionally used creates lowered response rates, while the time between data collection and data reporting limits the real-world utility of the results when it comes to making timely course corrections. In the case of the CSI, a customer could have received service in December 2011, been surveyed in October 2012, and had her results included in a report released in March 2013—15 months later! Similarly, the SSI data collected in the April/May time frame is reported the following November. Thus, while data collected by third-party companies can provide insights, truly understanding the quality of the customer experiences that your company is delivering may require the development of your own tracking tool that aligns with your customer journey and key performance indicators. The critical element in creating an effective measurement tool involves real-time assessment of your customer's satisfaction at key moments in his journey with your brand. These measures often start out being very transactional in nature (for example, how did we do at greeting you upon arrival?) but ultimately shed light on service moments that are most salient to the customers when they gauge the overall health of their relationship with your brand, as well as their likelihood of repurchasing and making referrals on your behalf.

The limits of third-party metrics were the driving impetus that led the Customer Experience team at Mercedes-Benz USA to develop a proprietary customer feedback tool that would gather input in real time. The leaders sought a measurement instrument and process that could assess baseline satisfaction at all the key contact points delineated in the sales and after-sales customer journey wheels. They also wanted a steady stream of customer information that would enable dealerships to respond quickly to specific concerns of individuals and more broadly add to the "refinements" envisioned by Steve Cannon in "The Standard." If done well, the newly created metrics and processes would also prove helpful in addressing the types of factors that contribute to success on external metrics such as the annual J.D. Power and Associates surveys.

Seeking a Strong Partner

Early in the process of exploring customer surveying options, the leaders at Mercedes-Benz USA concluded they would benefit from the expertise of a company with a track record of providing enterprisewide solutions that could take customer listening to the next level. They were looking for a partner that had a customer experience management (CEM) background extending beyond the automobile industry and that could facilitate the comparison of MBUSA customer experience data with data from high performers in other industries.

Upon tendering a request for proposals in August 2012, the Customer Experience team vetted qualified suppliers and chose Medallia, a customer experience management software company that had worked with clients like Apple, Nike, Fidelity, Verizon, and Four Seasons. Medallia brought a comprehensive package of solutions designed to administer and analyze surveys and react to the information. Leaders at Mercedes-Benz USA understood that they needed more than just a survey tool; those can be found online at a very low cost through companies like Survey Monkey. Rather, they needed the ability to collect survey responses and effectively get data into a customer experience management system that allowed the data to be used and leveraged quickly to help individual customers and make effective process improvements.

Upon selecting Medallia in October 2012, the Customer Experience team was given an aggressive target start date for deploying the yet-to-be created instrument—some four short months later, in February 2013. As you will see throughout the book, the Mercedes-Benz leaders often deliberately create urgency by setting timelines that stretch but don't overwhelm their staff. This leadership skill should not be overlooked, as it is clearly a component of the energy that fueled progress on the Mercedes-Benz transformation journey. In essence, it is in keeping with American composer Leonard Bernstein's observation that "To achieve great things, two things are needed; a plan, and not quite enough time." The Customer Experience team forged its plan and delivered the tool on time.

As Gareth Joyce, vice president customer services at Mercedes-Benz USA, was helping the mapping team simplify the customer experience map into the first customer experience wheel in anticipation of the March 2013 National Parts & Service Managers Meeting, Medallia was working with members of the Customer Experience team to develop MBUSA's approach to customer experience management: the Customer Experience Program (CEP) and the attendant sales and service metrics, or Customer Experience Indexes (CEIs). The areas of customer inquiry addressed in the sales and service CEIs align directly with the phases of the customer journey wheels. For example, the service CEI is a cumulative score based on responses to questions about satisfaction with key transactions at each phase of the journey depicted in the service wheel. Specifically, the CEI measures how effectively the dealership's service department has been able to "Win the Business," "Start on the Right Foot," "Keep <Its> Promises," and "Create Lasting Memories." Individuals at Medallia worked with the Customer Experience team to determine not only what questions should be asked but also the relevant weight that should be given to each area of the journey in relation to the customer's overall perceived experience.

Using the service journey as an example, you can see here how the Customer Experience team built the areas of inquiry and weights for components of the experience into the CEI and how the entire assessment links directly to the phases and touchpoints of the service wheel. Whether you are running a mom-and-pop dry cleaner, a midsized company, or a multinational business, effective customer listening requires a detailed understanding of the customer journey, an estimate of the relative impact of high-value touchpoints in that journey, and a disciplined process for consistently capturing and documenting customer feedback as it relates to your performance at key interactions.

Win the Business

Repair Selection Factors

Ease of driving in and out of the dealership (3.2%)

Ease of parking at the dealership (3.2%)

Overall cleanliness and appearance of the dealership (3.36%)

Dealer waiting room (6.24%)

Dealer Contact

Simplicity of scheduling appointment (7.26%)

Dealer's ability to accommodate your schedule (5.72%)

Start on the Right Foot

Identifies Needs

Courtesy and respect of the service advisor (7.91%)

Vehicle Check-in

Drop-off process (9.02%)

Keep Your Promises

Vehicle Repair

Attentiveness and fulfillment of requests (3.42%)

Thoroughness of maintenance/repair (12.18%)

Status Update

Ability to keep service within time estimate (8.7%)

Create Lasting Memories

Predelivery

Thorough explanation of work (6.67%)

Fairness of charges (4.2%)

Vehicle Pickup

Pickup process (5.55%)

Helpfulness of staff at pickup (5.25%)

Condition of vehicle (8.12%)

In addition to the range of questions presented to customers to generate the Mercedes-Benz service index (CEI service), the dealership's ability to meet specific existing service standards was also evaluated through a series of diagnostic questions:

- Time waited to speak to a service advisor (target: within 2 minutes)

- Time it took to get into alternative transportation (target: within 5 minutes)

- Did the service advisor keep you informed of the status of your vehicle?

- Was all of the authorized work completed right the first time?

- After service, did somebody explain the actual work performed?

- After service, did somebody provide a thorough explanation of charges?

- Total time to complete pickup process (target: within 6 minutes)

- Vehicle delivered back to the customer cleaner than it was dropped off?

- Were you contacted via phone or e-mail after service was completed?

The aggregate CEI creates a maximum possible score of 1,000 for each customer; average customer scores are provided in a dashboard that can be accessed online and via a mobile application by both dealers and MBUSA associates.

The maximum score and score range of the CEI allow for comparisons with the J.D. Power Customer Service Index. The CEI produces a cumulative score that can be compared loosely to the J.D. Power CSI. While the tools are not identical, they measure similar aspects of the customer journey. The CEI tool's ongoing data collection provides trend indicators that signal "likely" performance on the annual J.D. Power CSI study. Results can also be examined in the context of each specific phase of the customer journey and its corresponding touchpoints, as well as by individual items involved in measuring the touchpoints. In addition, the data can be analyzed at the dealership level, with specific sections directly corresponding to specific individuals or areas within the dealership. For example, one dealership can be compared to another based on the overall CEI, relative strengths in winning the business, and ability to keep time estimates, while an individual service advisor could be compared to other service advisors with regard to performance on items such as "keeping customers informed of the status of their vehicles." Over time, the summary data of responses was enhanced to include qualitative data, such as "verbatim" or free-form customer responses, such as these positive reviews received at Mercedes-Benz of Virginia Beach:

> Very nice service agent Carl puts my needs first, has a rental ready for me, and I am in and out in less than 15 minutes.

> Jeff has a pleasant professional character. It's a pleasure having him as my Service Advisor. I really appreciated the itemized price list of services under the A/B Maintenance checklist that he gave me as a reference to the services I might need. I feel at home in the guest lounge :-) Keep up the awesome service, MB of Virginia Beach!

> Great experience at pickup. . . . I had called ahead and let the cashier know I wanted to purchase an item from the gift shop, and she had it waiting for me! I just had to grab the bag and go.

> I was very impressed when the service advisor walked me to my vehicle parked in front of the building and discussed

with me the repairs and asked if I had any questions.
Well Done.

Other verbatim comments reflect opportunities to continue to elevate the customer experience, including the processes by which information is solicited:

> This has to do with this survey and the fact of having to answer all questions even when you may not have used that part of the dealership; example—I drop my car off and leave; I do not use the customer waiting area Wi-Fi, etc; how can I rate something I don't use? Please fix this.

A similar customer feedback tool, the sales CEI, was also created in alignment with the phases and key touchpoints depicted in the sales wheel. For example, in the Create Lasting Memories phase of the sales journey, in the section of the wheel labeled "Take Delivery," the customer feedback tool included questions asking the customer to rate how effectively the vehicle's features were explained, the amount of time spent during delivery, whether an overview and an introduction to the service department was made, whether technology like an iPad or tablet was used during the delivery process, and a series of other related questions. Such was the case for all other components of a customer's sales journey.

In addition to aligning the newly evolving sales and service CEI tools to the customer experience journey map and wheels, Harry Hynekamp, general manager of the Mercedes-Benz USA Customer Experience team, notes, "We primarily wanted the tool to measure our customer experience and allow us to make real-time improvements, but we also wanted to be number one in customer experience on metrics like the J.D. Power survey as well as ACSI, Pied Piper, and others. So we thematically incorporated some of the questions from these surveys into our internal CEI instruments."

As the CEI was being created and the technological infrastructure was being installed throughout Mercedes-Benz USA and the dealership community, the process of surveying customers was also being defined. Ultimately, it was determined that Mercedes-Benz USA customers would receive the newly created CEI surveys 15 days after purchasing a vehicle and 10 days after having a vehicle serviced. These time intervals were chosen so that dealers had ample opportunity to take care of any unresolved customer needs before a scored survey was sent out. The timetable also offers customers the opportunity to accurately answer questions like "Was all of the authorized work completed right the first time?" When the prior Customer Satisfaction Program (CSP) survey was received 48 hours after a service event, customers might not have had enough driving time to answer such a question accurately.

While the CEI survey is sent out at 15 days for sales and 10 days for service events, dealers typically follow up directly with customers within 48 hours. This outreach serves three important functions: (1) to thank customers for their business and demonstrate proper follow-up and caring, (2) to identify any immediate or unresolved needs, and (3) to alert customers that the CEI survey will be forthcoming from MBUSA. A key aspect of the overall customer relationship management strategy deployed by MBUSA was providing dealers with easy access to information about communication between their dealership, MBUSA, and the customer. They receive service alerts when customers require attention and can escalate issues to different departments to make sure that the customers receive the care that they need. Michael Dougherty, who was the department manager customer experience metrics & insights during the creation of the customer relationship management tools, notes, "An early follow-up communication message lets the customer know that we want to make sure we didn't miss anything. If they tell us they want to be contacted, we ask, 'Do you want sales or service to call you? What's the best time to reach you?

Please provide us with some information about your situation.' The customer's response is routed back through the customer relationship management tool and gets fully integrated. Alerts are generated to management to say somebody just raised their hand and they need your assistance. We have alerts dashboards that guide a timely and appropriate follow-up response." In a published Mercedes-Benz USA case study, Medallia notes, "Mercedes-Benz USA needed a solution with core 'off-the-shelf' business intelligence capabilities, but also flexible enough to develop and map to the unique organization of a dealership model. Furthermore, the company wanted a true enterprise solution and a team willing to creatively tackle the specific requirements of the automotive industry. . . . Customized dashboards engage dealers by presenting them with the right and relevant information to manage experiences and to close the loop immediately with customers. . . . With mobile reporting, dealers can connect with actionable customer data on the go, crucial for a proactive dealer who is rarely bound to a desktop. . . . Medallia also worked with Mercedes-Benz USA to develop a multi-step, closed-loop program designed to engage with customers about issues before it's too late."

Steve Earwaker, vice president at Medallia, shares an experience that demonstrates the cutting-edge effectiveness of the Mercedes-Benz customer experience program. A representative of another automobile manufacturer was visiting Steve to explore the possibility of hiring Medallia to create a customer feedback tool for that brand. Steve was struck by how much the prospect knew about Medallia's offerings, so he asked the potential customer how he had learned so much about the company. The prospect shared that he had been visiting a friend, and his host, a Mercedes-Benz owner, showed him an e-mail he had just received from his Mercedes-Benz dealership. The e-mail contained a quick pulse feedback question asking if the service work completed earlier that day had been to the customer's satisfaction. As it turned out, the dealership hadn't checked a backseat seatbelt issue, so the host simply clicked "no" in response to the question. According to Steve, "My prospective client shared that not even 10 minutes later, his host received a phone call from the Mercedes-Benz service manager asking if he could come over to my friend's home and immediately address the seatbelt issue. He said, 'When that happened, I knew I had to find out what was going on there. How could such a response be possible? I knew if I could get my dealers, my dealer managers, and my service managers to embrace customer feedback that sincerely, that quickly, and react that appropriately, it would transform our brand the way it has for Mercedes-Benz.'" Are you delivering that kind of responsive service experience? What are your customers sharing about you with their dinner guests?

Cases in which recurring immediate requests for follow-up are received shortly after purchase or service are viewed by Mercedes-Benz USA leaders as opportunities for targeted training. For example, if a number of sales customers from a specific dealership say that they want someone from the service department to contact them regarding the use of their navigation system, management can identify a systematic problem in the actual delivery of the vehicle. As a result, dealership-level management can reemphasize delivery staff training that will allow them to educate new owners on their navigation system in ways that serve to reduce the confusion those customers are experiencing shortly after driving off the lot.

Future chapters will address additional tools and training that Mercedes-Benz USA provides to dealerships in keeping with the final promise of "The Standard." However, for the purpose of this discussion, suffice it to say that the CEI surveys and the integrated customer experience management process (CEP) created at Mercedes-Benz USA offer robust and powerful data that can be used at the corporate office, by the field teams, and at the dealership level.

At the 2014 Mercedes-Benz National Dealer Meeting, CEO Steve Cannon reflected on the strides the company had made in its ability to gather and learn from the voice of the customer, noting that the CEI "tool has gotten feedback from 600,000 service customers and 200,000 sales customers since its inception." The timely and actionable responses of those 600,000 service customers are far more valuable, from an operational perspective, than the 3,700 J.D. Power CSI surveys collected during the same period. Similarly, it takes a regularly acquired and large data set like that collected from sales customers in response to the sales CEI to garner insights that can guide process changes and training.

While the Mercedes-Benz customer experience indexes provide an important view of the experiences of sales and service customers, leaders at Mercedes-Benz USA understand that customer experience success is not about numbers on a feedback instrument. To be a customer experience leader, Mercedes-Benz USA—or any business, for that matter—will have to use metrics as a yardstick and catalyst for action. Numbers, by themselves, should not be confused with customer intelligence. For data to be valuable, it has to be analyzed in a way that makes it leverageable customer knowledge. While the adage might say that "knowledge is power," your well-analyzed customer knowledge is only as good as the action you take on it.

At Mercedes-Benz USA, the effective use of data was achieved when dealers were aligned with the customer experience and accountable for using and driving improvements through that program. The tools needed to achieve alignment, commitment, and accountability at the dealership level are the focus of the chapter ahead.

➤ It pays to measure your baseline customer experience carefully prior to launching new customer experience initiatives.

➤ While data collected by third-party companies can provide insights into the customer experience you are delivering, it is often difficult to discern what will help you deliver great experiences day in and day out.

➤ Survey management is not the same as customer experience management. Strong external partners can customize "off-the-shelf" integrated customer listening, reporting, and tracking systems to assess the specific customer journey(s) you are providing.

➤ In measuring the voice of the customer to assess the strengths of your customer experience delivery, it is important to assess the relative importance or weight of various components of the delivery.

➤ Drive progress toward elevated customer experience by artfully setting timelines that stretch but don't overwhelm your staff. Remember the wisdom of Leonard Bernstein, when he noted, "To achieve great things, two things are needed; a plan, and not quite enough time."

➤ Solid customer management systems collect large quantities of customer feedback (both quantitative and qualitative). That data can be readily understood and leveraged both at a macro level to achieve process changes and at a micro level to address the needs of individual customers.

➤ Data collection is *not* the objective of effective customer listening. Translating the voice of the customer into aligned and accountable customer-focused action is the goal!

Teamwork is the ability to work together toward

a common vision. The ability to direct individual

accomplishments toward organizational

objectives. It is the fuel that allows common

people to attain uncommon results.

—Andrew Carnegie

Alignment, Accountability, and Tools for the Front Line

L et's assume that, like the leaders at Mercedes-Benz USA, you have carefully detailed your customers' journeys and translated those journeys into an understandable model for everyone involved in delivering customer care. Let's also assume that you have created a customer experience management system that converts the customer's voice into actionable intelligence and, more broadly, creates a platform for customer experience process improvements. How do you get those customer journey models and measurement tools into the hands of the front line? More important, how do you get everyone in your organization to embrace and be held accountable for the customer experience in the context of your journey maps and voice of the customer metrics?

If you are going to provide a world-class customer experience, everyone in your organization must understand and take responsibility for meeting and exceeding customer needs. Before launching the customer experience wheel and customer experience index tools at the dealerships, Mercedes-Benz USA needed to ensure that its business partners (the dealer principals) were fully willing to support and take responsibility for the success of the customer experience. As in every true partnership, where risk and reward are shared, the Mercedes-Benz USA leaders engaged in negotiated give-and-take discussions to secure an agreement with the principals/owners of the dealerships that would link their profitability to customer experience excellence (as measured by the customer experience index).

Whether it is an employer/employee, franchisor/franchisee, or distributor/dealer business model, gaining buy-in for performance measurement systems involves demonstrating the relevance of the items being measured to the well-being of the business. Buy-in also depends upon the person or persons being measured knowing that they can affect a positive outcome. Additionally, buy-in hinges on the fairness of the connection between performance levels and consequences and rewards. Without buy-in on a performance measurement system, employers may be able to hire, fire, and set performance criteria for employees, but they won't get maximum effort toward realizing the leaders' priorities.

In a distributor/dealer model like that of Mercedes-Benz USA and its dealer partners, the leadership has no control over dealership employees; MBUSA is legally bound by the franchise/dealership agreement when it comes to what can be "required" of dealership owners (and, by extension, their employees). MBUSA must negotiate changes and updates to dealer financial incentive packages with an elected group of dealer representatives (the Mercedes-Benz Dealer Board). To understand the process involved in the negotiations related to customer experience measurement and performance, it is helpful to look at the recent history of the dealership margin agreements forged by Mercedes-Benz USA.

Profit and Dealer Performance Margins

Since 2010, there have been two pivotal and transformational agendas put forward by the Mercedes-Benz USA leadership. As mentioned in Chapter 1, the first was the elevation of the physical environment of dealerships through the Autohaus program. The second was Steve Cannon's commitment to delivering a world-class customer experience as outlined in "The Standard." In each case, the MBUSA leaders went to the dealer body and negotiated financial terms that would propel the transformation forward.

Before I get into a discussion of the negotiated agreements between Mercedes-Benz USA and its dealer principals, I should highlight the inherent challenge involved in dealing with these types of financial issues. As is the case with most manufacturer/ distributor models or franchisor/franchisee arrangements, there are two separate business entities that rely on the revenues generated from customers. Often the franchisor and the franchisee both view the customer as being "theirs." In essence, the question is: Is the customer connected to the brand or to the local distributor of the brand? Furthermore, these arrangements pose challenges when determining how the manufacturer and the distributor should share the revenues derived from the customer. So as not to burden you with the details of the negotiations between Mercedes-Benz USA and its dealer principals, I will focus on how the resultant financial agreements propelled a transformation of the customer experience at the dealership level.

It should be noted, however, that the journey to the Mercedes-Benz USA agreements with its dealers has not always been smooth, nor was it a linear process (instead, progress was made, regression occurred, and then more progress was achieved). In these instances, leaders at Daimler AG, MBUSA's parent company, also had to agree with the financial terms. In general, change is hard for everyone. It implies that there must be something you are not doing well enough, so an altered path is needed. It also suggests that your life is going to be disrupted. It raises questions like: Will this disruption be purposeful? How will this new arrangement adversely affect me?

When money is involved, even more effort has to be exerted to keep all parties constructively moving forward, manage overt conflict, and quell passive resistance. Across all the changes identified in this book, and particularly in areas that directly affect the amount of money received by dealers, pushback occurs. Executives and employees become frustrated, the directions of the change initiatives are challenged, and meetings become contentious. In the end, when effective leaders present a compelling vision, craft solutions that are win/wins, and achieve a tipping point for buy-in, negotiated agreements are successful. Such has been the case for Mercedes-Benz USA and its dealer partners.

In 2012, MBUSA asked its dealers to connect a sizable component of their margin from the sale of a vehicle to customer-facing and experience-related performance criteria. Niles Barlow, general manager strategic retail development, notes, "The first line in the sand was drawn in the fall of 2007, when planning for the new Autohaus dealership facility concept was just under way. Historically, to comply with dealer franchise agreement terms, every dealership had to have a certain minimum square footage and minimum acreage, along with specific signage, or 'corporate identity,' as it is called. With regard to the architectural design of the facility and the look and feel inside and out, this was left up to the individual dealer and generally reflected his individual creativity and taste— what the dealer wanted, not necessarily what would appeal most to our customers. The result has been a menagerie of everything from Southwest Pueblo architecture to archaic urban showrooms to personal monuments. From a franchising perspective, it was controlled chaos, at best, and from our customers' perspective, nothing was recognizable in their travels across the country except perhaps a few common pylon signs and the three-pointed star."

The scope of the Autohaus transformation was daunting, with the objective being to have every Mercedes-Benz dealership in the United States either built anew or substantially renovated to meet a specific set of standards for space, flow, feel, function, facility design, furniture, signage, and other factors. The projected investment, estimated to be in excess of $1 billion, would occur in phases over a set number of years of design and construction, and while the dealers were still selling and servicing vehicles.

A template was tendered to the dealers by Mercedes-Benz USA, with 2008 being the planning year and 2009–2010 being the years during which Autohaus would be brought to life. The MBUSA proposal included a "historical ask" for dealers to meet the new Autohaus brand standards and other operational priorities in order to achieve a "dealer performance bonus," or margin. Niles notes, "The elements of the Autohaus initiative specifically included an 'accrual bonus,' set up by MBUSA, which rewarded every dealer who committed to and built an approved facility—a bonus of $400 per unit sold for calendar years 2008–2010. These dealers also received an additional allocation of vehicles commensurate with their investment, as well as help in supporting the anticipated sales volume increases the new stores would generate. The 2008–2010 dealer performance bonus margin system effectively focused the dealers on specific operational requirements as well as new brand standards. By installing operational necessities in the margin system, MBUSA had everyone's attention: the dealers, the MBUSA field teams, the headquarters folks—everyone knew exactly what the company's focus was to be for the next three years. We were all collectively focused on constructing new buildings, adding capacity, entering the pre-owned business feet first, and further penetrating the new vehicle market."

Through the performance bonus financial structure, each dealer could earn the full performance margin, but detailed thresholds tied operational excellence to the margin system in an unprecedented way. Scorecards were developed so that all dealers knew exactly where they stood on all the operational aspects within the margin. It was a groundbreaking, transparent, and straightforward approach to the business.

The dealer performance bonus and Autohaus were huge successes, driving over $1.6 billion of combined MBUSA and dealer capital improvement investment, all of which occurred in the midst of an economic recession. Michael Cantanucci, dealer principal of the New Country Motor Car Group, Inc., and a member of the Mercedes-Benz Dealer Board at the time of MBUSA's Autohaus initiative, notes, "The dealer performance bonus worked well. Mercedes-Benz USA had a well-thought-out strategy where they offered financial assistance to dealers who were willing to invest in Autohaus. It was tied into the margin, and Mercedes-Benz USA employed an effective approach to reward dealers for investing in the Autohaus facility program." Much of the success of the dealer performance bonus was a result of rewarding stores that excelled more than those that didn't, thus creating a stratification within the dealer network.

Niles Barlow explains how the dealer performance bonus also played into negotiations for elevating the customer experience by noting, "We have typically negotiated margins with the dealers in three-year increments. That gives them enough time to plan and run their businesses. Typically, changing the margin too quickly affects dealers disproportionately, as they have to change their compensation plans and the like. After the success of the Autohaus margin, we negotiated a new margin for 2011, which was supposed to be in place through 2013. However, when Steve Cannon became CEO in January 2012, he offered such a clear vision of the future that, in partnership with the Dealer Board, we renegotiated the margin in 2012 to align with all the elements of our customer experience initiative, particularly performance on the Medallia-aided CEP tool and the result of dealership employee engagement surveys. That margin structure was set in place for the period of 2013–2015." (More on employee engagement at dealerships in Chapter 7.)

Without getting into the details of the margin structure, it is important to understand that some of the negotiated dealer margin structure is fixed (not subject to the specific requirements of dealership performance) and some of it is variable, based upon criteria agreed to by the Dealer Board and Mercedes-Benz USA. In the renegotiated deal for 2013–2015, dealers agreed to shift about 30 percent of their fixed margin to variable, in order to enhance the portion attached to customer experience.

Harry Hynekamp, general manager customer experience, elaborates on the sizable portion of dealer margin that was directly linked to customer experience in the renegotiated deal: "Throughout 2012, there were many meetings between Mercedes-Benz USA leaders and Dealer Board members. It was this constant dialogue that secured a new margin structure that started January 1, 2013. Through that agreement, a sizable portion of the dealer margin structure was anchored to performance on customer experience standards, training that affects customer experience delivery, and use of the latest technologies and standards for customer care."

As is the case in any negotiation, Steve and his leadership team not only had to sell the customer experience vision to dealers but also had to "give to get." In the negotiations, Niles Barlow made a rather unusual offer, and Steve Cannon backed that offer with bold action. To "get" the shift of a sizable portion of the dealers' fixed margin into the variable customer performance–based column, Mercedes-Benz offered to "give" an all-new leadership bonus.

Michael Cantanucci explains the leadership bonus concept: "As dealers, we accepted that customer experience needed to be our focal point, but we had to put a percentage of our fixed margin at risk in order to support the customer experience transformation. As it turns out, a percentage of the variable margins typically were not paid out because some dealers did not meet the quarterly performance criteria. That unused money was considered 'breakage' and was historically retained by Mercedes-Benz USA. At Niles's suggestion, Steve went to Daimler headquarters in Stuttgart, Germany, to champion the idea of placing that breakage money in a pool to be distributed to dealers who performed the best in customer experience delivery. Stuttgart was convinced by Steve's case, and agreed that MBUSA could pay out the breakage money as a 'leadership bonus' to dealers who were achieving the highest levels of customer experience performance. That breakage money was tens of millions of dollars—a large amount for Daimler and Mercedes-Benz USA to give up." Michael continues, "The reliability of the fixed margin that dealers had received with no strings attached provided a comfort level. Making a change and giving that up in return for more performance metrics was concerning to the dealer body, but Mercedes-Benz USA's offer to pay out the breakage money was well received. It gave the dealers yet another reason to elevate their game and delight customers—so that they could participate in this extra profit source through the leadership bonus."

Whether you are negotiating with employees, unions, leaders, or distribution partners, a compelling vision, coupled with fair metrics and a willingness to make compromises for the greater good, consistently proves to be a formula for success. Niles Barlow succinctly describes the benefits derived from such an approach at Mercedes-Benz USA: "We really capitalized on having a very high-functioning Dealer Board. We used the word *co-creation* a lot. We co-created much of the aligned compensation and performance package. It's a lot about vision, openness, transparency, and an understanding that dealers want to make money first and sell cars second, whereas Mercedes-Benz USA wants to sell cars first and make money second. That may seem like a small nuance, but dealer profitability is absolutely key, and we needed to design that into the dealer margin."

The Mercedes-Benz USA leadership bonus is calculated at the end of every quarter. Each dealer is stack-ranked based on CEI performance, from the highest- to the lowest-performing dealer. Mercedes-Benz leaders draw a cut line around the 70th percentile on the CEP survey. So, the top-performing 70 percent of dealerships (who are also Autohaus-compliant and who meet brand standards and experience-related qualifiers) participate in the leadership bonus; the bottom 30 percent do not.

On April 15, 2014, Mercedes-Benz paid out $44 million in leadership bonuses to the top-performing 70 percent of dealerships in customer experience. Steve Cannon shares, "I am fine with people not sharing the benefits if they don't take care of their customers. The great news is the consistency and quality of customer experiences is improved and improving at small, medium, and large dealerships. Our dealer partners are paying attention, and the margin structure brings it home."

One of the foundational components of a successful customer-centric business is the ability to align rewards and compensation with the feedback received from customers. While it can be uncomfortable to think that customers will determine a portion of employees' compensation, it is becoming fairly well accepted that the voice of the customer and customer choice drive sustainable success. Whether it is "value-based purchasing" in healthcare, where insurance compensation is contingent in part on patient satisfaction, or the tip received by a server at a restaurant, the customer experience often dictates financial gain. Bold leaders, like Steve Cannon and those at Mercedes-Benz USA, are increasingly making similar links in their organizations. How about you?

Unlocking the Customer Wheels, CEI, and the Customer Experience Management System for Dealers

In Chapter 3, I deferred a discussion of the functional role of a number of members of the Metrics and Insights subteam within the Mercedes-Benz Customer Experience team. I noted that the role of these team members was inextricably linked with a powerful voice of the customer tool, which you now know is the Customer Experience Program (CEP). In fact, three individuals on the Mercedes-Benz Metrics and Insights team were responsible for launching the CEP sales and service survey platforms and are responsible for the ongoing training, deployment, execution, rules, and policies of the CEI tool, as well as connecting it to the dealer performance margin and leadership bonus. These team members not only oversee dealer scorecards but also link performance on the CEI to important KPIs for the brand.

For example, Tomas Hora, then general manager parts logistics, looked at the speed of inventory turns and found that those dealers who were most effective at parts inventory management also had higher scores on the CEP tool. Accordingly, Tomas looked for ways to improve inventory management throughout the dealership community, ultimately focusing on the creation of a new type of order, a "modified return policy," and relevant performance indicators associated with inventory and customer level fill rates, as well as proposing a new Dealer Inventory Management System. By using customer feedback data to guide inventory practices, Tomas was able to drive process changes, important business performance metrics, and ultimately further improvements in the CEP customer feedback tool itself. In essence, Tomas leveraged customer input to get the right parts to the right customer at the right time to achieve the best possible customer experience.

In addition to offering training on the customer experience wheels, the effective use of the CEP tool, and how to use other information generated through the customer experience program, Mercedes-Benz team members have developed Best Practice Guides to improve dealer performance on the sales and service CEIs (and ultimately on the J.D. Power SSI and CSI studies). Ellen Braaf, then MBUSA product manager after-sales service programs, after-sales business development, notes: "We used to say to dealers, 'You need to improve the customer experience,' but we didn't do a great job of telling them how to do it or what was in it for them. Now, based on the data from the CEI, we can cull the best practices that lead to significant increases in CEI performance. We can show how greeting a customer within two minutes can improve your result on metrics like the CEI or a J.D. Power survey by 130 points. Because we have the margin behind us, dealers can see that if they make small changes, or in some cases big changes, across multiple areas of the customer experience, the benefits for customers and for the financial well-being of the dealerships are significant."

The Sales and Service Best Practice Guides are detailed and specific to the important touchpoints that customers encounter throughout their journey. For the purpose of our discussion, I will give you a flavor of their content by highlighting a single best practice outlined in the Mercedes-Benz Sales Experience Best Practice Guide. From this example, you will see the tight linkage between the guide, the customer journey wheel, the Sales Customer Experience Index, and even projected performance on the J.D. Power Sales Satisfaction Index.

Best Practice 6 appears in the section of the guide that refers to the "Create Peace of Mind" phase of the sales customer journey wheel. It focuses on one critical touchpoint in establishing peace of mind—namely, the time involved in negotiating a vehicle's purchase price. Specifically, Best Practice 6 is "Completion of Negotiation in Less than 15 Minutes." In support of this best practice recommendation, the guide offers the following empirical information: "Based on the 2013 J.D. Power Sales Satisfaction Index results, a customer's overall satisfaction significantly decreases the longer the negotiation process takes, dropping 75 points when it takes 'more than 30 minutes' vs. 'less than 15 minutes.'" The guide also graphically depicts the impact of protracted negotiations (see Figure 6.1).

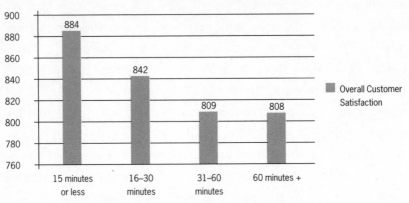

Overall time spent negotiating

Figure 6.1 Overall Time Spent Negotiating,
Taken from MBUSA's Sales Experience Best Practice Guide

The Best Practice Guide goes on to look at the questions on the Mercedes-Benz Customer Experience Index (CEI) that relate to negotiation length (for example, respect for the value of your time) and reminds the reader that at the dealership a customer's response to these types of questions has a sales CEI impact equivalent to 6.93 percent of the total survey. In a nutshell, if you develop processes that keep negotiation time under 15 minutes, you will delight your customers, drive CEI results, advance toward earning the dealer performance and leadership bonuses, and perhaps even contribute to the brand's success in the J.D. Power and Associates Sales Satisfaction Survey.

In addition to tools like the Best Practice Guides (which can favorably affect the performance of most dealerships), Mercedes-Benz

USA leaders offered additional in-store consulting in 2013 to approximately 120 of the more than 370 Mercedes-Benz dealers. In those cases, Mercedes-Benz USA staff originally provided that coaching to the dealerships at no expense. However, as the in-store coaching program has evolved, Ellen Braaf notes, "We've contracted with J.D. Power and Associates to provide customer experience assistance to dealerships that are not making the leadership bonus and not performing satisfactorily on customer experience targets as evidenced by the CEI. We have now shifted the cost of the services to the dealerships. We realized that we couldn't subsidize enhanced tools to help some dealers perform well enough to earn the leadership bonus and in the process knock out other dealers."

I have been sharing the Mercedes-Benz customer experience elevation efforts in the context of traditional car sales to consumers—a business-to-customer (B2C) model. However, it should be noted that all the approaches written about up to this point in the book have also been deployed on behalf of Mercedes-Benz business-to-business (B2B) customers.

Commercial vans are becoming increasingly important to MBUSA's parent company, Daimler AG. According to *Forbes* magazine, vans were responsible for approximately 9 percent of Daimler's net revenues in 2014. Through 2015, Mercedes-Benz has offered only a large-sized van in the United States: the Sprinter. The United States is second only to Germany in Sprinter van sales. It is estimated that in 2014, Mercedes-Benz van sales in the United States increased 20 percent year over year. End-of-year U.S. sales for the Sprinter approached 26,000 units in 2014, with sales of 50,000 units expected in 2016. This sizable increase will probably come from economic conditions that favor small business owners as well as the introduction of a midsize cargo/passenger van called the Metris. If there was any doubt about Daimler's commitment to the U.S. commercial van market, it was erased by the company's $500 million investment in Sprinter van production in South Carolina.

Bernhard Glaser, vice president and managing director DVU (Daimler Vans USA), notes, "Business customers are often neglected in conversations about the customer experience. However, from the onset of the transformation, we believed that it was as important to drive delight for them as it was for our luxury car purchasers. Whether it is a Sprinter or an S-Class, we are all selling a product bearing a shining star. We are still selling the brand Mercedes-Benz."

Customer segments in the Mercedes-Benz commercial business are quite varied, with about half of the sales going to small business owners (for example, a plumber with a single Sprinter van equipped with specialized shelving for daily needs) and half going to fleet purchasers like PepsiCo, FedEx, and Frito-Lay. Despite the scale differences, Bernhard notes that business customers often have similar yet different needs from luxury car purchasers. "Commercial Mercedes-Benz Sprinter buyers aren't necessarily looking for amenities like a customer lounge where they can sip coffee. They might enjoy all that, but they often don't have time for those things, since their time is their money. They need to get out of our service area to keep their business running. So customer experience on the commercial side is expressed in different ways, such as totally flexible service hours. Say you run your vans overnight. You might need us to do an oil change at 8 p.m. so that you can be back out on the road at 10 p.m."

Bernhard emphasizes that while the needs of business customers are different, the process for driving consistent high-quality experiences at the dealership level is the same for every consumer. "Like retail, all of our commercial sales and service go through our dealer network. About 200 of our Mercedes-Benz dealers have a commercial franchise. We are small compared to other players in the commercial van space, as we go up against Ford Transit, Chevy, and GM with networks of 3,000 dealerships across the country." On the product side, Sprinter competes with larger commercial sales networks by having a product with exceptional quality, excellent safety features, and the lowest cost of ownership. On the customer experience side, the Mercedes-Benz van division competes, according to Bernhard, "through a network of dealers who listen to customer feedback and link a portion of their compensation to their ability to deliver the experience that commercial customers need and expect. Unless our Sprinter dealers meet certain brand standards and perform well on measures of customer experience, they forfeit portions of the margin to top-performing dealers in a way similar to what happens on the passenger-car side of Mercedes-Benz." Whether your customer is someone in another business or is a traditional retail consumer, they are *all* customers. Business owners and consumers look for responsiveness to their unique needs and expect you to find ways to align those who represent your brand to perform at the highest levels possible in terms of serving those needs.

I have offered a high-level overview of the Mercedes-Benz USA dealership margin structure and some of the tools used to help dealers on both the B2C and B2B sides of the Mercedes-Benz business to succeed. My hope is that you see the need to anchor the voice of the customer to a fair performance evaluation system. That system should inspire people to act in ways that continually improve behavior in all phases of the customer journey. In addition to aligning customer experience and performance rewards, great leaders offer tools and extra incentive(s) to ensure added commitment toward a shared objective.

As I have done in each previous chapter, I will close with Keys to Driving Delight. Additionally, since this wraps up the section of the book pertaining to "The Standard," I will also offer a 10-point summary checklist (not unlike a multipoint automobile inspection) that you can use to diagnostically compare your customer journey efforts to takeaways from Mercedes-Benz USA leadership.

Your 10-Point Standard Section Checklist

Have you:

1. _____ Defined a clear, customer-centric leadership vision?

2. _____ Shared that vision widely with all stakeholders in word and visual form by mapping the journey ahead?

3. _____ Made a bold set of disciplined promises as to how you will reach your desired destination?

4. _____ Delivered on promises by creating an organizational and leadership culture that mobilizes your people in the direction of your objectives?

5. _____ Taken the time to assess all key interactions between your customers and your brand?

6. _____ Translated your customer journey map into language that is understandable to stakeholders?

7. _____ Trained people throughout your organization on the journey your customers take across your brand?

8. _____ Developed a measurement tool and customer experience management system to assess the voice of the customer in a timely and actionable fashion?

9. _____ Created performance expectations and reward systems that were measured by the voice of the customer throughout his journey with your brand?

10. _____ Generated best practice tools to help your team consistently deliver elevated customer experiences that meet and exceed your performance targets?

➤ Success in customer experience execution can come only when everyone in your organization understands and takes responsibility for meeting and exceeding customer needs.

➤ When developing performance measurement systems, consider and communicate the relevance of the items being measured to the well-being of the business, ensure that those who are being measured can create positive changes in the metrics, and be vigilant about the fairness of the rewards and consequences associated with your desired performance levels.

➤ Effective negotiations concerning compensation for performance are complex, are often fraught with conflict, evoke fear of change, and require extra effort and patience to achieve success.

➤ At the center of aligned action is a compelling vision, fueled by honesty and transparency, that drives trust through a win/win opportunity for all key stakeholders.

➤ Once incentives are aligned with important performance drivers like customer satisfaction and engagement, leaders need to create empirically derived best-practice tools to guide consistent behavior and the achievement of performance targets.

What's important is that you have a faith

in people, that they're basically good and

smart, and if you give them tools, they'll do

wonderful things with them. It's not the tools

that you have faith in—tools are just tools.

—Steve Jobs

7

Delight Is a
People Business

◇◇

A s you have seen in prior chapters, Steve Cannon and other
leaders at Mercedes-Benz USA invested in an array of tools
to produce customer-focused changes at the iconic brand. However, Steve realized from the outset that the newly created customer experience resources would be only as good as the people
who had the task of using them.

Steve also understood that staff members at Mercedes-Benz
USA and the teams at the dealerships had to be both passionate
about and fully engaged in the delivery of world-class customer experiences or no set of tools would be transformative. In early 2012,

at his initial National Dealer Meeting, Steve noted, "This challenge of delivering a 'best or nothing' customer experience every time will involve people, process, culture, and passion . . . behind great products are great people."

Both this chapter and the one that follows highlight some of the most significant efforts aimed at engaging and empowering the people associated with Mercedes-Benz in the United States. These "people" chapters will be followed by "process" and "technology" chapters. As you move through these sections, you will come to appreciate how the leaders at Mercedes-Benz USA took a multifaceted approach to organizational change by leveraging human factors, technology, process excellence (or a continuous improvement focus), and business infrastructure.

While I will make an effort to offer a chronological perspective on the timing of the initiatives in this and the following chapters, it should be noted that many of these programs took place simultaneously, thanks to the efforts of individuals throughout MBUSA. In the customer experience war room at MBUSA headquarters, for example, there are three large charts filled with people, process, and technology projects outlined by year. This chapter in particular looks at three foundational cultural approaches initiated at the outset of the customer-centric effort. They were targeted at winning the hearts and minds of Mercedes-Benz USA employees and dealership personnel. These efforts are categorized as enhancing the emotional connection to the Mercedes-Benz brand, maximizing the engagement of employees, and benchmarking world-class customer experience providers.

Enhancing the Emotional Connection to Your Product and Brand

At some point, you have undoubtedly received service from a disengaged or disgruntled employee. Maybe it was a server at a restaurant who couldn't provide a meaningful opinion about a food item because he had "never tried it," or possibly it was an employee who made no effort to disguise her disdain for her employer. In my books about companies like Zappos, Starbucks, and The Ritz-Carlton Hotel Company, I examined how leaders have gained a competitive business advantage by getting more from their people than their competitors did. In essence, leaders at those brands empower, engage, and ignite a passion for both their products and the importance of creating engaging experiences. When leaders talk about and demonstrate a passion for their company's products and service, it affects the entire organization. When staff members hear their leaders talk about delighting customers and see those leaders act in ways that accord with their words, those employees, associates, and partners put extra effort into customer care. As your team members offer that extra discretionary effort, your customers become more emotionally engaged and loyal.

Leaders at trendsetting customer experience brands actively foster cultures of product enthusiasm and corporate zealotry. At Starbucks, for example, corporate rituals like coffee tastings offer an opportunity for staff members at all levels of the organization to gain product knowledge and develop a passion for all things coffee.

At Mercedes-Benz USA, the leaders started cultural initiatives early in their transformational journey. Five months after Steve Cannon's first National Dealer Meeting, he discussed several culture-enhancing efforts at an additional Mercedes-Benz National Dealer Meeting held in Las Vegas in October 2012. At that Las Vegas meeting, Steve highlighted a culture survey that had recently been launched in dealerships, a new program that was later referred to as the Mercedes-Benz Way (both of which will be addressed later in this chapter), and a program referred to as Drive a Star Home, or DaSH (the word *Star* in the program's title is a reference to the brand's star-shaped logo). Specifically, Steve noted, "We are launching Drive a Star Home to give your employees the opportunity to drive our amazing products, and in doing so, gaining a deeper insight into our brand and our customers."

Through the DaSH program, Mercedes-Benz USA provided its dealer partners with more than 700 vehicles so that every dealership employee could drive a Mercedes-Benz for a two- or three-day period. While some dealership staff members already owned a Mercedes-Benz vehicle and others routinely experienced them as a part of their job function, an initial survey showed that a surprising 70 percent of retail employees had *never* been behind the wheel of the very vehicles being sold at their dealership.

While a program like DaSH is intuitively compelling and seemingly easy to execute (how hard could it be to let members of the retail staff drive a Mercedes-Benz, given that the dealership is chock full of them?), creating and executing the program was a logistical challenge.

Michael Doherty, then department manager retail training at Mercedes-Benz USA, played an integral role in the conceptual development and rollout of DaSH. Michael notes, "We looked at the total number of employees in our 370-plus dealerships and then worked out how many cars would be needed in order to give every employee a two-day drive within a 90-day time window. We then determined how many cars we would need per dealership. At that point, we had to innovatively explore how we were going to address cost and liability issues." In an effort to essentially "loan" vehicles to dealership staff members for 48 hours, MBUSA had to consider how those vehicles would be licensed and insured and what would happen if any of the vehicles were involved in an accident. The company also had to consider how to maintain the value of the vehicles after their "loaner" period was over. Ultimately, the leaders at Mercedes-Benz turned to Hertz to help with the program. Michael Doherty explains, "We asked Hertz to purchase 709 Mercedes-Benz vehicles with a guaranteed 100 percent rental return for three months, which would be significantly higher than their normal 65 percent rental utilization. After much negotiation, we secured the deal, sold the vehicles to Hertz, and distributed them throughout all the dealerships in the country."

As negotiations with Hertz were moving forward, Mercedes-Benz USA staff members were also developing processes to get dealership employees into their driving opportunity swiftly and easily. According to Michael, "The guiding principle that I reinforced with our team was that the process had to be easy and turnkey for all our customers—both the dealers and the dealerships' employees. It had to be enjoyable. It couldn't be a chore. Because if we put people through the wringer, they're going to say, 'To heck with it; I'd love to drive the car, but it's just not worth all the hassle.' The process had to be simple for the employees and for the dealers. And it was."

To maximize MBUSA's return on investment from providing the 700-plus vehicles to dealers, instructional designers and trainers at MBUSA developed modules that made the DaSH experience an immersive learning opportunity. Those modules were integrated into a three-part program broken down into prelearning, the drive, and postlearning. Training materials in the prelearning stage addressed Mercedes-Benz "basics" like the high-performance navigation and entertainment systems, practical information on how to adjust seats and electric mirrors, and important safety, performance, and innovation information. Upon completion of the prelearning stage, dealership staff members scheduled their extended test drive. This scheduling occurred through a DaSH coordinator who was available at each dealership.

After the multiday drive, participants had approximately 30 days to learn more about their vehicles through an e-learning module and to share what they had gained from the experience. Dealerships were given incentives by Mercedes-Benz USA to ensure that every employee had the opportunity to Drive a Star Home. As a result, the participation level of dealership staff and the overall engagement level of participants was tracked. Lin Nelson, then certification & recognition specialist in MBUSA's learning & performance department, reported, "Quantitatively, 18,387 dealership employees (93 percent of dealership staff) drove Mercedes-Benz vehicles through this program. Of these employees, 99 percent recommended the program, and 97 percent said it was a valuable use of their time."

Additionally, qualitative feedback from dealership employees was routinely captured and shared throughout the dealer network. A compendium of some of the stories from DaSH participants can be found at www.driventodelight.com/DaSH. But for our purposes, I will offer just a couple of the comments provided by those who Drove a Star Home:

> Working in the finance department, I only get to talk about the vehicles. It was a pleasure to be able to put my hands on one and get to know the product. It was a great experience getting to know the capabilities of these cars from the technology to the handling and performance—it was all good!

> It was great to take this vehicle home and show it to my neighbors, who have been curious about the GLK. I was able to demo the vehicle from home, and my neighbors made an appointment for the weekend to come in and test drive one.

> What an awesome experience! (I'm in tears! How crazy is that?!) Before, it was about the "brand;" now it's about the "car"! It's about the comfort. It's about the performance and handling. It's about how my 11-year-old son said "he felt safe in it." Because of what I've learned, I was able to explain to him just how safe the car really is and what goes into building the vehicle to make it safe. Yes, it is a luxury car,

but now, to me, it is so much more! Thank you so much for the opportunity to drive a Mercedes-Benz!

The success of DaSH at the dealership level prompted the expansion of the program to Mercedes-Benz headquarters—interestingly enough, as the result of a suggestion by an MBUSA Customer Experience Champion (a participant in the Mercedes-Benz Customer Experience Champions program referred to in Chapter 3). DaSH likewise spread to MBUSA's financing partner, Mercedes-Benz Financial Services (MBFS).

Brian Fulton, vice president, Mercedes-Benz Financial Services, shares the importance of aligning programs that inspire staff at both MBFS and MBUSA. "Through the eyes of our customers, Mercedes-Benz USA and Mercedes-Benz Financial Services are seen as one brand, not two companies. This is why we've set, and held ourselves accountable to, the highest standards for customer experience. At MBFS, Customer Focus has always been a Core Value in our organization, and 'Driven to Delight' is a promise that we make to our customers as a brand. We are continually taking steps to further elevate the experiences that we deliver to our customers. Those steps include continuous improvements for our fellow colleagues, who we view as internal customers, as well as the external customers, our dealers and our retail consumers. For anyone that we at MBFS interact with, every experience matters, which is why we strive to make every interaction with our customers a delightful one."

In order to make DaSH a reality at both MBUSA and MBFS, the leaders dedicated significant resources to a seemingly simple idea: make sure everyone who represents your brand has had an opportunity to enjoy the products you sell. An innovative partnership with Hertz, coupled with process infrastructure and learning tools, enabled participants to experience a Mercedes-Benz vehicle and literally be brought to "tears" by the experience. What are you doing in your business to help your people fully connect with your products or services and to build passion for the experiences that your customers can and do enjoy?

While DaSH allowed dealership employees to experience the craftsmanship, safety, and enjoyment of driving a Mercedes-Benz, it ultimately evolved into a more sustainable and comprehensive program referred to as the Brand Immersion Experience. The Mercedes-Benz Brand Immersion Experience will be explored in detail in Chapter 8.

To Drive Customer Delight, You Must Drive Employee Engagement

In Chapter 1, I noted that employees at Mercedes-Benz USA's corporate headquarters bounced back from morale problems that occurred in the 2005–2006 time frame. In response to lower morale, the MBUSA leaders who were in place at the time began focusing on product quality, employee empowerment, and restoring pride. That generation of leaders was responsible for helping the company become the first and only original equipment manufacturer (OEM) to make *Fortune* magazine's "Best Companies to Work For" list. Steadfast commitment to the engagement of MBUSA employees has earned MBUSA a consistent place on this prestigious list. Steve and others on his team understand that leaders are responsible for the engagement level of their employees as well as connecting that engagement to workplace productivity. Mercedes-Benz leaders champion the importance of employee engagement, knowing that happy employees are productive employees. In keeping with that perspective, research from Gallup shows that in the United States alone, productivity losses due to employee disengagement are estimated to be between $450 and $550 billion per annum.

Steve reflects on the process that helped restore trust and passion in the days after the failure of the Chrysler merger. "The first thing we did was take a hard look at where we stood with all of our employees, and that look started with an anonymous, in-depth survey. In it, we encouraged our people to honestly tell us what they thought, and they didn't disappoint us. In fact, we got frank messages that essentially suggested management was unapproachable, not seen as treating employees fairly, not providing clear communication, and not listening. So we as a group worked through those results and confronted the problems that led to that feedback."

Based on the honest appraisal that the leaders received from the MBUSA workforce and the leadership training, communication efforts, and employee recognition efforts that followed, the culture at Mercedes-Benz USA turned around. In fact, the company showed double-digit gains on employee engagement metrics, improved verbatim comments on surveys, and sustained accolades from independent evaluators. Had it not been for the high levels of engagement at MBUSA, the leaders could not have initiated the massive customer experience transformation involved in the Driven to Delight leadership agenda.

While the state of the Mercedes-Benz USA workforce was strong, transforming an iconic, product-focused brand into a provider of world-class customer experiences would depend largely on the engagement level of the employees at Mercedes-Benz dealerships. Did those employees feel sufficiently cared for by their managers that they would exert the effort needed to delight their customers? More important, how could Mercedes-Benz USA positively enhance the engagement level of dealership employees?

Steve shares, "We learned a lot from the way we improved culture and employee engagement from 2007 to 2013 at Mercedes-Benz USA, and we wanted to share our lessons with our 370-plus dealer partners." The first component of that sharing involved asking those dealer partners to survey the 24,000 people they employed. Since employee engagement surveys can shine a light on many overlooked management problems, it was important that the initial dealer employee engagement surveys be both voluntary and done in partnership with the dealer principals.

Of the host of vendors considered to guide the dealer employee survey process, the Mercedes-Benz Dealer Board and Mercedes-Benz USA chose Lior Arussy and the Strativity Group. As you will recall, Lior earned the trust and respect of dealers and of MBUSA at the time of the Driven to LEAD training program. He needed to leverage that trust to help dealers address the employee concerns and issues identified through the engagement survey process. Lior and Strativity also brought with them a model of employee engagement that appealed to both Mercedes-Benz USA and the dealer community. That model defines staff member engagement across four dimensions—Individual, Manager, Customer, and Organization (IMCO). The Mercedes-Benz dealership survey assessed employee perceptions across these four dimensions, including the degree to which an employee:

Individual

- Feels that his work effort makes a difference.

- Experiences work/life balance.

- Can take ownership of issues he routinely encounters.

Manager

- Views the distribution of work as manageable and fair.

- Is inspired by his direct supervisor.

- Feels appreciated by his supervisor.

Customer

- Concludes that his dealership creates great value for customers.

- Perceives the leaders at the dealership as making customer-centric decisions.

- Is empowered to do what is right for customers.

Organization

- Has confidence in the vision and strategy of leadership.

- Views leadership as effective communicators.

- Feels connected to the overall success of the dealership.

To get maximum participation in the employee engagement survey, dealers and their staff members had to trust that the information they offered would result in positive changes for their organization. The survey was independently administered and analyzed by Strativity. Lior and his group reported only participation levels and summary engagement scores from participating dealerships to the Mercedes-Benz USA leaders. Similarly, while a detailed report of the group's findings was provided to the leaders at each dealership, individual staff members were guaranteed that no identifying information would be shared and that only aggregate results would be presented to the dealer leaders.

These safeguards notwithstanding, why would a dealership want to go through such a comprehensive analysis of staff engagement voluntarily? Lior suggests that the answer is partly financial in nature. "We actually built a very sophisticated calculator that allowed us to show that a 10 percent improvement in employee engagement would result in a $367,000 impact on the bottom line of the average MBUSA dealer. We then would plug in information like the dealer's specific sales data, number of employees, and average employee salary to show the likely profitability impact of improved employee engagement on that specific dealership."

Efforts to build a business case for measuring and enhancing employee engagement, coupled with strategies to protect the privacy of respondents, resulted in an impressive 71 percent response rate (almost 16,000 dealership employees) on a fairly in-depth (28-question) dealer engagement survey. However, in order for the data to be meaningful, action had to follow from the survey results. To that end, the Mercedes-Benz USA leaders worked with Strativity to produce an "Engage in Action" guide that offered dealership leaders best practice recommendations across the four areas of engagement identified in the IMCO model. That guide provided hundreds of suggestions for leaders on everything from employee selection, participatory management, employee recognition, and performance review processes to inspirational leadership and effective communication of vision and strategy.

Web conferences were also conducted with dealers to explain the IMCO model, clarify how engagement results should be interpreted, and aid in the use of the Engage in Action guide. Additionally, Mercedes-Benz USA hired Strativity to provide in-dealership consulting, face-to-face with the leadership teams. Lior explains, "We would come the night before our full-consulting day and do an employee focus group to find the specifics that were behind the dealership's scores. The following morning, we would present a combination of the dealership's engagement scores and the qualitative examples we picked up from the focus groups. Then we moved into an action planning process that first allowed leaders to express how they felt about the results. In fact, we mapped all the emotional responses on a reaction map." According to Lior, some leaders were initially enraged, some felt betrayed, and others viewed the problem areas identified as exaggerated. In any case, the training process let leaders cleanse themselves of their initial responses so that they could deal with the real issues and get to root causes as well as action steps.

In describing the sobering results of the first year of dealer employee engagement surveys, Steve Cannon notes, "We found that 37 percent of the total employee base across U.S. dealerships were either not engaged or actively disengaged. We knew we couldn't deliver world-class customer experience if only 63 percent of the people in Mercedes-Benz dealerships felt a strong emotional connection to their leaders, their customers, and the brand. If that information wasn't troubling enough, we also found that the least engaged group in our dealerships was our service technicians, with 55 percent being *dis*engaged. This group frequently felt unappreciated or underappreciated." Steve adds, "Service technicians reported that their typical interactions with leaders in the dealerships occurred only when things went wrong, and there was little recognition for what they did well. They are the very people we rely on to get our customers' cars repaired right the first time. All of this pointed to the importance of the tools and coaching we were offering dealers. To be one of the best customer experience providers, MBUSA has to help grow leaders and engage all team members at the dealership level."

In addition to providing tools for dealers to use to engage service technicians, MBUSA has developed a Sales and Service Laureate program. This program recognizes and rewards the very best dealership employees who consistently provide outstanding customer experiences. Laureates receive recognition from MBUSA, a trophy, and a trip to Germany to tour Daimler's manufacturing facilities and museum and also experience the many people and places from which the brand began. On a more informal but equally important scale, Steve Cannon recognizes individual customer experience excellence during his frequent dealership visits, when he personally presents a President's Coin in gratitude and appreciation of the outstanding care the recipient consistently provides.

Mercedes-Benz USA continues to coordinate employee engagement surveys for dealerships. Leaders at MBUSA are walking a fine line between respecting the dealer principal's autonomy in dealing with his employees and offering structure and encouragement for those who wish to genuinely listen to their people.

Lior Arussy reports significant improvement in employee engagement from the baseline surveys to the annual follow-up. "MBUSA saw a 10 percent increase in employee engagement across the dealer community, with a 20 percent increase in targeted areas like technician engagement. Some dealers had lower engagement scores after baseline, and anecdotally, it appears that in many of those cases, employees were reluctant to share their true feelings the first year of the survey. However, as those employees saw the process unfold, they became more willing to provide genuine feedback."

Annual dealership employee engagement surveys will continue, and Engage in Action guides will support the dealership action planning process. Mercedes-Benz USA won't be providing one-on-one consulting for employee engagement action planning, since dealerships have already been exposed to those tools; however, dealerships can seek that type of consulting independently. In lieu of coaching support, Mercedes-Benz USA has broadened its leadership development focus from simply guiding leaders to offering dealers a more robust leadership-training model—the Mercedes-Benz Leadership Academy (the academy will be discussed in detail in Chapter 8).

Are you genuinely listening to the needs of your people and developing action plans to increase their engagement at work? Do you have a competitive advantage because your people are formally and informally recognized for their commitment to others? Do your team members feel that they work for leaders and an organization that care about their input as well as their growth and development? It is impossible to deliver sustained customer experience excellence if you don't listen to, acknowledge, and drive the engagement of your employees. Furthermore, it is impossible to deliver employee engagement unless you train managers to build emotionally rewarding work environments.

Studying the Best and Learning from Setbacks

At Mercedes-Benz, "Driven to Delight" means being the best customer experience provider, irrespective of industry. To be the elite experience brand, leaders at Mercedes-Benz first sought to learn from admired experience providers and then tried to define a unique Mercedes-Benz version of the best-of-the-best sales and service experiences. Leaders at Mercedes-Benz wanted to inspire staff members at both MBUSA and Mercedes-Benz dealerships through stories and examples from companies that are known for their customer experience excellence. Leveraging that inspiration, leaders hoped to create the "Mercedes Benz Way"—a branded customer experience template that could be delivered by everyone in the organization.

The journey to developing a unique Mercedes-Benz Way (or MB Way) of customer experience delivery started with benchmarking recognized service companies and sharing their branded experience touchpoints and processes. In addition to providing inspiration, examples of quality from other businesses could demonstrate the powerful human impact of customer experience excellence. To initiate this benchmarking process, the MBUSA leadership asked its advertising agency, Merkley+Partners, to identify brands that were leading the way in customer experience delivery. As part of that outreach, leaders at those world-class customer experience brands were invited to share how they created consistent and unique experiences for their customers. Mercedes-Benz videotaped the interviews and used them to further excite passion and paint a human picture of customer experience excellence. Some of the brands that were included in the videos were the Mandarin Oriental Hotel Group, Starbucks, and Nordstrom.

"The Mercedes-Benz Way" video was presented across MBUSA and shared at key events like the National Parts & Service Managers Meeting and the National Dealer Meeting. Along the same lines, I was involved in a benchmarking project with Mercedes-Benz USA in 2013 where I arranged and facilitated a panel discussion involving leaders from The Ritz-Carlton and Zappos along with MBUSA's CEO, Steve Cannon. That panel discussion was presented live to members of the Mercedes-Benz USA corporate and field teams and was archived for other internal uses.

The benchmarking phase was a success, and it helped employees throughout the organization understand the unique execution of superlative customer experiences that takes place at other legendary brands. However, the journey toward defining a specific Mercedes-Benz Way was not as fruitful. As a more formal step in defining the Mercedes-Benz Way, Strativity conducted a two-and-a-half-day workshop in Las Vegas with some of the Best-of-the-Best employees from Mercedes-Benz dealerships. Harry Hynekamp, general manager customer experience, describes the event: "When participants arrived at the workshop, they walked through a box—so that they could literally be thinking outside of the box. We instantly got people in the mindset of innovating the future of the Mercedes-Benz experience and bringing our performance to an even higher level in terms of customer delight. This event was about breaking down different parts of the customer experience and really ideating innovations. We were looking beyond satisfying customers or meeting expectations at touchpoints. We were focused on what it would take to deliver true *delight*." In addition to developing ideas concerning the Mercedes-Benz customer experience, participants had assignments to shop and dine at an array of luxury and nonluxury retailers and restaurants in Las Vegas. As they were having these experiences, participants literally cataloged their feelings and emotions and filtered everything through their five senses as active customers.

While the Mercedes-Benz Best-of-the-Best customer innovation event produced many great insights, it didn't define a distinct Mercedes-Benz Way of service delivery. In essence, the leaders were struggling to find something that I call the "*so* effect." For example, if a retailer starts a generous return policy, someone might say, "That is *so* Nordstrom." If another business begins to encourage its people to remember the names and orders of repeat customers, someone might say, "That is *so* Starbucks." The *so* effect means that a brand is known for being so excellent at an aspect of experience delivery that consumers almost see that area as signature behaviors for the brand.

The Mercedes-Benz Way became a project to identify, develop, and train methods for delivering signature customer experiences across both sales and service. Much as the Apple Store experience was a vast departure from other existing retail environments (no paper signage, greeters who triage customers, sleek and sophisticated design), Mercedes-Benz USA was looking to define ways to deliver memorable moments, unique actions, and innovative processes that would elevate experiences beyond the satisfactory and into a realm of extraordinary delight that was "*so* Mercedes-Benz." To achieve this differentiated and higher-level experience, leaders at Mercedes-Benz USA initiated a pilot training program that they expected to be rolled out across MBUSA and the dealer network. Mercedes-Benz leadership tendered a request for proposal, selected a vendor, and launched a pilot at the company-owned Manhattan dealership.

Unfortunately, the pilot program didn't effectively communicate a unique Mercedes-Benz Way of delivering customer experiences. Rather than going forward systemwide with a flawed version of Mercedes-Benz Way training, the leaders at Mercedes-Benz pulled the plug on the program after the pilot. Steve Cannon explained the decision to end the project in a letter to stakeholders by noting, "For months I've talked about the MB Way program we were launching as part of the 2013 customer experience offering. This was going to be our largest platform of the year and we put a lot of money and effort into building it. We had even hired a vendor to help execute our plan. Unfortunately, that plan proved too complex to deliver at the 'Best or Nothing' level we expect. Thus, after months of effort, MB Way was shelved before it ever launched. We swung for the fences and came up short. It hurt to see us fail, especially with something as close to my heart as our customer experience journey. Through that process of failure, I learned. Everyone involved learned and no one lost their job."

How refreshing it is to hear a senior leader at a major corporation not "spin" a defeat—to acknowledge that an effort was unsuccessful. If your people are going to stretch for greatness, not everything will go as planned. In fact, if you are not hearing about breakdowns, either your culture is risk averse or people are investing energy into keeping those breakdowns from ever reaching your awareness. When leaders admit miscalculations, avoid placing blame, and learn from those experiences, people throughout the organization feel safe in thoughtfully attempting to drive change.

While the intent of the MB Way training was sound, several building blocks necessary for the project's success seemed to be missing. Harry Hynekamp notes, "In analyzing our efforts to create and train a Mercedes-Benz Way, it became crystal clear that our concepts were before their time. We needed to do more foundational work on improving our overall experience before we started to define ways to create unique Mercedes-Benz experiences that differentiated us from our competition. We were still so far from where we wanted the training to take us that we were putting seeds in less than fertile ground. The training initiative was a failure in the sense that we spent money going after something that couldn't yet begin to grow organically within the network at that time. So we came to a crossroads after that pilot. We knew that we were improving customer experiences, but we still had gaps to fill before we could formally train on a branded approach to delivering delight."

As suggested by Steve Cannon, the leaders at Mercedes-Benz USA looked at lessons learned from the MB Way training stumble, identified the gaps that needed to be filled, and changed course in the direction of two truly innovative and comprehensive initiatives, the Mercedes-Benz Brand Immersion Experience and the Mercedes-Benz Leadership Academy, that I will outline in Chapter 8.

Human Lessons and Your Business

While the automotive business is product-based, the sales and servicing of that product depends solely on people. The critical importance of the human element is probably true for your business as well. To enhance the human experience for the people in dealerships, leaders at MBUSA gave those dealership employees the opportunity to enjoy the engineering, safety, and driving experience that are unique to Mercedes-Benz vehicles. Additionally, MBUSA leaders capitalized on the power of storytelling to inspire service excellence through lessons from some of the world's most customer-obsessed brands.

I have long said, "All business is personal." As leaders, we have the task of improving the lives of the people we call customers by inspiring and empowering the people we call employees, staff members, or team members. In the chapter ahead, you will see how Mercedes-Benz USA and its dealer partners made significant long-term investments to elevate leadership skills, employee service behaviors, and passion for the brand on behalf of the people who represent the brand.

➤ "Best or nothing" customer experiences involve people, process, culture, and passion.

➤ Unless your staff members are passionate about your products, your brand, and your leadership, there will never be enough "tools" to create sustained customer experiences and profitability.

➤ Gallup estimates losses of $450 to $550 billion each year as a result of lost productivity from disengaged workers in the United States alone.

➤ To the maximum degree possible, encourage all of your people to experience the products and services that you offer.

➤ Measure employee engagement on a regular basis. Seek both a quantitative and a qualitative understanding of employee feedback and develop tools for managers and leaders to help them take action based on that feedback.

➤ Continue your commitment to study industry leaders in the area of customer experience delivery. Select impassioned service professionals to help you brainstorm ways to create an innovative, branded experience that is uniquely your own.

➤ Realize that not every effort you undertake will be a success. Admit miscalculations. Be willing to curtail unproductive or ill-timed efforts and correct your course quickly. Benefit by learning from setbacks, apply that learning to the establishment of new directions, and remain steadfast in forging ahead.

icies but it must also represent the people behind th
ven to delight. it is not just a phrase. it is a path, a prom
elief. it is a commitment to creating positive relationsh
making people smile and to leaving them with a sens
mplete trust. driven to delight means exceptional pers
atment. it is a reminder that the journey is never done.
re is always a more thoughtful way. and throughout e

If your actions inspire others to

dream more, learn more, do more and

become more, you are a leader.

—John Quincy Adams

ven to delight means exceptional personal treatment. i
minder that the journey is never done. that there is alwa
re thoughtful way. and throughout each interaction we
member that the best or nothing cannot just be a descripti

Fully Committed to Growth and Development

◇◇

The success of the Mercedes-Benz DaSH program, the dealer engagement surveys, and the benchmarking efforts outlined in Chapter 7 created excitement and enthusiasm across Mercedes-Benz USA and among the dealership employees. Despite the setback associated with the efforts to create the Mercedes-Benz Way, the leaders established momentum by educating, emotionally engaging, and inspiring people to see the value of being driven to delight.

Because they were attempting a dramatic cultural and behavioral transformation both at headquarters and across the dealer network, the leaders at MBUSA were eager to capitalize on their positive forward momentum. Bestselling leadership author John Maxwell wrote about the importance of leveraging constructive energy by noting, "While a good leader sustains momentum, a great leader increases it."

Steve Cannon and his leadership team accelerated forward, creating the Mercedes-Benz Brand Immersion and Leadership Academy programs. Speaking about Brand Immersion at the 2014 Mercedes-Benz National Dealer Meeting near the Mercedes-Benz U.S. International (MBUSI) plant in Vance, Alabama, Steve shared, "Starting in September, this will not only be the site of a world-class production facility, it will be the site of a world-class learning program. For two days, your teams will be immersed in our brand to a level that we've never done before. They will tour the factory, they will drive our cars, and they will learn about the greatest automotive brand in the world. Winning people over is always about hearts and minds. And, ladies and gentleman, we will be going after both. I consider this program an absolute foundation of our success." The Brand Immersion Experience would also inculcate those associated with the brand on Mercedes-Benz values and customer experience standards, expectations, and responsibilities

At that same National Dealer Meeting, Steve provided the thinking behind the Mercedes-Benz Leadership Academy. "This program rests on a very simple premise: leadership matters! You and your leadership teams are the critical link. Leaders create culture, leaders inspire teams, and leaders get results." During the remainder of that event, Mercedes-Benz dealers attended breakout sessions that provided more detail on Brand Immersion and the Leadership Academy. Additionally, they engaged in activities that were essentially a preview of some of the experiences their teams would encounter at Brand Immersion (for example, an MBUSI plant tour and on- and off-road drives that showcased the performance, innovation, and safety features of Mercedes-Benz vehicles).

The remainder of this chapter will offer an in-depth view of the Mercedes-Benz Brand Immersion Experience and the Mercedes-Benz Leadership Academy. Since you may not be in a position to build programs on the scale of Brand Immersion or the Leadership Academy, special attention will be given to how you can extrapolate the objectives of each program and modify the scale of your efforts to achieve similar results.

Brand Immersion

If you ever want to do a case study on the rapid evolution of cultural change, you need look no further than a comparison of the DaSH program and its successor, the Brand Immersion Experience. Without question, DaSH (the Drive a Star Home program, discussed in the previous chapter) was a major success in giving dealership employees an opportunity to personally experience the cars that their dealership was selling and servicing each and every day. So why not just keep the program running year after year?

The leaders at Mercedes-Benz learned a great deal from DaSH and considered making a few adjustments in order to roll out a DaSH 2.0-type program. After thoughtful consideration, however, it was determined that a bolder and more innovative initiative was in order. The new program should capture the best parts of DaSH—experiential hands-on learning—and add an even broader set of scalable and sustainable learning opportunities. The newly evolving Brand Immersion Experience would be aimed at giving staff members a way to explore more than a few rides in a Mercedes-Benz automobile. It should showcase all aspects of the brand (performance, safety, engineering, and, yes, customer experience). Therefore, Brand Immersion was designed to bring dealership staff members to a centralized Brand Immersion Center rather than bringing the program to every dealership. By investing in a state-of-the-art learning center and placing it near other brand assets like the Mercedes-Benz U.S. International production facility and various driving courses, leaders at Mercedes-Benz created an unparalleled learning experience.

Having participated in the design of the customer experience component of the Mercedes-Benz Brand Immersion Experience and having been a participant in its first-ever class, I will try to use restraint in explaining the intricate details of the experience and in expressing my strong opinions about the remarkably unique approach that Mercedes-Benz took in sharing the specialness and direction of the brand. Therefore, allow me to put you in the shoes of a participant.

Assume for a moment that you are an employee at a Mercedes-Benz dealership somewhere in the United States and you are scheduled to attend the Mercedes-Benz Brand Immersion Experience. As your first day of training approaches, your dealership arranges for you to fly to Birmingham, Alabama. Upon arrival, you are transported to a nice hotel in a dynamic area of the city. At the hotel, you are given access to a Mercedes-Benz reception lounge on the hotel property in preparation for the start of your event the next day. At the same time, you receive a tablet device for use during the Brand Immersion Experience. That device will not only allow you to capture pictures and notes throughout the experience (which will be sent to you after you return to your dealership) but also provide you with enriched, interactive curriculum materials and opportunities to "explore more" than is covered during the formal training time.

The morning of the first day of Brand Immersion, you and your fellow participants are shuttled to the dedicated Mercedes-Benz Brand Immersion Center on the site of the Mercedes-Benz U.S. International production facility in nearby Vance, Alabama. The Brand Immersion Center is a mix of training classrooms, touchscreen interactive learning stations, a museum of vintage and historic Mercedes-Benz vehicles, and areas dedicated to showcasing the many safety and engineering innovations pioneered by Mercedes-Benz.

Upon arrival at the Brand Immersion Center, you participate in a general session and watch a videotaped welcome message from MBUSA president and CEO Steve Cannon. That message sets the tone for the activities that you and your fellow participants will encounter over the next two days. It outlines the opportunity you will have to see the precise engineering involved in designing and building Mercedes-Benz automobiles, highlights the appreciation you will gain for the legacy of the brand, and emphasizes the expectation that you will clearly understand what it takes to be Driven to Delight. To make the experience more intimate, you and your colleagues will be broken into subgroups for some of the activities planned for the immersion experience, while at other times your subgroup will join with the rest of the participants for a shared presentation or wrap-up event.

In your case, the first activity will be a tour of one of the most advanced automotive manufacturing plants in the world, run by Mercedes-Benz U.S. International. It has built M-Class automobiles since the plant opened in 1997 and was the first full-production Mercedes-Benz plant outside of Germany. In addition to the M-Class Sport Utility, the Alabama facility produces the GL-Class luxury SUV, the C-Class Sedan and Coupe, and the GLE Coupe SUV. In the plant, which spans over 5 million square feet (approximately 86 football fields), more than 230,000 vehicles (with 300,000 expected in 2015) are assembled annually for distribution to 135 countries. During your tour, you are exposed to precision production processes that result from both technological and human efforts. You experience well-coordinated teamwork, extraordinary supply chain management, and an uncompromising commitment to quality and safety.

Your next activity represents one of three modules dedicated to the desired customer experience for Mercedes-Benz USA. The three modules are:

- "Understanding Extraordinary." This is an interactive educational experience in which you are given an opportunity to understand the transformational journey of the brand as it shifts from being vehicle-centric toward a customer-obsessed focus.

- "Listening and Empathizing." This module offers an opportunity to enhance your ability to listen effectively for understanding and emotionally place yourself in the position of your customer before offering solutions.

- "Adding Value and Delighting." This module gives you exposure to tools that help you effectively provide uniquely human value and to go one step beyond what is expected in order to delight those you serve.

Please note that the Mercedes-Benz leaders resisted the urge to introduce a new set of concepts or terms in pursuit of this customer experience training. Instead of inundating participants with new acronyms or models, the framework from prior training programs (LEAD) was retained to serve as the foundation for personally driving delight across every human interaction. LEAD behaviors had been established years earlier and resonated well with dealer participants. This new round of cultural immersion training leveraged that existing platform and deepened the skill sets involved in listening effectively, empathizing, adding value, and delivering delight for customers.

As your first day of Mercedes-Benz Brand Immersion comes to a close, you are briefed on how you can use the LEAD format to observe and review your evening's dining experience in the restaurant district near your hotel in Birmingham. You and your colleagues will be going to one of an array of restaurants and not only enjoying a sumptuous meal but also looking at the entire dining experience, from arrival to departure, through the lens of how well the restaurant staff demonstrated LEAD behaviors. Ultimately, you will share your observations at the kickoff to day two.

As day two progresses, you will participate in unique driving experiences that showcase the safety and performance aspects of Mercedes-Benz vehicles, engage in a module on the innovative nature of the brand, and have a closing evening ceremony at the nearby Barber Vintage Motorsports Museum. From the standpoint of understanding how Mercedes-Benz leads through innovation, you will freely explore the Brand Center, with its displays of classic Mercedes-Benz automobiles and numerous automotive breakthroughs. You will have the task of taking pictures of specific innovations, understanding the vision involved in identifying the customer problem that needed to be solved, and appreciating the action that was taken to create an innovative, customer-based solution. Additionally, you will be given a glimpse into the brand's future, including its commitment to emission-free vehicles as well as accident-free and autonomous driving.

From a driving perspective, you will encounter both off-road and on-track performance aspects of Mercedes-Benz vehicles. For the purpose of this description, I will provide just a portion of your off-road experience in the GL-Class SUV. While navigating an obstacle course of wobbly bridges, switchbacks, and river runs, you will encounter a pinnacle moment when your professional driver yields control to the Downhill Speed Regulation (DSR) feature of the GL as you look down a road with an extremely steep 70-degree slope. During the descent, DSR maintains the vehicle at a steady speed by coordinating the engine, gear controls, and braking system. By the time you have experienced the banked curves, rock climbs, water holes, potholes, offset railroad ties, and other obstacles along your path, you will thoroughly appreciate the level of safety and stability that has been built into the vehicle, even though it will seldom, if ever, be required under normal driving conditions. A similar respect for the performance aspects of Mercedes-Benz cars emerges after you are given a chance to drive them for yourself in optimal racetrack driving conditions.

I think you now have a feel for the participant experience at MBUSA's Brand Immersion, so let's take you out of the participant role and begin to look at the lessons that can be derived from this very special offering. The Mercedes-Benz leaders did not seek to create an "orientation" program. Those programs are probably taking place based on the policies and procedures at the dealerships. Instead, Mercedes-Benz USA has developed a place and a set of experiential learning opportunities that saturate participants in the history and richness of everything that makes up the Mercedes-Benz brand.

All too often, employees or representatives of a brand are given little information about the meaning, purpose, and uniquely special aspects of the brand or the desired service experience at the company they are hired to represent. We have all seen situations where a person is selling toasters at Brand A one day and selling computers at Brand B the next day. After recruiting someone from another company, managers often fail to help their new employee understand the history and legacy of the organization he has just joined. Moreover, they seldom explain the way they want customers to be served in their organization. No wonder customer experience is fairly unremarkable from Brand A to Brand B.

The Mercedes-Benz Brand Immersion Experience represents, on a rather grand scale, what all of us should seek to create for our team members—namely, a context that builds a unique connection to the brand and the organization as a whole and that validates our team members' choice of employer. Our efforts to emotionally connect our people to our brand may also reap the additional benefit of creating a sense of psychological well-being.

Psychologist Martin Seligman, Ph.D., has theorized, and much scientific research has affirmed, that authentic happiness emerges, in part, from "attachment to and service of" something larger than oneself. Whether it is a Brand Immersion Experience or some other ongoing effort that you create, driving happiness for your employees is a noble goal. If you help your people foster an attachment to your brand and inspire them to be of service to others in a way that is consistent with the aspirations of your company, you are serving both your people and your customers. Ultimately, leaders at Mercedes-Benz demonstrate a commitment to driving the delight of customers by building delight in the people who represent their brand. Brand Immersion plays a significant part in that delight infusion process.

Leadership Academy

Many leaders might look at an existing successful program and ask, "How can we make this even better?" However, the leaders at Mercedes-Benz USA look at programs like employee engagement coaching and ask, "How can we make it the 'best or nothing'?"

Steve Cannon received extensive training on leadership as a cadet at West Point and throughout his military career as a U.S. Army Ranger. Steve knew that coaching might help leaders improve scores on employee surveys but wouldn't necessarily address the broader issues of leadership philosophy and skill. In fact, during employee engagement coaching sessions, Lior Arussy, president of Strativity, notes, "We were uncovering issues that reflected a lack of leadership development. We had breakdowns occurring with leadership basics like welcoming and orienting new employees to dealerships. As an example, we heard about a situation at a dealership where a new valet began parking cars on his first day of employment, only to be arrested several hours later. The employee hadn't been to an orientation, nor had he been introduced to anyone else at the dealership. A receptionist saw this 'stranger' walking around with Mercedes-Benz keys and driving cars, so she called the police. Clearly, some of the fundamentals of leadership were missing."

Dianna du Preez, general manager, Mercedes-Benz Academy, was largely responsible for creating the Leadership Academy and explains the thinking behind it: "We understood that leadership is the main driver of a company's culture. Employee engagement obviously stems from culture, and engaged employees are critical if you want to deliver extraordinary customer experiences. To truly achieve our transformational customer experience goals, we needed to focus more intently on the 4,000-plus leaders in our dealerships and help them broadly develop themselves and their people. Therefore, the Leadership Academy was a very focused initiative unlike anything ever seen in the automotive industry."

While automobile manufacturers often provide e-learning and other impersonal leadership development tools, Mercedes-Benz wanted to change the nature and level of training for both senior leaders and frontline managers at Mercedes-Benz dealerships. Dianna notes, "We have individuals throughout our dealer network who are highly educated and have substantial levels of leadership understanding and training. But in general, there was a significant lack of understanding concerning the importance of the role that leadership plays in shaping and feeding culture in an organization. Even in a pilot session with our Dealer Board, there was a lot of conversation about the fact that sales managers, service managers, or parts managers are often appointed because they are the best at what they do. The best parts advisor becomes a parts manager. The expectation is that outstanding performers just need to continue doing what they were doing, and they will be able to also manage people and receive a higher salary." Dianna continues,

"Unfortunately, the best salesperson isn't always the best sales manager. That's why the curriculum for the Mercedes-Benz Leadership Academy focuses on what it takes to be a successful leader and not on technical responsibilities. We don't address how to sell more cars or how to sell more parts. The focus is on understanding what it takes to lead a great culture. For example, the Leadership Academy explores how to create clear performance expectations and makes distinctions between coaching, mentoring, and managing. Our program connects the well-being and motivation of dealership associates to customer experience and, ultimately, to higher sales."

The Mercedes-Benz Leadership Academy was developed to serve two groups of leaders: dealership executives and managers. While much of the training is similar, a more strategic and enterprisewide focus is offered in the executive-level curriculum. The Leadership Academy is designed to be a continuous leadership development process, delivered in phases. The first phase, called "Lead Yourself," is centered on helping participants understand their leadership style and leadership philosophy; it has been delivered to more than 600 executive-level participants and more than 3,000 managers since 2014. The Lead Yourself curriculum will continue to be offered and will serve as a prerequisite for attending future leadership development training courses. The next planned training phase is called "Lead Your Team." It builds on insights gained in the previous phase and will enhance participants' understanding of how to lead teams and influence talent effectively. The course after Lead Your Team will be "Lead Your Organization," which will address how to sustain performance success and lead effectively across the entire organization.

The Lead Yourself training involves the completion of a pre-event self-assessment tool on leadership style, travel to a training location in either Chicago or Dallas, and two days of structured learning. In addition to opportunities for networking, the experiences include deep exploration of each individual's predominant leadership style, with an appreciation for the need to be adaptive in leading and communicating with others. Participants are exposed to "Leadership Lessons from the Blue Angels," an examination of the mindset of high-performance teams like the U.S. Navy's elite flight demonstration squadron. Participants are also given information and experiences that show them how to expand energy to enhance productivity and how to leverage tools, practices, and methods to shape a dealership culture that drives both employee and customer engagement.

Participants in Lead Yourself are also guided through an exercise that helps them define their own list of leadership beliefs. This list is not about finding the "right" leadership approach but rather focuses on finding the tenets of leadership that each participant wants to use as the foundation for her unique leadership approach. As an example of using beliefs to shape a career, Steve Cannon's leadership beliefs were shared with participants. They are:

- Create a compelling vision.

- Listen more than you speak.

- Ask 1,000 questions.

- Set ridiculously high standards.

- Be visible. . . . No one wants to follow someone they don't see.

- Culture eats strategy for breakfast.

- Be nice!

- Your team watches everything you do, so make sure your words and actions align.

- The best feedback is fast feedback.

- Never undermine a person's dignity.

- Be present or don't show.

- The glass is always half full.

At the end of the Lead Yourself training, each leader makes a 90-day commitment to focus on one specific leadership action. To create "accountability partners" for their leadership growth, participants share their commitment with others in their training class. Results from the first phase of training at the Leadership Academy have demonstrated meaningful shifts in leadership behavior, with participants acknowledging the value of the training and their commitment to growth objectives. From a qualitative perspective, participants in the executive sessions noted:

- "I hope that the dealer body as a whole embraces the spirit of the program and modifies it to suit their dealerships."

- "Great new ideas and skill sets. Really made me take a very introspective look on how I can become a better leader and person."

- "I can't wait to send my management team."

Similarly, participants in the manager sessions shared:

- "I am excited to see the effects of this in our dealership."

- "The event kept me engaged and allowed for purposeful thinking. I look forward to taking these lessons back to my team."

Drew Slaven, vice president marketing at MBUSA, notes that programs like the Mercedes-Benz Leadership Academy are so representative of the brand's cultural change efforts that "I have invited leaders of our advertising agencies to participate. In addition to our dealership partners, I want the people who help create our customer messaging to benefit from Leadership Academy offerings such as Brand Immersion. We should provide opportunities to educate all of our business partners on what it means to us to be Driven to Delight and what it means to develop leadership skills in pursuit of that objective."

The Mercedes-Benz Leadership Academy offers insights into how each of us can develop an ongoing leadership training program at our business. But more important, it demonstrates that in order to treat customers well, we have to develop and grow leaders. In keeping with management consultant Peter Drucker's words (and one of Steve Cannon's leadership beliefs) that "Culture eats strategy for breakfast," the leadership team at MBUSA has invested in programs to build leadership talent within Mercedes-Benz dealerships.

The shift from customer experience consulting (described in Chapter 7 and provided earlier in the transformation journey) to the Mercedes-Benz Leadership Academy reflects the importance of being proactive. Leadership development can't be solely reactive (for example, fixing problems identified in annual employee engagement surveys). It must anticipate leaders' needs and help them understand what it takes to develop high-performance cultures. Great leadership development programs give participants the tools to build and motivate team members for sustained excellence.

While you may not be able to develop programs on the scale of the Brand Immersion Experience or the Leadership Academy, it is worthwhile for you to think about how you can infuse passion for your products and your brand legacy into your employee base. For example, how can you afford opportunities for your people to experience—rather than hear about—your products or rich components of your history? What are you doing to explain what it truly means to be of service in your business? What skills are required to ensure that your customers feel the way you want them to feel after interacting with your brand? From a leadership perspective, what ongoing programs do you have in place to make leadership development a never-ending process in your business? Are you promoting people based on technical skill, or are you addressing leadership behavior as well? Finally, do you truly believe that your sustained profitability is linked to customer care? If so, is that customer care a by-product of your team's level of engagement and the overall skills of your leadership?

Clearly, Steve Cannon is driving a revolution at Mercedes-Benz aimed at influencing the hearts, minds, and skills of individuals in all parts and at all levels of the organization, both at Mercedes-Benz USA and Mercedes-Benz Financial Services and at the dealerships as well. As a result, from the onset of programs like Brand Immersion, staff members from Mercedes-Benz USA and Mercedes-Benz Financial Services have attended alongside dealership staff. Similarly, Mercedes-Benz executives, senior managers, and managers have attended the Mercedes-Benz Leadership Academy alongside dealer leadership and dealer principals. In essence, Steve and his team at MBUSA understand that effective culture change doesn't occur because an edict is sent down from a manufacturer, franchisor, or boss. It happens when people throughout an organization are exposed to and adopt new attitudes, behaviors, and skills. In the chapter that follows, we will look at how Mercedes-Benz USA supported these people initiatives through process improvements designed to streamline work flow and make it easier to delight customers.

➤ In the words of John Maxwell, "While a good leader sustains momentum, a great leader increases it."

➤ To truly win the hearts and minds of team members, training can't simply be didactic; it must be experiential, hands-on, and memorable.

➤ Employee orientation generally offers a basic overview of a company or a job, while full brand immersion typically requires a greater investment to drive connection, meaning, brand pride, and, ultimately, deep passion.

➤ It is imperative that you help every employee understand how you want customers to feel and what it means to serve them well in your business.

➤ Resist the urge to follow the latest customer service or customer experience trend. Success comes from having a consistent customer experience template (at Mercedes-Benz, it is Listen, Empathize, Add value, and Delight), not from changing to newly packaged concepts.

➤ Immersive programs help employees find purpose and context for their work, which in turn fuels their attachment to, and service of, something larger than themselves—ultimately contributing to authentic happiness.

➤ Some leaders ask, "How can we make this better?" Others leaders ask, "How can we make this optimal?"

➤ Customer experience excellence depends on the level of employee engagement. Employee engagement levels, in turn, are determined by the health of your culture and can be traced back to the quality and development of your leadership talent.

➤ Leadership development is not a "one and done" phenomenon. It is a never-ending process that offers perspective and insights on what it takes to motivate and drive sustained human performance, and tools to carry it out.

➤ In the words of John Quincy Adams, leadership is about inspiring others "to dream more, learn more, do more and become more."

Innovation is the only insurance against irrelevance. It's the only guarantee of long-term customer loyalty.

—Gary Hamel

9

Driving Process and Technological Change

A longstanding management principle suggests that if you take good people and subject them to bad processes, the processes will win every time. However, senior leaders at Mercedes-Benz USA challenge that belief. In fact, Steve Cannon and his team emphasize the importance of inspiring people to drive necessary process changes. MBUSA's leadership approach hinges on the idea that good people should and will modify business systems that are out of step with the company's ultimate transformational objective (in this case, delivering world-class customer experience). Furthermore, team members should leverage the best available technologies in mission-centric ways. This chapter and the one that follows will look at changes made in the infrastructure of business execution at Mercedes-Benz USA.

In Chapters 7 and 8, you saw how early initiatives to inspire and engage the staff at Mercedes-Benz dealerships (DaSH and employee engagement surveys) evolved into more sophisticated and sustainable solutions (the Brand Immersion Experience and the Leadership Academy) designed to build a lasting culture of customer obsession. Similarly, the early process improvements and technology enhancements outlined in this chapter serve to facilitate the complex, integrated processes and technological solutions discussed in Chapter 10.

Bringing Technology and a More Desirable Experience to the Showroom

What are your childhood memories of automobile showrooms? For me, the showroom was the end of a ritualized journey. In what became an annual event, my father would wait for the new Ford models to arrive at the dealership. We would enter a balloon-filled building, be greeted quickly by an eager salesperson, and typically be handed a brochure before we approached the new models. If my father was contemplating a purchase that year, we would test-drive the cars, haggle with a salesperson (often making offers and counteroffers scrawled on a piece of paper), and possibly continue those negotiations with a sales manager. Assuming that a deal was concluded, we would wait for a finance officer, be subjected to aggressive efforts to upsell service/maintenance options, sign copious numbers of financial documents, and finally be handed the keys. Years later, when I purchased my first car, the experience was not substantially different, nor has it been for most of my purchases thereafter.

While the dealership experience has remained fairly constant for decades, there have been rapid changes in customer behavior and customer demographics in the last few years. For example, millennials (alternatively referred to as gen Y), that cohort of more than 100 million consumers born between 1982 and 1997, have been raised with instant access to information and omnipresent computer-aided resources. This segment of the population, which is expected to be purchasing 75 percent of all vehicles by the year 2025, has very different expectations for the car-buying experience. In fact, David Barkholz, writing for *Automotive News*, notes that millennials "are coming of age. And they demand a level of transparency, tech savvy and barter-free buying unseen in previous generations."

These millennial consumers, and much of the rest of the population, for that matter, have been exposed to price transparency, easy online transactions, and technology-rich, innovative retail experiences like the Apple Store. As a result, when they enter a world where pricing is vague, sales staff are aggressive, and technology is absent, they become underwhelmed, frustrated, and ripe for innovative alternatives.

While small in scale, Tesla Motors created a disruption in the automobile showroom experience by moving its dealerships from the periphery of town into shopping malls. Tesla's store designs are in keeping with Apple's retail approach, complete with interactive touchscreens and a direct-to-consumer model. The resistance of the automobile industry to these types of changes can be seen in the lawsuits brought against Tesla from groups like the Massachusetts State Automobile Dealers Association. While much of the litigation centers on a car manufacturer circumventing traditional franchised dealership-based distribution, it also highlights the tension created as brands look to lure customers away from a showroom experience that is sometimes ranked below "going to the dentist."

Early on, the leaders at Mercedes-Benz USA realized that world-class experiences require a consistently appealing dealership environment. Enterprisewide dealer upgrades were well under way through the Autohaus program (discussed in Chapter 1) before the Driven to Delight transformation. Accordingly, Steve Cannon and his leadership team focused their efforts on modernizing technology, streamlining the customer journey, and making the experience as easy as possible for customers in Mercedes-Benz dealerships.

The efforts outlined in this chapter have been well received by Mercedes-Benz customers such as Dr. Wendell McBurney, who notes, "I bought my M-Class in 2012. I had spent four hours at a Cadillac dealership looking at the SRX and had to go through all sorts of contortions to get them to focus on my needs rather than their needs. I had to meet the sales manager and the service manager. I had to meet this person and that person. I had to jump through hoops in order to get to the bottom line. In fact, I never did get to the bottom line. After giving up and going to the Mercedes-Benz dealership, it took only 30 minutes to agree upon our new M-Class."

Similarly, Mercedes-Benz owner Paul David notes, "My wife and I spent a lot of time researching our car purchase online. Since Mercedes-Benz offered more videos than any other car manufacturer, we appreciated Mercedes-Benz technology and learned a great deal about the safety of their vehicles. In fact, Mercedes-Benz provided heartwarming, personal videos about people, their cars, and how the safety of their vehicle saved them in accidents. After researching over the Internet, I went into the dealership and took a test drive. That's when I realized that even the amazing videos did not do the cars justice."

Mercedes-Benz owner Steve Levine also appreciated the substantial amount of information he received as part of his Mercedes-Benz online experience, as well as the proactive nature of the dealership staff. "A couple of months before the lease was up on my Mercedes-Benz, my salesman called and asked me to come in to talk. I went into the dealership, the salesman showed me a couple of cars, we drove the new model, we talked for about half an hour, and two hours later I walked out with a new car. We basically traded keys. They made me such a good deal, and without haggling and without involving the sales manager. The salesman had the authorization to go ahead and make the deal. I've never bought a car so fast in my life. That was a really great experience."

Before I launch into the specific early programs and technologies that have generated such laudatory comments from customers like Wendell, Paul, and Steve, it might be worthwhile to take a moment and think about the timeliness and relevance of the experiences you are providing to your different consumer segments. Are the look and feel of your service environment and the relevance of your products appealing to baby boomers (the approximately 78.2 million consumers born between 1945 and 1964), generation X (constituting roughly 70 million customers born between 1965 and 1981), and generation Y/millennials? Have you upgraded and refreshed your processes and technology components to meet the changing purchase behaviors of all relevant consumer segments, most notably those customers who will ensure your long-term success? Have you taught your people how to deliver service experiences that connect technology with the wants, needs, and desires of different consumer segments?

Brands often spend large amounts of time, money, and effort on developing products for and marketing to large customer segments like generation Y. They spend significant amounts on product development, advertising, and social media campaigns, but they fail to invest in the environmental and service aspects or technologies that would make the experience connect with customers or even be on a par with the quality of the products they sell.

In 2013, Erin Shea, writing in *Luxury Daily* about the soon-to-be-released 2014 Mercedes-Benz CLA, noted, "Mercedes-Benz USA is opening up the brand to a younger consumer group with new promotions for its CLA model, which has a sticker price of less than $30,000. . . . Social media is the main tool that Mercedes is using to drive its CLA campaign and communicate with its target audience." Given that a new "target audience" would be entering dealerships, Mercedes-Benz USA also had to work with dealers to ensure that they would offer an experience that was welcoming and relevant to that customer segment.

Drew Slaven, vice president marketing at Mercedes-Benz, notes, "If you have a brilliant product and you deliver it with a great customer experience, you begin to diminish the very need for marketing." Drew cites Apple as an example of a product company that has innovated a relevant, technologically rich customer experience that has put the company in a position where it "could shut down its consumer marketing tomorrow and still sell as many iWatches and other innovative products as it does now with advertising. It is the combination of product and relevant, engaging experiences that authentically connects you to your desired customers."

As you will see, the people at Mercedes-Benz USA took charge of changing and improving a broad suite of programs, processes, and technologies geared to connect with the discerning Mercedes-Benz customer base. In fact, Dietmar Exler, vice president sales, notes, "We saw two trends coming together—increased information availability and a strong desire on the part of consumers to have unpressured product access. A long time ago, you had a limited amount of information available on new cars, so the dealership was the place to go to learn about a vehicle. Today, everything about a car can be found online. However, it is one thing to read about a car's benefits and features and quite another thing to experience them. We have generations of people wanting to come in to experience what they have read about and seen online. They don't want to be sold. They want to go from information to experience."

While the "what" of MBUSA's efforts to take customers from abundant information to hassle-free sales and service experiences will apply most directly to the automobile industry, the "why" and "how" of these programs and technologies will offer insights that are widely applicable across business landscapes.

Positioning People to Affect Processes

Some managers believe that if you want to jump-start improvements in customer experience delivery, you need to hire more people. Certainly, work groups frequently clamor for "increased head count" to deliver customer care at the levels sought by senior leaders. As you have seen from the decisions discussed in earlier chapters, the leadership team at Mercedes-Benz doesn't see staffing increases as the initial step in creating success with customers. In fact, as evidenced by the way in which the Customer Experience team was created, leaders at Mercedes-Benz are more likely to first realign existing staff around a common mission and then maximize the discretionary effort of the existing workforce by driving engagement and brand passion. Staffing increases are considered when aligned and engaged staff members can't sufficiently meet the volume of customer need.

In two specific cases, the MBUSA leadership saw specific unmet support needs that directly affected the timely responses of customer service solutions at dealerships. As MBUSA's customer-focused transformation progressed, its expectations of the dealer network relative to the customer experience steadily increased. With increasing sales and service volume and an expanding product lineup, dealers, in turn, wanted Mercedes-Benz to provide faster responses to the more challenging technical cases that arose in their service departments. Dealers spoke; Mercedes-Benz leaders listened; and additional field support staff were hired.

Harry Hynekamp, manager of the Customer Experience team, notes, "We actively seek and receive feedback from our dealers, and we heard very clearly that we were not providing them with enough field and product technical specialists to support their efforts to serve their customers better and more efficiently." So what is a field technical specialist? Suppose your car is in for service, and the dealership technician has done everything in accordance with Mercedes-Benz work instructions, but the repair efforts have not resolved the issue. At that point, the technician will probably have the shop foreman troubleshoot the issue. If the shop foreman can't resolve the problem, a technical case is opened and assigned to an MBUSA field technical specialist. The field technical specialist helps identify the root cause of the problem and works with the technician at the dealership to resolve it. After the repair is made, the field technical specialist loops back and debriefs the shop foreman and the technician on any resource needs or processes that will address similar issues in the future.

Let's compare that field technical specialist to a product technical specialist. If the field specialist cannot resolve a problem, it is referred to a product specialist, typically an engineer, at the Mercedes-Benz USA home office. Given the complex nature of the problems they address, product specialists often create solutions that modify overarching repair processes that are used throughout the dealer network. Based on the feedback of dealers and the important role that field and product technical specialists play in addressing the most challenging service situations, Mercedes-Benz USA hired more people for each of those positions. Dealership service teams now have more technical resources, challenging service needs are resolved more swiftly, customers are happier, and dealers are more likely to earn the leadership bonus.

Mercedes-Benz owner Nancy Rece shares a situation in which her local dealership interacted with Mercedes-Benz USA team members to provide her with the expedited resolution that she desired: "My husband purchased a new M-Class diesel model and picked up the car in late November. When the engine was cold, it would start up okay. But we'd be half a minute away from the house and the choke and idle would act up; the car would shake, and it would cough for a few minutes, then it would be okay after it had warmed up." Nancy notes that her husband contacted the dealership to determine the source of the vehicle's problems, and the dealership contacted Mercedes-Benz USA. Nancy continues the story by noting, "Mercedes-Benz USA had to work with Mercedes-Benz in Germany to come up with a solution to the problem. Then, once they thought they had a solution, they had to run it through the U.S. EPA. Then our local Mercedes dealer, Mercedes-Benz of West Chester, made the change to one of its vehicles to make sure that the fix worked. Throughout this whole process, they were in constant contact with us, making sure that everything else was okay. They were very apologetic. And when they were finally able to make the fix, the problems were solved." Because of the swift initial response of MBUSA support, constant communication with the customer, resolution of the problem, and service recovery gestures, Nancy concludes, "This could have been a very negative experience, but the process and communication . . . was very acceptable. It turned out to be a good experience."

In a similar vein, Mercedes-Benz USA added resources and enhanced the customer resolution capacity of other areas of corporate support, including the Customer Assistance Center (CAC)—the arm (and voice) of the brand and the area with which customers interface when they contact corporate headquarters. The Mercedes-Benz leaders first changed the philosophy at the CAC to empower the CAC agents, then added agents as needed.

In the not-too-distant past, the Mercedes-Benz USA Customer Assistance Center would respond to customer complaints with a fairly impersonal letter that essentially said, "Your matter is best handled by your dealer." Not only was such a response unsatisfactorily dismissive, but it often increased the aggravation of individuals who had already addressed their issue or concern with their dealer unsuccessfully. Karen Matri, then department manager customer advocacy at MBUSA's Customer Assistance Center, explains the perspective and process shifts that have occurred: "We stopped sending letters and began offering innovative solutions. We worked on developing our agents to review all the facts of a case, employ empathy, educate customers, reach agreement as needed, and generate creative solutions." Mercedes-Benz owner Bill Faulk shares how empowerment and coordinated follow-through pay dividends in customer loyalty. "I called the Mercedes-Benz customer service number and asked if there were any rebates or incentives for current lessees. They said there were not. So, I started venting, telling them they should do something for a customer who wanted to stay a customer and not give him the same deal that anyone walking in off the street could get. I left it at that and hung up the phone. I went to my dealer and cut a deal for a new vehicle, getting a price I was fine with. That was it. I was supposed to pick up the car on a Friday. On the prior Wednesday or Thursday, I received a call from someone at Mercedes-Benz corporate offering me a $2,000 incentive. He said they wanted me to be a customer for life. You know what? He's right. Because they went out of their way, took care of me, and did the right thing, they have a customer for life. When this car goes back off-lease, I'll buy another one. To me that was a 'wow moment.' Who does that? When does a call to a contact center result in someone from a corporate office calling you? It just doesn't happen—ever."

Stories like the one shared by Bill reflect customer "wow" moments resulting from an empowerment shift at the Mercedes-Benz Customer Assistance Center. Although the CAC agent could not resolve Bill's need initially, that agent "advocated" for Bill and accessed resources that secured Bill's loyalty. But doesn't a customer advocacy mindset and increased employee empowerment increase customer resolution costs? In my experience, these types of concerns frequently surface as brands seek to manage the "gray areas" of customer wants and needs in an innovative way. As an effective transition occurs, however, customer assistance staff members learn how to balance the immediate needs of customers with broader business objectives and financial prudence. Staff members learn that monetary compensation is an appropriate first response, but they find ways that don't overcompensate customers. Instead, they listen, understand what a customer needs, educate the customer on what is realistic, and find innovative ways to create solutions that are fair to both the customer and the business. Brandon Newman, case manager, customer advocacy, notes, "I have been entrusted to creatively deliver an outstanding customer experience. When I am listening to customers, listening to dealers, and looking for solutions, I am always balancing what the customer needs with how I can resolve that need using the appropriate resources. I want to do what's right for the customer and be a good steward of our company's assets. Often, solutions have nothing to do with money—they involve making sure a customer is heard, understood, and valued. When money is involved, fairness and respect are key. The ultimate component of that respect is to close the loop with the customer. Even when customers don't get everything they want, they need to feel that a fair resolution was achieved and gain closure. Listening to them, understanding them, and making an empathetic effort to gain a fair resolution leads to a customer experiencing delight."

Karen Matri notes that the empowering changes made at the CAC certainly exceeded any and all perceived risks. "We now see customer problem resolution that is timely, well researched, and aligned. By educating our customers, they understand our goodwill criteria and are less upset. On-the-spot decisions regarding less expensive issues create amazed customers. Most important, I am proud of the creative spirit of our CAC agents. For example, when there was no resolution for an eight-year-old, out-of-warranty vehicle, our agent seized the opportunity to delight a customer by donating $50 to a No-Kill animal shelter because that customer's dog had spent eight wonderful years in the backseat of that car."

Hmm . . . a letter saying, "We can't help you; go back to your dealership" or a well-staffed call center with empowered employees looking for ways to connect, listen, empathize, educate, innovate solutions, and delight customers. Which of these would you rather experience? More important, what are your customers experiencing? To be truly successful at customer experience delivery, you can't continue to operate with processes that were originally designed to make it easy for you to conduct business. Your people should be encouraged and empowered to build processes that make it easier for customers to be served by you.

Elevated and Consistent Processes

A shift toward customer-focused processes led to positive changes at the Customer Assistance Center. Similarly, philosophical shifts and process improvements occurred across the Mercedes-Benz dealership network with regard to another essential process, the service loaner vehicle or alternate transportation experience. I use the phrase *alternate transportation* to reflect the way the program was often referred to prior to a mind shift that resulted in what is now known as the Mercedes-Benz Courtesy Vehicle Program.

Prior to 2012 and the evolution of the Courtesy Vehicle Program, there was no consistent, uniform way of securing a loaner vehicle across the Mercedes-Benz dealership network. In some dealerships, you could drop off your Mercedes-Benz for service and drive away in another Mercedes-Benz "loaner" while your vehicle was being serviced. In other cases, your loaner car would not be a Mercedes-Benz. In those instances, it would probably be a car from another manufacturer that the dealership group represented. The process of securing your loaner vehicle was also highly variable; some dealerships had a rental car counter in their service department, while others required their customers to go to a rental counter somewhere other than the dealership. In some cases, the loaner vehicle was presented to the customer in a very professional manner: cleaned and washed, with a bottle of water in the cup holder and a full tank of gas. In other situations, the customer was handed the keys to whatever car was readily available, no matter what condition it happened to be in.

Given the inconsistent nature of loaner car offerings across Mercedes-Benz dealerships, the MBUSA leadership set out to develop a courtesy vehicle program that would deliver a vastly improved customer experience. To make this happen, MBUSA would need to require its dealers to maintain a Mercedes-Benz loaner fleet specifically for that purpose. In partnership with the dealers, Mercedes-Benz USA deployed existing resources to defray some of the cost of the new Courtesy Vehicle Program, and dealers secured a representative cross section of Mercedes-Benz models (both entry-level and high-end) for their courtesy fleet to address all the travel, car seat, strollers, hauling, and other purposes for which customers used their vehicles.

To ensure the success of the program, MBUSA support staff developed the processes and procedures needed to execute it consistently. Those guidelines included defining the nature of the fleet the dealers were to have on hand, the technology platform they would need to manage the fleet, a streamlined process for delivering the courtesy vehicles to customers, and the process by which the loaner cars would be returned to retail (as pre-owned) and be supported in that marketplace.

The changes made to the Courtesy Vehicle Program have delighted customers. Mercedes-Benz owner Steve H. notes, for example, "The service department at Beverly Hills Mercedes is amazing. I took my car in for a regular planned service call. They gave me a loaner car that was much nicer than the car I brought in for service. It was a brand-new E-Class. Not only was it a nice gesture, but it also was a great marketing tool for someone who was almost done with payments on the current car." Changes in the Courtesy Vehicle Program have resulted in a more consistent experience across the dealership network. In Steve's case, the loaner also enticed him in the direction of purchasing a new vehicle that might have been outside of what he would typically have considered.

The evolution from an extremely variable alternate transportation experience to a consistent and convenient Mercedes-Benz Courtesy Vehicle Program would not have been successful without all the foundational pieces discussed in prior chapters (a compelling vision to be a world-class customer experience provider, leadership actions that instilled trust between MBUSA and the dealer community, and efforts to engage and inspire staff members, both at Mercedes-Benz USA and throughout the dealer network). Similarly, without a consistent Courtesy Vehicle Program in place, Mercedes-Benz USA would not have been able to take on far more complex customer-facing challenges, such as an integrated online scheduling platform referred to as Digital Service Drive (more on that in Chapter 10). Moreover, the leaders at Mercedes-Benz USA would not have succeeded in providing consistent loaner vehicle experiences had they not financially invested in partnership with their dealer partners.

The approach that the Mercedes-Benz USA leaders took in creating the Courtesy Vehicle Program closely parallels their response to another product: prepaid maintenance. The creation of the prepaid maintenance program and its associated processes was inspired, in part, by a customer need that was being addressed by a number of Mercedes-Benz competitors who claimed to offer "free maintenance." Rather than rushing out with a similar program, the leaders at Mercedes Benz USA sought to create a series of offerings and related processes that was in keeping with their overarching vision to be a world-class customer experience provider. Through this filter, the prepaid maintenance program would have to respond to the consumer's desire for choice, pricing transparency, value-based options (up to 30 percent savings compared to purchasing maintenance as you go), and packages that were customized for different customer driving patterns and the unique requirements of each vehicle. Since "free" maintenance programs are free in name only (maintenance costs are built into the "below-the-line" vehicle purchase price) and typically have substantial exclusions, the leaders at Mercedes-Benz USA crafted a program guided by the desire to offer customers truly worry-free care. That care would come with visibility concerning exactly what customers were paying for (something that is increasingly important to younger customer segments) and assurance that the covered services would not result in any hidden out-of-pocket fees.

Mercedes-Benz leaders knew that customers appreciate an honest message about maintenance costs and a clear, robust set of prepaid maintenance options. In fact, in the year following the launch of the Mercedes-Benz prepaid maintenance program (and every year since), the J.D. Power results show higher satisfaction scores with the Mercedes-Benz USA program than with so-called free alternatives. These results verify that Mercedes-Benz leadership has filled a gap for customers by giving them the ability to get reasonably priced options for worry-free driving.

From my perspective, the mindset and processes involved in developing the Mercedes-Benz prepaid maintenance program are very consistent with innovations in other industries, such as the Amazon Prime program. At Amazon, customers had traditionally experienced a recurring annoyance at the end of each purchase—the payment of shipping costs. Thus, a "prepaid" shipping value program reduced that recurring irritant and gave economic price advantages to those who committed to prepayment. Research conducted by Consumer Intelligence Research Partners on the Amazon Prime program has shown that Prime not only improved customer loyalty but resulted in Prime customers spending on average $1,500 with Amazon as of December 2014. That is $625 more than their non-Prime cohorts.

As you look at your business, are there parts of the customer experience that are repetitive and unpleasant? This can be as simple as making your customer repeat his name and service need to each new person he encounters rather than having that information seamlessly shared internally through a revised process. Additionally, how might you bundle—and price—service options that remove annoyances or provide an elevated level of care? Think of this as being like the "fast pass" option at an amusement park, where guests can choose to pay more to skip the wait and move to the front of the line. How might programs such as these enhance your customers' loyalty and increase their spending with your company?

Give Me Technology—Give Me Mobile

Without question, Mercedes-Benz vehicles are technological marvels, born from a legacy of engineering innovation. But even with all the cutting-edge, high-tech systems that are onboard a Mercedes-Benz, it was not all that long ago that the dealerships selling and servicing them had a veritable dearth of technology in customer-facing areas. That was all about to change with the corporate staff's focus on updating processes and technologies that were out of step with customer needs and expectations.

In order to begin the journey toward a more consistent technology presence in the dealerships, Mercedes-Benz USA championed a Digital Dealer Network initiative in 2010. That program required dealers to purchase a high-definition touchscreen monitor and place it in their showrooms. The monitor was connected to a Mercedes-Benz intranet that allowed video updates on Mercedes-Benz products to be downloaded onto the monitor. Given the interactivity of the touchscreens, a salesperson could co-create a vehicle with the customer before the customer even walked out to the lot or took a test drive. In essence, the technology facilitated a conversation concerning customer needs and served to shape an understanding of what the customer was looking for in a Mercedes-Benz vehicle. Additionally, the salesperson could quickly and interactively present vehicle options that might interest the customer. In essence, these large, interactive showroom screens facilitated the assessment of a consumer's needs, product exploration, and the ability to presell a vehicle before a test drive occurred.

With the rise of tablet technology, in 2011–2012 Mercedes-Benz shifted its focus away from hardwired Digital Dealer Network monitors to a dealer iPad initiative and iPad product applications. Also, many of the "build your own" vehicle options migrated to the Mercedes-Benz USA website, as customer shopping behavior increasingly began online, prior to a showroom visit. In support of tablet technologies, MBUSA required dealers to buy a set number of iPads based on their sales volume. These tablets were to be used at various stages of the sales process. At the launch of the iPad initiative, two product apps were available; additional apps subsequently became available for virtually every Mercedes-Benz model. The leaders at Mercedes-Benz USA encouraged dealers to use these apps to explain product features—especially those features that were difficult to demonstrate live, like Blind Spot Assist.

Dealers swiftly embraced the mobile technology, purchasing far more iPads than MBUSA required. Findings from J.D. Power research suggest that customers significantly value the use of iPad technology during the automotive sales experience and even spend more money on a vehicle when these types of technology are used.

Given the successful deployment of tablet technology in support of the sales process, leaders at Mercedes-Benz USA maintain an ongoing exploration of ways to use mobile technology to enhance customer experiences throughout the entire customer journey. For example, the Mercedes-Benz USA Dealer Delivery app, which has gone through multiple updates, was created to establish a consistent approach to explaining brand benefits and vehicle features at the time a customer takes delivery of his vehicle. The presentations provided through the app are specific to the customer's model and equipment package. A "delight" feature of the app includes the ability to take a picture of the customer with his new Mercedes-Benz and e-mail it automatically at the end of the delivery process. This personalized e-mail includes further explanations of the vehicle features and links to MBUSA.com "How To" videos. These videos, in turn, provide even more detailed information for the customer to access at his convenience. Kristi Steinberg, then department manager, retail business development at MBUSA, shares that the success of the Delivery app "results in noteworthy improvements on both our internal customer experience index and our syndicated J.D. Power Sales Satisfaction Index scores. The right technology available at the right time deployed by the right people is a winning formula for us."

This combination of having the "right technology available at the right time deployed by the right people" continues to evolve at Mercedes-Benz dealerships. For example, leaders at MBUSA are looking for ways to seamlessly integrate appropriate technological solutions throughout customers' financing and service experiences. Since complex integrated service solutions will be discussed in detail in the next chapter, I will simply offer one more example of how tablet technology and a financing and insurance (F&I) app have been deployed to expedite and enrich the F&I journey at Mercedes-Benz dealerships.

Greg Gates, then senior manager marketing, Mercedes-Benz Financial Services, describes the thinking behind the F&I app: "Our customers have busy lives, and the last thing they want to do is sit and wait for a finance manager to free up. When we created the iPad application, we wanted to value our customers' time, provide them with helpful information, and give them something fun—or at least different—to use when they would otherwise be waiting. Rather than taking the customer's time to respond to verbal questions that we can collect digitally, the F&I manager can more effectively craft finance options that best suit the customer's need." With the introduction of the app, customers are given iPads (with a menu of F&I-related content and digital forms). Once the customer has digitally provided the needed financial information, she walks into the office of a finance manager, who has received and reviewed the information and can customize lending, leasing, payments, and other options expeditiously. In a short period of time, Mercedes-Benz has gone from limited customer-facing technology in its dealerships to being the manufacturer acknowledged by J.D. Power as leading the industry by using iPads and other technology tools most frequently in both sales and service.

Implementation of new products, processes, and technologies is always filled with challenges, not least of which is the need to continuously upgrade and improve technology platforms. Not surprisingly, many of the process and technological interactions at Mercedes-Benz are continuing to evolve and will probably be replaced by a new generation of breakthroughs. Wisely, leaders at Mercedes-Benz leverage process innovation and technology consistent with the guidance given by Tim O'Reilly, the computer expert who popularized the term *open source*. Tim suggests, "What new technology does is create new opportunities to do a job that customers want done." At Mercedes-Benz, customer experience technology is not there for technology's sake; it is present to drive delight for increasingly technology-savvy consumers.

As you look at your business, are good people at the mercy of bad processes, or have your people been inspired and empowered to drive customer-centric change? Are your customers experiencing more customized solutions and an ease of doing business with you? Are you updating your customer-facing technologies to remain relevant and do the job your customers want done?

➤ Innovation is your only insurance against irrelevance.

➤ When good people encounter bad processes, the bad processes should not win. When people see the vision for transformational change shared by senior leaders and are encouraged to modify processes and leverage technology, successful change is achievable.

➤ Service delivery processes often change more slowly than consumers do. Evaluate how well your service programs and products address the needs of existing and emerging generations of consumers.

➤ Before you think technological upgrades, have you addressed the basic appeal of your physical environment?

➤ Adding staff members does not necessarily result in improved customer experiences. However, in some instances, elevation of the customer experience can't be achieved without hiring more people in service and support functions.

➤ Often the greatest impact on the customer experience occurs not because of increased staffing but instead from a perspective shift that allows existing team members to be empowered to innovate solutions in response to the "gray" areas of customer need.

➤ Well-trained and empowered team members balance customer needs with overarching business objectives and financial prudence, thus creating wins for both their customer and their company.

➤ Effective customer-facing technologies educate, engage, and expedite service processes.

➤ Look at your service processes from the perspective of your customers to identify recurring annoyances they encounter. Consider giving them the opportunity to prepay costs in order to have some of those annoyances removed. Use Amazon Prime or Mercedes-Benz prepaid maintenance as examples to fuel your creativity.

➤ Are you adding technology innovations for the right reasons? Do you view technology as creating new opportunities to do jobs that your customers want done?

Complexity that works is built up out of

modules that work perfectly, layered one

over the other.

—Kevin Kelly

en to delight. it is not just a phrase. it is prom
elief. it is a commitment to creating po onsh
making people smile and to leaving the sens
aplete trust. driven to delight means e persc
tment. it is a reminder that the journey ne.
e is always a more thoughtful way. a ut e

10

Integrating Processes into Enterprisewide Solutions

◇◇

I f you were a fan of the television series *Seinfeld*, you will probably recall a scene in which two of the show's main characters, Jerry and Elaine, approach a rental car counter to pick up a midsize car. The rental agent confirms Jerry's reservation, but tells him that there are no midsize cars available. Jerry is confused and explains that he made a reservation and that a reservation should keep a midsize car available for him. After some additional banter, Jerry sums up the situation in a nutshell by noting that while the company is great at making a reservation, they "just don't know how to hold the reservation."

en to delight means exceptional personal treatment. it
inder that the journey is never done. that the s alway
e thoughtful way. and throughout each interaction we r
mber that the best or nothing cannot just be a descriptio

Many customer experience failures—like Jerry's carless reservation—result from organizations, process gaps, or technological systems that are not integrated to help the customer move across a business. Online rental reservation systems may function perfectly, but when the vehicle is not available, the customer doesn't care how easy it was to book the car online.

This chapter explores a series of ways in which the Mercedes-Benz leaders have made improvements in the customer experience—not by trying to take care of a particular pain point during a transaction but by aligning people, processes, technology, and systems. It is through this effort that Mercedes-Benz has provided streamlined customer interactions.

From my perspective as a customer experience consultant, the types of integrated human and technology platforms discussed in this chapter represent best-in-class approaches to customer experience excellence. While there are countless examples that could be discussed, this chapter will look at how groups of people at Mercedes-Benz link together to deliver seamless and delightful experiences.

Philosopher and historian Bertrand Russell noted that it's healthy "to hang a question mark on the things you have long taken for granted." While working with the leaders at Mercedes-Benz USA, I've had the opportunity to hang a number of question marks along their transformational customer experience journey. Some of the questions I asked in 2013 resonated strongly with Gareth Joyce, vice president customer services, and his team.

Specifically, I asked Gareth to look at the improvements that had been made so far and determine which of them had produced more than incremental progress. As the MBUSA leaders looked to the future of customer experiences, how could they steward the brand in fundamentally different, innovative, new, or groundbreaking ways?

When one is fortunate enough to ask the right leaders the right questions at the right time, it is amazing how creative solutions emerge. However, never in the course of my consulting career have I seen the magnitude of innovation that was unleashed at MBUSA. Much of the remainder of this book looks at fundamentally different—and groundbreaking—initiatives such as MB Select and Digital Service Drive.

MB SELECT

Tylden Dowell, former customer experience specialist at Mercedes-Benz USA, describes MB SELECT as a group of initiatives originally created from the premise "The answer is yes; now what's the question?" MB SELECT was initiated in the fall of 2013 to support the launch of two vehicles: the CLA, which is the car that serves as the new entry to the Mercedes-Benz brand, and the redesigned flagship, the Mercedes-Benz S-Class. The major components of MB SELECT were (1) a cross-functional task force that met daily during critical vehicle launch periods to proactively monitor and address (within 24 hours) any issue that would adversely affect customer experiences and (2) a cache of monetary resources that was made available to "delight" customers following the purchase of a CLA or S-Class.

Participants in the cross-functional "rapid response" team represented virtually every facet of the automotive business; they included president and CEO Steve Cannon, vice president of sales Dietmar Exler, and vice president of customer services Gareth Joyce, as well as sales representatives, finance and insurance professionals, dealer participants, field technical support staff, and individuals from the Customer Experience team. Despite their varied titles, the team members operated as equals. From a process perspective, the group met every day during the vehicle launch window. It closely tracked social media posts, customer surveys, and service department data, looking for any issues that surfaced repeatedly on these newly launched vehicles. When issues did arise, the group did not seek to ascribe blame but rather tried to find solutions; to that end, participants were expected to research issues that touched their areas and provide answers to their fellow team members at the next daily meeting. Decisions were made quickly, based on information garnered from all available forms of data, customer feedback, and the input of dealers and Mercedes-Benz field representatives.

An excellent example of how the rapid response team operated and the results it generated is found in the corporate response to the missing CLA "brushed aluminum floor pedals with rubber studs." Listed as a feature of the Edition 1 option package, the floor pedals added a sporty touch to the vehicle's interior, in keeping with its distinctive exterior styling. The rapid response team became aware that the initial Edition 1 CLA vehicles did not, in fact, have the studded pedals, although the feature was listed on the window stickers. The labels were inaccurate.

In prior launches, if the style of a vehicle's floor pedals wasn't a safety concern (and the CLA's studded pedals were not), a more reactive posture might have been considered appropriate. Early purchasers who did not get the studded pedals they were expecting would probably have received a formal apology and an item like an iTunes gift card to acknowledge their inconvenience. However, in this case, the rapid response team leveraged all resources within the company to make sure that going forward, every incorrect CLA label was replaced with an accurate one. Furthermore, the team problem-solved a viable solution for the very small number of individuals who had purchased Edition 1 vehicles. Instead of a service recovery solution like an iTunes gift card, the team secured a supply of the studded pedals (which are a feature of the

AMG version of the CLA) and installed them on the affected vehicles. Through the collective knowledge, speed of response, and resourcefulness of the team members, widespread customer frustration was averted and a relevant service recovery was achieved.

In addition to developing expedited resolutions to emerging issues, the rapid response team was able to bring together disparate parts of the automotive business. Leaders at Mercedes-Benz were able to react nimbly to customer and dealer feedback. Participants in the rapid response team were not representing their corporate departments—they were representing the imminent needs of CLA and S-Class customers.

In business today, many customer service delays occur because employees fear that they will be chastised for any problem that occurs when they are pursuing a customer solution. Time is spent justifying actions and averting blame. Corporate distrust permeates each work area—as if the people in another department are less responsible or lack commitment. Leaders have the opportunity to break down those geographic or departmental silos by developing cross-functional teams with the common purpose of finding quick and effective customer solutions. How well does your business erase the naturally occurring silos that interfere with a rapid systemic response? Do you observe people justifying and defending their actions through long e-mail treatises, or are your people rising above the blame game to swiftly and collectively focus on solutions that will improve the service experience or enhance service recovery?

The second key component of MB SELECT was making financial resources available to address the needs of new CLA and S-Class customers. Steve Cannon shared the logic behind this important part of the integrated solution: "I was returning from Germany after having meetings with some of the product engineers for the S-Class. They had said that with every product, there are going to be some start-up issues. So I began thinking about how we can address those occasional issues at the launch of the best automobile in the world and assure dealers and customers that we at MBUSA are truly committed to the best customer experience journey. Over the years, we had heard customers and dealers tell us they wanted to have problems resolved immediately and not wait for responses that had escalated up the Mercedes-Benz USA ladder. As such, MB SELECT was about us collectively trying to raise our game. Why not give dealers the power to immediately do the right thing for an S-Class customer instead of taking two weeks to solve a problem with us? So that led us to build a goodwill package into that S-Class launch and into the launch of our CLA as well."

The "goodwill package" that Steve Cannon is referring to was an allocation of meaningful discretionary financial resources to be applied for each S-Class and CLA automobile. Dealers could use those resources provided by Mercedes-Benz USA—with no strings attached—on a case-by-case basis to immediately respond to a particular customer's need and/or to enhance the overall customer experience. While dealers had to document the use of those funds, no permission was required and no reimbursement request was challenged. In essence, dealers were given the authority and discretion to use corporate resources, when needed, to enrich the experience of CLA and S-Class purchasers.

Unless your business is structured differently from mine, you have to be wondering where all those resources came from. As you will recall, in Chapter 3, I mentioned the savings made by Gareth Joyce's strategic planning process when he realigned resources associated with the Roadside Assistance program. The savings resulting from that scope change were funneled into MB SELECT. Other cost savings efforts associated with parts delivery efficiencies also provided funding for the MB SELECT program. Resources (and budgets) are finite, so great leaders find different ways to utilize their people and dollars so that they can maximize profitability, sustainability, and customer loyalty.

Given the benefits of the rapid response team and the goodwill package, both programs have been extended well beyond the CLA and S-Class launches. For example, the rapid response team is now deployed for every Mercedes-Benz launch, but it also meets in between launches to address issues concerning existing vehicles. The team constantly listens to the voice of the customer on social media and solicits the input of dealers and field staff. Similarly, MBUSA's allocation of discretionary financial resources has been extended to every Mercedes-Benz vehicle.

MB SELECT has been positively embraced by dealers, as evidenced by the comments of individuals such as Pat Evans, Mercedes-Benz of Virginia Beach service manager, who notes, "MB SELECT is a wonderful program, allowing us complete freedom to use designated resources to make things right for customers, to brighten their day, or to 'wow' them. We can use MB SELECT to repair a car or to address inconveniences—whether we caused them or not. In essence, MB SELECT helps us to provide the highest level of care and exceed customer expectations."

Mercedes-Benz of Alexandria general manager Pete Collins shares an example of how MB SELECT goodwill resources were used at his dealership as part of resolving a very unfortunate situation. "We had a client who was in transit. He had bought a new C-Class Coupe at his home in Florida. During a multistate trip, his engine began making an odd noise, and he brought his car in to us in Alexandria, Virginia. We put him in a courtesy vehicle, and our service technician did a road test to try to duplicate the customer's complaint. In the process of that road test, our technician got sideswiped in the customer's car. The front bumper was ripped off the brand-new car that the customer had owned for less than a week. As you might suspect, he was understandably furious. After we calmed him down, he told us he no longer wanted that particular vehicle. Although his lease contract was already in place, I tried to find him a replacement car at our dealership, but we couldn't find one to fit him. We ended up extending his time in our courtesy vehicle, fixing the damaged car by putting a brand-new bumper on it, and shipping that car back to Florida, where the dealer exchanged vehicles for him. MB SELECT supports dealers in doing the right thing and encourages us at the dealer level to put our own money into the equation in partnership with the investment MBUSA has made in the program."

The innovative ways in which customers are delighted by the MB SELECT program are chronicled and shared throughout the dealer community on a monthly basis. Periodically, "best of the best" customer delight stories are selected and recognized. Here are a couple of examples:

> Our customer's GLK recently left her stranded on the expressway. It turns out she was also nearly nine months pregnant and on the way to her baby shower. We immediately sent two drivers and delivered a loaner to her, right on the expressway. She was delighted to find, in the loaner vehicle, a Mercedes-Benz gift bag filled with baby clothes, blankets, and a teddy bear we had quickly picked up at the gift store at the dealership. We also sent an Edible Arrangement to her baby shower for the whole party to enjoy! Our customer stated that she is now a lifelong, loyal customer to both our dealership and Mercedes-Benz.

> A first-time customer recently came into our service drive with an issue, and we provided him with alternate transportation. I noticed a car seat in the backseat, and the salesperson informed me that our customer has a four-year-old son who loves Mercedes-Benz as much as his father. We repaired the vehicle and got it back to him before the holiday. We pulled a red Mercedes-Benz pedal car from Accessories. We wrapped up the pedal car and put it under the tree in

the showroom. When our customer returned for pickup, we let him know there was something for his son under the tree. He was noticeably touched.

We recently helped a new customer with a check-engine light in his CLA. It illuminated only two days after driving off the lot. Once the vehicle was in for service, we happened to discuss this particular customer with his salesperson. We discovered that the customer had been asking about the illuminated grille star for the CLA; it had not been available at the time of purchase. We decided to special-order the star and had it installed. We delivered the CLA back to our customer at dusk, with the star illuminated as he walked up. His face was brighter than the star! He was so excited that we had recalled his interest in the accessory and had installed it for him as a surprise. We now have a customer for life!

Dealerships have taken the MB SELECT resources and augmented them with their own operational resources to "do right" for the customer. Through MB SELECT, the MBUSA leadership has emphasized that creating Mercedes-Benz customers for life is far more important than simply driving today's transactional profit.

While it is not easily monetized, investing in customer loyalty through programs/initiatives like MB SELECT can, at times, produce immediate results. Anecdotally, stories emerge throughout the dealer network. An example is a new S-Class purchaser who had his door dinged in a parking lot. When he brought the car into the dealership, he expected to be charged for the repair. MB SELECT money was used not only to fix the door but to purchase Mercedes-Benz logoed items that were placed in his vehicle after the repair was complete. Shortly after being "delighted" by the unexpected level of service, the man came in and purchased another S-Class for his wife.

The ultimate goal of MB SELECT, however, is not to prompt short-term sales, but rather to deliver a world-class experience befitting the luxury and engineering of the products delivered by the brand. In the context of that experience, short-term costs must be looked at as investments in longer-term loyalty building. The adage goes, "You have to put your money where your mouth is." The money invested in MB SELECT is evidence that MBUSA is investing in actions that support corporate aspirations to deliver world-class experiences.

Even if you do not have substantial resources to spend on enhancing the customer experience, small investments do make a difference. As inspiration, think of independent hotels that provide guests with a map of nearby restaurants with staff recommendations, or retail shops that offer customers a complimentary beverage while they are shopping. If you have a mechanism for tracking the loyalty and purchase patterns of your customers, you can tailor your service enhancement and service recovery investments to the demonstrated spend of customers. Examples of these types of investment include loyal dry cleaning customers receiving free home delivery or loyal shoppers at an art gallery being invited to an exclusive showing. If an investment in customer delight is evidence of a business's purported commitment to being customer-centric, what proof can you point to for your business?

mbrace

In Chapter 9, we touched upon how Amazon removed pain points and increased customer spend by developing the Amazon Prime program. Similarly, Amazon was heralded in 2013 for building live chat support into Kindle Fire tablets through a function that

Amazon referred to as "Mayday." In a *PC Magazine* review of Mayday, Sascha Segan touted Amazon's rich integration of cutting-edge technology and human service components: "Mayday is the new tablets' most flashy feature. By hitting a button on a pull-down menu, you can start a video chat with an Amazon support rep who has the ability to control your tablet." Sascha goes on to describe how the Amazon support representative can press virtual buttons and draw on the customer's tablet. Additionally, these representatives do more than answer customers' questions. They frequently serve to fuel customer discovery by making suggestions on books to read and apps to loan on the Kindle Fire. According to Sascha, Amazon targeted "no more than a 15-second wait time for anyone requesting Mayday assistance." Mayday is in keeping with a type of human/technology integration developed by Mercedes-Benz called mbrace.

Leveraging off of breakthroughs in telematics (an interdisciplinary field that includes telecommunications, road safety, electrical engineering, and computer science), Mercedes-Benz vehicles allow for communication beyond a simple "mayday" or emergency response button, including a suite of products that delivers true concierge service. While some Mercedes-Benz vehicles were equipped with mbrace technology (safety, security, and travel assistance) as far back as 2009, upgrades were introduced in model year 2013 to deploy a new generation of technology and ensure that every Mercedes-Benz vehicle would have mbrace as a complimentary feature for the first six months of ownership.

In its most basic form, mbrace provides customers with the security of knowing that a specially trained Mercedes-Benz agent will swiftly dispatch a Mercedes-Benz technician to address roadside assistance needs. That same agent can summon emergency personnel in response to the driver's touching a button or as a result of automatic crash notification functions built into the telematics system.

Historically, owners were given complimentary access to a suite of mbrace subscription services, as well as Mercedes-Benz apps that enabled them to use telematic functions from their smartphones. This service (referred to as mbrace PLUS) was designed to integrate telematics technology with personal concierge support 24 hours a day, 365 days a year. The mbrace PLUS subscription service was best described in the narrative presented in the online video promoting it:

> One of the great perks of staying in a luxury hotel is the concierge. Wouldn't it be nice to take that service with you? With mbrace PLUS, personal assistance is just a button's push away. The button in your Mercedes-Benz connects you to an mbrace customer specialist ready to fulfill just about any request, from planning a trip to a special night out. We do it all—travel reservations, tickets to an event, a seat at a hot new restaurant—your personal mbrace agent can make it happen. We will even download directions directly to your car's navigation system. Your concierge is also a resourceful personal assistant, helping you with almost anything you need. And if they don't have the answer to your question, they will do the research and get back to you. And with the mbrace mobile app, you even have access to concierge services on your smartphone. With mbrace PLUS, you've got the right connections. Just ask, and mbrace PLUS delivers.

Whether car owners make phone calls to receive roadside assistance, report an accident to a Mercedes-Benz agent, or push the button in their Mercedes-Benz to have an agent make a reservation and download directions into the car's navigation system, all the technological solutions facilitate human care. For example, if a customer simply chooses to use a Mercedes-Benz Roadside Assistance app on a smartphone rather than relying on the telematics system on board the car, that customer is assured a timely roadside response from a Mercedes-Benz certified technician. The car owner can also locate a dealer. The app uses location services to find the customer, and once contact is made, it provides confirmation that a technician is on the way. The app offers fast, accurate help and creates more efficient call handling for roadside assistance. This technology-rich platform has essentially reinvented the Mercedes-Benz Roadside Assistance customer experience. Similarly, when a customer leverages technology to connect with a Mercedes-Benz agent, that customer is interacting with an individual who has been selected for service talent and who has been acculturated to drive customer delight in the context of the desired Mercedes-Benz brand experience. The Mercedes-Benz customer is not talking to an offshore call-center worker who is restricted to the words on a script. Similarly, the technician who is being sent to the vehicle is from a Mercedes-Benz dealership, not a third-party vendor.

All vehicles that are routinely serviced by authorized Mercedes-Benz dealers are eligible for Mercedes-Benz Roadside Assistance. Beyond complimentary service, mbrace allows customers (aided by telematics) to select the level of care that best meets their needs. Mercedes-Benz owner Charlie DeFelice described multiple examples of the benefits he derived from his mbrace selection: "Because of severe weather, our roads have been hammered. I've used mbrace three times in the past three months, each time for a flat tire. The first time, I'd just gotten off a plane, and it was raining really hard. There was a traffic accident affecting my usual route, so I diverted and then had to pull into an industrial park with my flat tire. I pressed the mbrace button, and the agent asked my location.

I told them I had no idea. They then located me through the GPS on my car and told me to stay in the car and they'd be right there. And they were." A month later, Charlie hit a pothole on the way to a business meeting. He was able to contact a Mercedes-Benz Roadside Assistance agent through mbrace and have the tire changed while he was in his meeting. Finally, Charlie shares, "A month later, on a Sunday, my wife and I were driving to a business dinner and social gathering in Manhattan. It was raining very hard, and I hit a pothole on Eighth Avenue. Again, the indicator said "right front tire malfunctioning." I was thinking this was going to ruin my evening and I'd get filthy changing the tire. Then I remembered I had mbrace. I pushed the button and pulled into a parking garage. I gave the name of the garage and the attendant's name, and the mbrace rep said they'd take care of it. When I went back after the dinner, Roadside Assistance had changed the tire. Every time I've had to use that service, it exceeded my expectations and makes me more loyal to Mercedes-Benz."

In August 2015, Mercedes-Benz upgraded the mbrace system yet again. With further improvements in telematics, the latest version of mbrace offers all of the safety and connectivity features of prior versions along with an increased ability to not only interact with the vehicle remotely—locking and unlocking, starting, heating and cooling it via the mobile app or website—but also allowing an increased ability to receive direct assistance from the vehicle owner's dealership, and inspiring, personalized branded content. With the launch of the new mbrace technology, MBUSA moreover invested millions of dollars in order to give new vehicle purchasers five years of complimentary mbrace access with the option to purchase even more enriched subscription content.

I suspect your customers aren't particularly different from those served at Mercedes-Benz USA. They become increasingly loyal when your technologies help them to serve themselves if they wish. And those technologies further engage customers when the tool expedites contact with caring staff members on those occasions when your customers require human assistance. You don't have to be an iconic luxury brand to use relevant technology to deepen your relationship with your customers. So, what specifically are you doing to exceed the technology expectations of those you serve?

Premier Express

Gareth Joyce, vice president customer services, succinctly shares an important aspect of service integration efforts at Mercedes-Benz USA, "Yes, we are in the superior automotive technology business. But of equal importance, we are in the business of caring for customers and respecting their time. All of the early pieces in our customer-centric transformation—such as developing a uniform approach to our courtesy loaner car program or enhancing the empowerment of our agents at the Customer Assistance Center— were building blocks. Premier Express, and ultimately our Digital Service Drive, represents our willingness and ability to take on one of the most challenging issues in service delivery—a truly efficient, seamless journey for our customers that is in keeping with their lifestyle."

Mercedes-Benz was not quick to jump on the "express" service bandwagon. In fact, according to Harry Hynekamp, general manager of customer experience at MBUSA, "We were late to the party when it came to express service, in part due to internal perceptions of what it meant to deliver luxury. Some believed that our customers might not associate fast service with luxury service. However, consumer demand and the volume of our service business required us to rethink expedited service options and find a way to offer rapid, personalized care, including a high-quality express platform. When you grow a service business quickly, with further expectations of growth through 2020, you have to think about providing expedited operational approaches for your customers and your dealers."

Premier Express was developed to deliver that type of expedited and efficient service. This no-appointment, quick-service-delivery approach offers basic maintenance that can be completed in less than 30 minutes. The program, which was piloted in 2014, had its nationwide launch in the first quarter of 2015. Frank Diertl, general manager after-sales business development, and his team designed the Premier Express service program and helped hundreds of dealers deploy it at their dealerships. Since the initial Premier Express pilot, MBUSA has seen improved retention of service customers. While not all of that improvement can be attributed exclusively to Premier Express, it is clearly a significant contributing factor.

As Gareth suggested, the real business case behind Premier Express is a singular focus on honoring customers' time so that they don't seek routine maintenance services from national quick-service companies that don't offer Mercedes-Benz-certified technicians or genuine Mercedes-Benz parts. To make Premier Express work, the Mercedes-Benz leaders defined a new staffing model and process work flow. Dealerships offering Premier Express have two-technician teams that are dedicated to basic maintenance services. Customers can arrive without appointments and have these services completed in 30 to 70 minutes, depending on vehicle model, service interval, and whether the customer desires a complimentary car wash.

Changes in work flow can be challenging and costly, but the results from Mercedes-Benz Premier Express show increased customer satisfaction and a consistent ability to deliver services within the time parameters promised to the customer. Additionally, with the deployment of Premier Express, maintenance work flow became more efficient and cost-effective, since the most advanced (and expensive) Mercedes-Benz technicians were reserved for the most challenging (and expensive) repair cases and were not deployed in routine service maintenance tasks. Put in another context, Premier Express is a time saver for consumers, just like mobile ordering and mobile pay at Starbucks. Rather than waiting in line to order, brands like Starbucks use a human/technology interface that allows customers to order and pay in advance by using their mobile devices. Using Premier Express or Starbucks mobile ordering and pay as examples, think about the express services you could provide to your customers in response to routine requests.

Through streamlining of work flow, dealership costs are better managed (think fewer loaners needed), resulting in price offerings that make dealership services more competitive with less expensive service providers outside the Mercedes-Benz network. I wonder what cost-saving benefits you could derive from creating similar efficiencies?

Premier Express gives customers the option of increased service speed, helps dealers enjoy greater profitability by reducing costs, and attracts consumers who may have defected from the dealership service department. With each retained or rescued customer, Mercedes-Benz dealerships have the opportunity to build and maintain lifelong customer relationships. In essence, each well-crafted and well-executed service interaction is less about a specific oil change and more about future vehicles, parts, and services that will be purchased by that same loyal customer. Of course, loyal customers will also have ample opportunities to strengthen their relationship with service departments as they seek to care for and maintain their future purchases.

Digital Service Drive

Digital Service Drive is the pinnacle of MBUSA's cutting-edge integration of processes, technology, and human service. It is designed not only to set standards for what specific components of the Mercedes-Benz service experience should entail but also to technologically integrate various aspects of the customer's overall service experience. Before Digital Service Drive, for example, while most dealers purported to have "online scheduling," this could mean anything from state-of-the-art scheduling platforms with mobile integration and texting capabilities to making sure the service department phone number was on the dealership website so that customers could call in and make an appointment. The major elements of the Digital Service Drive program are:

- *Online service appointment scheduling.* Customers are given the opportunity to schedule their vehicle service needs and arrange a courtesy vehicle at any time using a smart device or computer. They can also automatically update customer information prior to a service appointment.

- *Service drive tablets.* The use of iPads and Digital Service Drive technology enables a service advisor to complete the write-up, vehicle history, walkaround, customer information collection, and loaner contract processes from the advisor's tablet. These activities all take place in the service drive without the customers having to leave their vehicles.

- *Status notification automatically sent via the customer's preferred communication method.* The customer receives updates on the service process and a summary of the work being completed in easy-to-understand language.

- *Flexible bill pay*

  - *Online bill pay.* This feature enables customers to use their devices to make self-service payments by delivering final parts and service invoices via text and e-mail. It also allows customers to pay anywhere and anytime that is convenient for them.

  - *Active service cashiering.* Service advisors can complete the payment process on the service drive via their tablet and enterprise payment system. Customers no longer have to go to a cashier (or wait in line) to pay.

From a dealer's perspective, Digital Service Drive (like Premier Express) results in greater customer satisfaction by providing customers with choices and offering cutting-edge tools that project a professional image for the dealership while also demonstrating its investment in progressive, technology-rich retail experiences. From the customer's vantage point, the Digital Service Drive simply means ease, convenience, and more productive use of his time at the dealership.

The Mercedes-Benz journey to the Digital Service Drive is largely predicated on addressing changing consumer expectations. Frank Diertl, general manager after-sales business development, notes, "The Digital Service Drive was designed to address the needs of customers who interact with brands through technology and to offer them tools that fit the way they go through their daily life. These consumers choose brands based upon the way those companies enable them to interact technologically. Not every customer fits into that higher-technology group, but its numbers are increasing. Today, many consumers are looking for ease and for an app that facilitates that ease. Our customer base is changing right before our eyes. Zappos, Starbucks, and even Domino's Pizza are setting the retail environment expectations that our customers are going to judge us by. Not only do we want to keep up with the way those other brands integrate people, processes, and technology, but we want to be a leader as well. Digital Service Drive is cutting-edge, and it is setting a new bar in our industry. The program is fully in keeping with the behavior and investments needed to be a truly world-class customer experience provider."

That brings us to an important question. Are your investments and behaviors in keeping with those of world-class customer experience leaders? By now, it should be obvious that Mercedes-Benz USA didn't crack the code on customer experience delivery *until* the leaders established it as a priority. The very fact that you are reading this book suggests that it is a priority for you as well. Turning your priority into action will probably involve systemic integration of technology, processes, and human service, much as Mercedes-Benz has done with MB SELECT, mbrace, Premier Express, and the Digital Service Drive.

Throughout this book, you have seen the tremendous amount of work everyone representing the Mercedes-Benz brand in the United States has done to achieve a transformation to customer obsession. While I alluded to the results of this transformation in Chapter 1, the upcoming chapter provides a detailed accounting of the customer-specific and financial gains Mercedes-Benz has realized from this unrelenting Driven to Delight journey. In essence, the next chapter answers the question "Is this major undertaking worth the effort?"

➤ World-class customer experience providers go beyond making transactional improvements at key customer touchpoints. Instead, they develop integrated human and technology platforms to make the customer experience as seamless as possible.

➤ One of the most important aspects of producing enterprisewide solutions to customer challenges is forcing people out of their silos and into face-to-face cross-functional teams that respond rapidly to customer needs.

➤ Healthy "rapid response teams" track feedback from all key stakeholders and anticipate potential emerging problems before they flare to crisis proportion. More important, participants on these teams have the task of circumventing blame and eliminating defensiveness in the pursuit of viable and expedited customer solutions.

➤ Creating customers for life is far more important than driving today's transactional profit.

➤ A successful customer experience typically involves great technology, streamlined processes, and impassioned people. Leaders in brands that provide great customer experiences must constantly work to link these success drivers together in order to make life easier for, and respect the time of, their customers.

➤ With each retained or rescued customer, you have the opportunity to build and maintain a lifelong customer relationship, which allows your business to craft sustained and sustainable revenue and profit streams.

icies but it must also represent the people behind th
en to delight. it is not just a phrase. it is a path, a prom
elief. it is a commitment to creating positive relationsh
making people smile and to leaving them with a sens
plete trust, driven to delight means exceptional

➤ Frequently, when work flow is redesigned around customer needs, efficiencies are achieved. Those efficiencies, in turn, result in cost reductions that make a business more competitive, while benefiting customers as well.

➤ Increasingly, consumers are choosing brands based upon how the brand uses technology. In essence, many customers are looking for easy interaction through technology, an app. They seek brands and companies that fit service into their busy and mobile lifestyle.

ven to delight means exceptional personal treatment. r
minder that the journey is never done. that there is alw
re thoughtful way. and throughout each interaction we
ember that the best or nothing cannot just be a descri

Much effort, much prosperity.

—Euripides

en to delight. it is not just a phrase. it is a prom
lief. it is a commitment to creating po onsh
making people smile and to leaving the sense
plete trust. driven to delight means e perso
tment. it is a reminder that the journey ne. t
e is always a more thoughtful way. ar ut e

11

Success Achieved

◇◇

You've seen the comprehensive and coordinated efforts of
the leaders at Mercedes-Benz USA as they have championed the consistent delivery of world-class customer experiences.
You have to be wondering, "With all that effort, did these leaders achieve their goal? Where's the proof that this large-scale investment of leadership capital, time, and money is paying off for
Mercedes-Benz USA in terms of sales and profit? Is this 'Driven
to Delight' transformation actually resulting in delight for customers? How is Mercedes-Benz gauging its customer-centric progress?"

en to delight means exceptional personal treatment. it i
nder that the journey is never done. that the s alway
e thoughtful way. and throughout each interaction we m
mber that the best or nothing cannot just be a description

203

Bringing it closer to your company, you might be thinking, "How would I evaluate the quality of customer experience elevation efforts in my business?"

Leaders like Steve Cannon are reluctant to claim "victory" on their transformation agenda, since they see many opportunities for growth ahead (see Chapter 12 for more on the future of customer-centric change at MBUSA). However, as someone who has watched and been part of the transformation, it is clear to me that MBUSA leaders and the dealer partners have made a radical culture shift and a dramatic change in the way customers experience the brand.

In this chapter, I will show you what Mercedes-Benz Driven to Delight success looks like from the perspective of MBUSA's internal customer experience measures as well as from the metrics of outside research firms. You will also see how transformational change is evaluated qualitatively through the shifting perceptions of staff members at dealerships, Mercedes-Benz USA, and Mercedes-Benz Financial Services. Former NBA star and U.S. Senator Bill Bradley once said, "Ambition is the path to success and persistence is the vehicle you arrive in." Steve Cannon and his leadership team have clearly set out to achieve an ambitious goal—to be the best customer experience provider, bar none—and their persistence has enabled them to "arrive in" a Mercedes-Benz world-class customer experience.

Broad Objectives Link to Customer Experience Delivery

As you will recall from Chapter 3, Steve Cannon's leadership team initiated its customer experience transformation agenda in conjunction with its long-range vision for business success. MBUSA leaders sought to be the most admired automotive brand, maximize customer loyalty, lead all premium brands in new vehicle sales, be the most profitable Daimler market, and enhance employee engagement.

Undeniably, many factors are involved in achieving success in brand admiration, profitability, customer loyalty, sales dominance, and employee engagement. Some of these factors include product desirability, product quality, advanced technology, creative marketing, and overall fiscal management. However, every one of the KPIs at Mercedes-Benz is also affected, at least in part, by the quality of the experiences customers have when they enter Mercedes-Benz dealerships.

Throughout this chapter, I will be sharing proof of the strong admiration that customers feel for the Mercedes-Benz brand and demonstrate the strong loyalty of those customers (as evidenced by the Polk Automotive Loyalty Award and other recognitions from industry experts). But let's take a moment to talk about the sales strength of MBUSA and the levels of employee engagement the company has seen during this transformative time.

Official figures for luxury new vehicle sales in 2012 show that both Mercedes-Benz USA (274,134 vehicles) and its significant competitor BMW North America (281,460 vehicles) posted double-digit increases and record sales when compared to 2011. In 2013, Mercedes-Benz overtook BMW for the U.S. luxury automotive sales title with 14 percent sales growth over 2012, ending the year with a record-shattering 312,534 vehicles sold (compared to the 9 percent increase for BMW, to 309,280 vehicles). In 2014, the seesaw battle for the top sales spot went back to BMW, with both brands continuing to experience growth and set sales records (339,738 BMW vehicles and 330,391 Mercedes-Benz vehicles sold).

Mercedes-Benz has not yet established runaway dominance in luxury car sales, but it has developed a leading position in a crowded field of premium automakers, including Lexus, Audi, Jaguar, Infiniti, Land Rover, Cadillac, and Lincoln. Perennially, a thin margin has separated Mercedes-Benz and BMW for the number one position in luxury auto sales in the United States.

Dietmar Exler, vice president sales at Mercedes-Benz USA, puts the competition to sell the most cars in the luxury category into perspective: "Customers don't decide to buy a car from us because we sold more cars than BMW in a given year. Winning the sales battle is of interest to automotive journalists and to the executives at our respective companies. We care about strong sales. Customers, however, care about quality vehicles and the nature of the care they receive from those who represent our brand."

The service and care that customers receive translates into profitability at the dealer level and has a positive impact on Mercedes-Benz. Harald Henn, vice president finance & controlling, Mercedes-Benz USA, notes, "We have compelling data showing that the engagement level of customers is positively correlated with dealer profitability. While it is slightly more difficult to link that correlation back to Mercedes-Benz USA, our business plan projects growth at the top line at 10 percent each year into the foreseeable future. Part of that growth comes from our commitment to a culture of service and a level of employee commitment that scores way above the national average."

Mercedes-Benz USA is unmatched in the automotive industry when it comes to employee commitment and engagement level and other measures of workforce health. Throughout the customer experience transformation, MBUSA has received various awards for its workplace culture and its highly engaged employee base. In 2014, Mercedes-Benz enjoyed a fifth consecutive year on *Fortune* magazine's "100 Best Companies to Work For" list and has been acknowledged by other work environment evaluators as well. In May 2014, for example, Mercedes-Benz was ranked number four among large companies on the annual NJBIZ list of "The Best Places to Work in NJ." In his response to that selection, Steve Cannon alluded to synergies that occur when sales numbers, employee engagement, and customer experience are strategic priorities. "We're four months into another record sales year at MBUSA, and that wouldn't be possible without the dedicated team of employees at our headquarters in Montvale and regional offices in Parsippany and Robbinsville. Their passion for the product and laser focus on delighting our customers is central to our business, and a great workplace culture is paramount to continued success."

In addition to its progress on sales and employee KPIs, MBUSA has improved in other areas as well. As measured by the internal Customer Experience Index (CEI) tools that we explored in Chapter 5, MBUSA has made enviable progress in customer satisfaction in both sales and service interactions.

Specifically, if you were to compare the baseline 2013 national average on the sales CEI to the 2015 national average, you would see a sizable increase (a baseline score in the 950s versus a current score in the 970s, out of a possible 1,000). Similarly, nationally averaged service CEI scores increased by approximately 20 points from 2013 to 2015.

These substantial improvements in real-time leading indicators of customer satisfaction and engagement suggest that the human, process, and technology efforts outlined throughout this book are having a marked effect on the way customers think and feel about the care they receive while they are buying or maintaining their vehicles. These internal findings represent feedback from a large number of Mercedes-Benz customers and are consistent with outside results and accolades from important experience evaluation firms, including J.D. Power and Associates.

Transformation Captured by Outside Measurement

To put it bluntly, performance on J.D. Power studies has long been a thorn in the side of the Mercedes-Benz USA leaders. As mentioned in Chapter 5, while J.D. Power results represent *indicators* of sales and service satisfaction, the MBUSA leadership is aware of the prominence of J.D. Power rankings in the marketing messages of the company's competitors. In the luxury category, Mercedes-Benz USA was not content with what Steve Cannon referred to as a "humiliating ranking of 22" in 2007 or even a middle-of-the-pack "mediocre number 6" in 2012.

Although the Driven to Delight transformation was never about being number 1 on the J.D. Power satisfaction studies, J.D. Power rankings should corroborate other indicators of customer experience progress. This type of corroboration is important in the context of MBUSA wanting to be credibly viewed as a world-class customer experience provider.

Anticipation was high in late 2014 when J.D. Power was about to release the results of its Sales Satisfaction Index (SSI) study. Mercedes-Benz had been ranked sixth in 2012 (the onset of the Driven to Delight transformation) and fifth in 2013. The 2014 results would be a timely gauge of progress as a result of contact point mapping, real-time customer listening strategies, investment in culture development, process improvements, and technology interventions. Rather than me telling you the results, I'll let Steve Cannon's written announcement to Mercedes-Benz dealers paint the picture:

> Congratulations to the #1 dealer body in the country! I am very proud to announce that for the first time in 24 years Mercedes-Benz has earned the number one ranking

on the 2014 J.D. Power Sales Satisfaction Index. All I can say is 'WOW . . . you did it!' . . . On behalf of the entire executive team and every MBUSA team member, thank you for embracing our goal of becoming the number one customer experience brand in the world! This is another step along that journey together. Each and every team member in your dealerships earned this award for Mercedes-Benz and we are extremely grateful for their dedication and determination. Most importantly, thank you for delighting our customers each time, every time, no exceptions! . . . Moving up from 5th place last year, our 33 point year-over-year improvement is the largest in the industry and the largest year-over-year lift in MBUSA's history. With a significant 12 point lead over the #2 ranked brand, we have opened an impressive gap ahead of our competition. We showed strong improvement in 100% of all survey categories and this was truly an inspiring victory! While we're proud of this great accomplishment and hope you fully celebrate it with your teams, we will not take our foot off the gas pedal. As we gain momentum, our competitors will continue to work harder to catch us and our customers continue to deserve "The Best or Nothing."

The 2014 J.D. Power Sales Satisfaction Index victory was not the only independent verification of the customer experience transformation that was occurring in Mercedes-Benz dealerships across America. In fact, Mercedes-Benz finished first in the 2014 American Customer Satisfaction Index (ACSI) automotive study for the second consecutive year. Looking across industries, in 2014 Mercedes-Benz also tied on the ACSI study with The Ritz-Carlton Hotel Company (the top performer in the highly competitive hotel sector). Additionally, the performance of Mercedes-Benz on the ACSI surveys in both 2013 and 2014 was comparable to highly regarded service companies such as Amazon, Nordstrom, Apple, and Starbucks.

These results on the ACSI reflect multiyear customer recognition that Mercedes-Benz was delivering the most satisfying brand experiences in the automotive sector. They also verify that Mercedes-Benz was truly providing "world-class" consumer satisfaction when measured against established customer experience leaders irrespective of industry.

Other consumer research results corroborate the ACSI findings concerning the loyalty of Mercedes-Benz customers. The Polk Automotive Loyalty Awards, presented by IHS Automotive, are based on the repurchase behavior of customers as reflected by state automobile registration and lease transaction data. In essence, brands that win the Polk Automotive Loyalty Awards have the highest percentage of households who remain brand-loyal when they return to market. In the luxury category, Mercedes-Benz was a Polk Automotive Loyalty Award leader in various categories in 2013 and 2014.

Many of the factors that lead Mercedes-Benz owners to stay loyal to the brand are clearly linked to the handling, style, quality, and safety of the vehicles, as well as the ownership experience. However, research from retention specialists like the Accenture group suggests that loyalty is often lost as a result of the way people are treated during sales and service interactions, not as a result of product issues. An Accenture report titled "Maximizing Customer Retention" notes, "The root causes of customer churn can be hard to trace. They may lie buried in negative experiences associated with any one of multiple interactions. In order to improve and sustain customer retention rates over time, companies must improve the customer experience of all these interactions." The Driven to Delight transformation agenda, with its heavy emphasis on improving the customer experience at all critical interaction points, certainly serves to reduce defections caused by negative interactions and enhance the type of loyalty recognized by the Polk Automotive Loyalty Awards.

Improvements in sales and service excellence at Mercedes-Benz are further validated by recognition from many others involved in assessing the automotive industry. For example, Mercedes-Benz dealerships ranked highest in the United States on the 2015 Pied Piper Prospect Satisfaction Index (PSI) for the seventh straight year. Pied Piper differentiates the PSI from other studies through its use of "mystery shoppers," who report their experiences with the sales process. The sales process, as defined by Pied Piper, is a series of specific steps that Pied Piper research has correlated with overall sales. Similarly, in 2014, Mercedes-Benz was named the best automotive brand for service by Women-Drivers.com, while also showing steady improvements on the J.D. Power Customer Service Index (more on CSI in Chapter 12 as we look at the future of customer experience elevation at Mercedes-Benz).

When your KPIs, overall sales, and internal customer experience metrics and the findings of independent evaluators all demonstrate that the customer experience is improving, your work is resonating successfully with customers and other stakeholders. For Mercedes-Benz USA, this means delighted customers who loyally buy more vehicles and happily service those vehicles at Mercedes-Benz dealerships!

Transformation as Heard Qualitatively Through the Voice of the Customer

While recognition and quantitative improvements are confirmation of the transformation of the Mercedes-Benz customer experience, a richer appreciation of the significance of that transformation can be gained through the voices and qualitative assessments of customers and other stakeholders. Many of their stories reflect substantial, almost heroic, acts of service excellence that are consistent with a commitment to be the best global customer experience provider. These actions are also similar to the stories I regularly encounter from customers of brands like The Ritz-Carlton Hotel Company, where the ladies and gentleman of The Ritz-Carlton go significantly out of their way to aid those they serve (for example, disassembling a commercial washer to look for a guest's ring that might have been lost in recently laundered sheets).

In the case of Mercedes-Benz, these large-scale efforts often involve multiple dealership staff members doing far more than a customer expects. Mercedes-Benz owner Alexander Blastos offers one such example. "I was driving from Dallas back to New Hampshire and was getting close to Memphis when I heard a troubling noise. It was a Friday about 4:00 p.m. I called the Mercedes dealer in Memphis, and they told me they were closing at 5, but to come in and they'd wait for me." In addition to being surprised that the service department would stay open just for him, Alexander explains the extra offers of service that occurred once the noise problem was diagnosed. "The technician found that my emergency brake had activated, and given that my vehicle has a huge amount of power and torque, the emergency brake was essentially obliterated."

Even though it was determined that it would be safe for Alexander to drive the car to his destination in New Hampshire and have it repaired there, the dealership in Memphis took action and offered to serve Alexander in ways that seemed extraordinary to him. "First, they got me a room for the night in Memphis, since it was late in the day. In addition to giving me the option of fixing my car as quickly as possible at their dealership, they also offered me the option to ship my car to New Hampshire, if I would feel safer taking another form of transportation." Alexander summarizes his delight with the extraordinary thoughtfulness of the Memphis dealership by asking, "What other car company would stay open after hours, put you up in a hotel, and do whatever it takes to make a person feel comfortable and cared for when it comes to repairs and travel needs? All aspects of that service experience were nothing short of spectacular." Maybe staying open later would have been enough to impress Alexander. Certainly putting him up in a hotel exceeded his expectations. But by listening, empathizing, and adding value with options like shipping his car, the dealership personnel in Memphis were driven to delight him.

Much of the time, customer delight is created by gestures that involve far less cost or effort—acts that reflect a willingness to say yes to a customer's need when most other providers either would not respond or would simply say no. Mercedes-Benz owner Donna Pompeo offers one such situation: "When I got my car serviced, I had some fur earmuffs in the back seat. They weren't extremely expensive—they cost about $50. But when I picked up the car, they were no longer there. I asked the dealership if it was possible they had fallen out when I got my things out of the car. I really never expected much to come of my inquiry, but to my pleasant surprise, I received a check for the earmuffs. I don't think that would have happened in other types of auto dealerships." Where might you cost-effectively say yes to your customers in ways that will surprise them, particularly given the standard of care they have come to expect from other service providers in your industry?

Often customers aren't looking for a yes to a tangible or material request. They simply want service personnel to give them their undivided and thorough attention during the time they spend at your place of business. As a result of the leadership's transformation efforts, Mercedes-Benz customers like Paul David are increasingly sharing stories of quality attention from dealership employees. "My salesman spent a good hour just going over all the features of the car. I would say I've never had that kind of detail or treatment across the 25 makes of cars that I've bought during my lifetime. It's amazing how a patient, knowledgeable, thorough, and professional approach can make such a difference." When product concierges and staff members are selected for their ability to care for others and are trained on the experience you want them to deliver, they can produce service moments unlike anything customers have encountered before.

Customer letters sent to the Mercedes-Benz corporate office are trending increasingly positive and demonstrate how not only caring *for* customers but also caring *about* them can have a multigenerational affect. Such was a letter received from Bruce Tanzi:

Dear Mercedes-Benz,

I wanted to write and thank your great folks who handle roadside assistance. It has made me a customer forever (even if I am still driving a 2000 [model] as my everyday car). I was on a road trip with my almost 17-year-old daughter when the car died in the fast lane on Broad Street in Philadelphia, Pennsylvania. We were eight blocks from the ballpark, and Philly is not my hometown.

Lost in South Philly and 30 minutes late for the Phillies/Red Sox game, the Roadside Assistance folks came to the rescue. They were polite, friendly, and very helpful. Not only did they arrange everything and make it worry free, the tow person dispatched was totally awesome and professional. The Cherry Hill dealership (also, not my regular dealership) was fabulous. I cannot tell you how great it feels to know you have such a great team on your side, especially with a young driver coming into the picture. She now has the (800) FOR-

MERCEDES number in her mobile phone, and I feel good about that. Thanks again for being customer driven and going above and beyond. While there may be an ultimate driving machine—I'm sure there is only one ultimate service team—THANKS MERCEDES!

When your customer spins your competition's tagline (in this case, BMW's "The Ultimate Driving Machine") in the direction of praising your organization's service, and when he claims to have been won over as "a customer forever," you know your transformation efforts are on the right track!

Winning Hearts and Minds Means Attitude Shifts and Behavioral Changes

Plato once said, "Human behavior flows from three main sources: desire, emotion, and knowledge." The leaders at Mercedes-Benz USA sparked a desire throughout the corporate and retail organization to delight their customers. These leaders helped the staff members understand the emotional benefits of striving for customer experience excellence, particularly as it relates to enjoying more purposeful work. In addition, the leaders provided the tools and knowledge necessary to delight customers through people, process, products, and technology.

This flow of desire, emotion, and knowledge was all geared to effect customer-centric behavior change at the dealership level. As you have seen throughout this chapter, transformation is being verified by a positive shift in quantitative data and in the qualitative voice of the customer. But do dealership staff members see themselves as behaving differently?

In Chapter 10, I talked about the portion of the MB SELECT program where Mercedes-Benz USA provides goodwill resources to help dealers delight customers. In that discussion, I explored how the program served to highlight thinking about not just the cost of transactions but the value of investing resources to fuel long-term loyalty. In many ways, MB SELECT served as a springboard for goodwill acts and behavior changes, leading the organization not only to consider but to prioritize the potential lifetime value of a customer at each transaction.

Here are three examples of the types of delighting and loyalty-building behaviors reported by Mercedes-Benz dealers:

> Our client purchased two 2014 S-Class vehicles within the last month. He brought in one of his new vehicles because the eyeglass compartment on the overhead control panel was not ejecting; the part was ordered on October 21st with an estimated time of arrival for November 15th. During a follow-up call regarding the ETA for the part, the client mentioned he would be playing golf at the Miami Beach Golf Club the following day. A fellow employee from Mercedes-Benz of Coral Gables was sent to purchase a $500 gift certificate at the golf club. This card can be used toward any services offered at the Miami Beach Golf Club. The certificate was handed to the client personally at his home along with apologies for the inconvenience and the delay for the part still not [being] available. The client was delighted with the personal attention to detail he received, along with sincere apologies on behalf of Mercedes-Benz of Coral Gables for the inconvenience.

> Mr. Y traded his 2013 S550 in [for] a 2014 S550 at his dealership, Astorg Motors, this fall and was thrilled with his new

car. Unfortunately, he had to make a 1 hour and 15 minute trip to complete the transfer of his old Sirius Radio contract to the new 2014 S-Class. Unobserved, the general manager saw Mr. Y wandering around the Accessory Boutique while waiting for the first service of his new car to be completed. Mr. Y spent some time looking at the all-season floor mats and then tried on a Mercedes-Benz vest but did not purchase anything. After Mr. Y left the Accessory Boutique, the general manager took the mats and vest and went to the shop to find the new S-Class, where he placed the vest on the passenger seat and installed the mats. When the customer was reunited with his clean car, he found the two accessories he had previously been looking at inside his new S-Class. He was so moved that he got out of the car and came back into the dealership to thank them. . . . He called his salesman again and said, "You guys are awesome; that's why I drive past two other dealers to come see you!"

Many of our clients are often pressed for time when dropping off their Mercedes-Benz for service. They are rushing to get in, outline their concerns with their advisor, finalize their loaner car arrangements, and then head off to their busy lives. Seldom are they able to stop in our café and enjoy a cup of coffee or get a bite to eat. To deliver the WOW effect, we have implemented the Breakfast Express. It's a rolling cart filled with prewrapped bagels, rolls, Danishes, fruits, and coffee. So while waiting with either their advisor or the transportation coordinator, the client can choose anything from the cart, we will bag it, and then they will be on their way. A seamless uninterrupted flow is the WOW for those on the go.

When your brand is represented by individuals who consistently act not just to satisfy your customers but to wow and delight them, you have joined an elite group of customer experience providers. The difference between "good" and "great" customer experiences often comes down to how well you and your team execute to deliver both practical and emotional value. It is rare for leaders to inspire their team members to consistently execute satisfying, memorable, and emotionally engaging customer experiences. In fact, most companies struggle to deliver anything more than reasonable satisfaction levels punctuated with intermittent customer delight.

Data, Customer Voice, Behavior Change, *and* a "Delighted" Workforce

As evidenced by the awards MBUSA has earned for creating a positive and inspiring work environment, the leadership at MBUSA continues to focus on engagement. Similarly, the improvements noted in Chapter 7 suggest that the process of conducting employee engagement surveys and offering tool kits to drive engagement is producing measurably positive outcomes at the dealership level. In addition to quantitative improvements in employee engagement and awards from outside agencies, let's see what Mercedes-Benz corporate employees are saying about how Driven to Delight has affected them:

> I start each day thinking about how I can make a difference to not only my customers but my colleagues as well. Every interaction we have is with a customer!

> The customer expectation is high—it always has been with our brand. Our customers are now receiving the experience they expect.

The notion that we must Listen, Empathize, Add value, and Delight our customers defines our existence.

There is no way to delight a customer unless you are feeling delighted yourself. I am proud of working for this company and feel that my team comes in delighted each day and ready to make a difference.

Steve Cannon recognizes that delivering a customer experience that is commensurate with our vehicles requires all of us—at every level and in every department at MBUSA. In my role as a trainer, I have seen the customer experience themes woven throughout our curriculum. As an MBUSA team member, I have watched as we worked to include the same high levels of customer care when dealing with one another. The quality of customer care is becoming part of our DNA and is no longer thought of only as the purview of our Customer Assistance Center agents or our dealer partners.

The positive impact of the Driven to Delight change initiative not only is being felt at the corporate office and field level but also is occurring in all areas of the dealerships (both customer-facing and non-customer-facing functions). This is exemplified by the following comments from dealership staff:

> I always thought we did a great job of taking care of customers, but in the last several years, I realize we did a lot of things that made life easier for us. I now know what it means to put the customer in the center of the experience.

> It's easy for anyone to say they care about delighting customers, but Mercedes-Benz has put the work into making those words come to life for us at the dealership and for our

customers. I am glad I have been challenged to drive delight for every customer, every time.

Things are different in my dealership today. I do administrative work and never thought of myself as a customer experience provider, but I have a whole new perspective now. It is my job to Listen, Empathize, Add value, and Delight everyone in my building.

When cultural-change programs take root in an organization, their impact can often be felt by other business partners as well. For example, individuals at Mercedes-Benz Financial Services report:

> We have our own customer-centric focus at MBFS, but clearly Steve Cannon and his team at MBUSA have led a rallying cry for customer care in ways that have changed the way our team looks at and delivers customer interaction.
>
> You can't help but be inspired to improve the way you relate to customers and coworkers when you see the steadfast commitment made at Mercedes-Benz USA. They have upped their game, and since we partner with them in the service of our shared customers, we've had to up our game as well.

Even vendors like Lior Arussy note, "The level of excitement for customer experience excellence is markedly different now than it was in my early involvement with the brand. It is energizing." As someone who has worked with senior leaders at Mercedes-Benz USA, I can also attest to the infectious nature of their customer-obsessed enthusiasm.

Success, however, can breed complacency, and it can give the sense that the customer journey is nearing its end. Lest you think that the leaders at Mercedes-Benz USA are content with their progress, let's look to the future. In Chapter 12, you will see the lofty aspirational goals the leaders have set for the future of customer-centric Driven to Delight experiences across Mercedes-Benz. More important, you will have opportunities to see how you can ensure that success won't hamper your motivation for a sustained customer-focused journey.

➤ Customer experience success is quantitatively and qualitatively measurable. The return on your time and resource investments should be found in key performance indicators, internal customer experience metrics, outside evaluations of customer satisfaction, customer and staff stories, and the internal perceptions of your people.

➤ True success in customer experience delivery requires a willingness to look for trends across diverse data sets, both internal and external.

➤ Customer loyalty is fragile and is often lost not as a result of product issues but as a result of the way people are treated during sales and service interactions.

➤ In keeping with Accenture's research, it is important to look for the root causes of customer churn, many of which are likely to be linked to negative customer experiences across one or many important contact points between the customer and your brand.

➤ A culture of customer experience excellence often produces customer stories of both heroic and relatively simple service acts. Heroic stories often involve large-scale efforts relying on the teamwork of many staff members working effectively to do far more than a customer expects. Simple service acts often come down to a single person saying yes to a customer request when customers typically would expect to hear no or not to be offered the courtesy of a response.

➤ Great leaders are story collectors, and they freely share stories of service excellence (both heroic and simple) across their organization to inspire their teams to action.

➤ Think about ways to cost-effectively say yes to the wants, needs, and desires of customers when they do not expect a favorable answer.

➤ Great leaders help their team think beyond the cost of service transactions and develop a mindset to invest in service that fuels long-term loyalty.

➤ When your brand is represented by individuals who consistently act not just to satisfy your customers, but to wow and delight them, you have joined an elite group of customer experience providers.

➤ Moving to a true customer-centric culture should produce increased engagement in your workforce and change the way your people think about and feel toward your brand.

➤ The impact of your culture will affect other stakeholders and partners who interact with your brand.

➤ Customer-obsessed brands never rest! Consumer behavior and technology are constantly evolving. Leaders must also reset short- and long-term strategic objectives to deliver relevant experiences to those they serve.

Without continual growth and progress, such

words as improvement, achievement, and

success have no meaning.

—Benjamin Franklin

cles but it must also represent the pe... ...d the
en to delight. it is not just a phrase. it i... ...prom
lief. it is a commitment to creating po... ...onshi
making people smile and to leaving the... ...sense
plete trust. driven to delight means e... ...perso
tment. it is a reminder that the journey ...ne. t
e is always a more thoughtful way. a... ...ut ea

12

How Good
Can Good Be?

A n article in the February 2015 issue of *Automotive News* began with, "Mercedes-Benz USA CEO Steve Cannon says the

brand plans to prod dealers to improve sales processes even though

Mercedes scored the top luxury-brand ranking" on the 2014 J.D.

Power Sales Satisfaction Index (SSI) study. The article goes on to

quote Steve as saying that he would continue to provide inspir-

ing programs to the top-performing dealers and require the low-

est performers to invest their own money in "process training to

get better." Specifically, this approach of "inspiring" the best and

"requiring" the rest involves the expectation that dealers who are

en to delight means exceptional personal treatment. it is
nder that the journey is never done. that the...s always
e thoughtful way. and throughout each interaction we mi

performing at the bottom of the network will have to pay consultants from J.D. Power to assist them in creating action plans, developing sales and service process skills, and engaging in customer care and follow-up. Harry Hynekamp, general manager customer experience, notes, "This approach is essentially an attempt to assist those dealers in making more money through both the margin structure and leadership bonus. We want to ensure that these dealers are keeping up with the top group in the network."

The need for continued progress is particularly relevant to the service side of Mercedes-Benz dealerships, whose performance is measured in part by the J.D. Power Customer Service Index (CSI). As suggested in Chapter 11, Mercedes-Benz dealers have made steady progress on the CSI. That improvement, however, hasn't paralleled the substantial increases in ranking achieved on the SSI.

For the service periods measured during Steve Cannon's tenure as president and CEO, Mercedes-Benz USA has held the following ranks in the J.D. Power CSI study: tenth in 2013, eighth in 2014, and seventh in 2015. The latest ranking drew the following reaction from Steve, which comes from a letter to Mercedes-Benz dealer principals and general managers. "[These] results continue to reflect positive momentum as our efforts move us ever closer to our ultimate goal, the #1 position." Steve also placed Mercedes-Benz service-related improvements on the CSI in perspective by noting that the overall score that Mercedes-Benz achieved "is not significantly different from that of a top five finisher, missing those rankings by only 4 points out of a possible 1,000."

As one looks closely at the most recent CSI survey results, many other positives emerge. For example, Mercedes-Benz improved in the majority of categories measured. Steve notes, "Specifically, service advisor ranks moved from ninth place to sixth (one point shy of the top four)." Scores for customers receiving routine maintenance service (68 percent of all interactions in Mercedes-Benz service departments) moved up from eighth to third, and customer ratings of repair services moved from a ranking of ninth to seventh. As was the case with sales transactions, customers viewed Mercedes-Benz as being the industry leader in the use of tablet technology during the service experience.

A head-to-head comparison with BMW, the primary competitor to Mercedes-Benz in the United States, was also heartening. As Steve notes, "Mercedes-Benz significantly distanced itself from BMW, with whom we were tied in 2014, and who declines year over year."

Another victory in the most recent CSI survey was that for the first time in 17 years, the Mercedes-Benz scores moved above the luxury-brand average. This data point, coupled with a third-place ranking on J.D. Power's version of a Net Promoter Score (which measures the likelihood of a customer recommending a brand), reflects important momentum in Mercedes-Benz USA's hunt for a first-place finish in a J.D. Power service study.

Gareth Joyce, vice president customer services at Mercedes-Benz USA, puts the J.D. Power CSI results in a much broader perspective. "It's evident in the CSI, as it has been through many industry surveys, that customers feel our service experience is improving. We also know that the J.D. Power service survey has the longest muscle memory of all those in the market. In essence, it's the dial that moves the slowest. So I am not concerned about our present placement, since results are looking back 12 months on a journey where we have been aggressively improving service behaviors across a network of more than 370 dealers with more than 28,000 people doing more than 2.2 million transactions a year. We know our CSI results will take time to be fully recognized."

Possibly the best news of all for Mercedes-Benz USA regarding the future perceptions of service customers (and the corresponding CSI results) falls in the areas where J.D. Power data indicates that the brand has the greatest opportunity for experience improvement. Those areas include ease of scheduling, honoring a customer's time throughout the service journey, providing status updates on repairs, and streamlining the service advisor cashiering process. Steve Cannon believes that the Mercedes-Benz USA "strategic initiatives focused on People, Process, and Technology are specifically addressing each of these opportunity areas. Many initiatives, such as Brand Immersion, dealer engagement surveys, Premier Express, and Digital Service Drive, have been executed swiftly and are just emerging in the marketplace. As a result, customer benefits from these programs will become apparent in future surveys."

Gareth Joyce is particularly pleased with the speed of execution on enterprisewide solutions that is occurring at Mercedes-Benz USA and the dealership network and cites Premier Express as an example. "For 2014 we ambitiously committed to and achieved a rollout of Premier Express to half of our dealerships within a 12-month period. In fact, we were able to bring it to life in more than 180 stores. That accomplishment reflects how our culture is mobilizing our vision to be Driven to Delight. Some competitors have tried similar programs with very limited success."

From Gareth's perspective, the core competencies required for rapid execution of customer experience strategy are a significant Mercedes-Benz advantage going forward. "When I talk about execution," explains Gareth, "I am referring to a level of commitment and success that is measureable. Even though some of our stores were initially hesitant on early initiatives, leaders in those businesses are seeing the significant improvement in customer experience and profits for their counterparts who were early adopters. For example, with Premier Express, dealers who were early to embrace the program have successfully managed to use it as a way to develop young technicians in the network. The Premier Express lane offers an environment where you can recruit technicians who have a great attitude, and then train them quickly. Premier Express exemplifies how we can deliver a more relevant customer experience, provide a profitable platform for dealers, and recruit great talent, even in an environment with a shortage of technicians in the United States." By developing compelling programs that offer wins for the customer, wins for the dealer, and wins for the brand, rapid deployment and brand alignment are quickly achieved.

Rapid deployment is also at play with the upcoming launch of the Mercedes-Benz Digital Service Drive. Gareth notes, "To match brands like Starbucks or Mandarin Oriental, we had to develop a stronger digital presence. In just nine months, we built a platform for our dealers that had not been available before. There are lots of traditional technology solution providers who have been playing in the automotive space for years. But to achieve the level of seamless integration we desire, we had to find entrepreneurial vendors to quickly build the solution that we needed and wanted. From our perspective, Digital Service Drive proves to our dealers that we can partner to develop software that serves the evolving needs of their customers." In the future, a portion of the dealer margin will be linked to a dealer's ability to deliver the service benefits associated with Digital Service Drive technology.

To further fuel change in the areas that are most relevant to customers (and that have the most impact on the brand's CSI ranking), the Customer Experience team continues to refine its internal measurement processes [the Customer Experience Index (CEI) tool described in Chapter 5]. Harry Hynekamp explains, "We started to plateau in terms of our own internal survey mechanism. So in 2015 we readjusted the questions we ask customers and changed the weight we gave specific questions to help our dealerships link their improvement efforts to areas of customer need. In essence, our adjustments will help dealers focus on the things that customers are telling us we can do better. These areas include such things as expediting the timeliness of our follow-up contact. Early on, our measurement feedback loop helped us take care of the low-hanging opportunities. Now we have to refocus and reweight our survey questions to take on bigger challenges that will produce important improvements in the customer experience in our internal and external measurements. In all cases, we want to create better experiences for our customers."

Moving forward, the Mercedes-Benz USA leaders not only are highlighting a different set of target behaviors but also are improving the process by which they seek the customer's feedback. As you will recall, the current process involves the customer coming in for sales and service and then receiving a thank-you e-mail letting her know a survey is coming from MBUSA. Harry Hynekamp explains how that process will be modified in the future. "The first change falls under the premise that 'we can only fix what we know about.' Since some customers don't voluntarily raise issues or don't want to 'bother' us with small problems, we need to let them know we are here to help and that we want to redeem ourselves if anything is missed. As such, we will be introducing a second, shorter e-mail that will trail our initial survey. That e-mail will ask four questions: 'We noticed you had an issue; did the dealer follow up with you?' Yes or no. 'Did they resolve the issue?' Yes or no. 'Are you likely to refer the dealer to a family or friend?' Yes or no. That's a question to get at a Net Promoter Score (NPS) calculation. And finally, 'Is there anything else we can do for you?'"

In the future, Mercedes-Benz USA will also be doubling the percentage of dealer margin directly linked to performance as measured through customer feedback. That feedback will be a combination of results from the reweighted internal metric (the CEI), a calculation of their customers' reported Net Promoter Score, and the customer responses regarding whether their issues ultimately were resolved. Basically, future margins for dealers will reflect customer-reported transactional excellence, loyalty, and advocacy. Harry Hynekamp notes, "We want part of our reward to dealers to be based on their follow-through. By introducing this 'redemption model,' we are giving added focus and benefits to those dealers that have a robust process to fully resolve customer needs." Harry describes the evolution of the customer experience performance aspects of dealer compensation as a stair-step approach: "Our first margin was all about surveys and success during customer transactions. Now we're blending in relationship tracking and ways to reward service recovery. This is leading up to the third step, which we will introduce sometime in the future. That step will be a true metric of loyalty and advocacy. We also will be expanding our performance metrics. Today we count only new car sales in the margin. That will change to include certified pre-owned and noncertified pre-owned sales as well. These customers are just as important to us as new car buyers."

When Harry talks about stair-stepping, I think of customer experience excellence as being much like the high jump in track and field. Once you clear a bar set at 7 feet 2 inches, the bar is raised to 7 feet 3 inches, and you are challenged to stretch your performance further. Mercedes-Benz USA has set goals for specific behavior and uses data to measure improvements toward those goals. Once service habits are developed to meet those performance goals, new goals are developed to stretch the enterprisewide ability to meet and exceed customer expectations. The bar is raised again to include additional metrics for relationship health and service recovery. Then the universe of products covered is expanded.

Drew Slaven, vice president marketing, adds perspective on the ceaseless pursuit of excellence. "If someone were to ask me, 'When will you know you have achieved your customer experience mission?' I would say, 'If you expect that job to be done, then you don't understand the job.' This isn't something that has a finish line. It's not a program. It's a mindset." How well are you raising the bar and stretching the mindset of your people? Are you shifting your experience targets to constantly improve the customer experience you are delivering to your customers? Are you continually refining the way you solicit input from customers and measuring transactional and relationship satisfaction, engagement, and loyalty?

Other tactical approaches that are slated to expand and improve the customer experience in the upcoming years at Mercedes-Benz include a new approach to training and competency building, the return of the Mercedes-Benz Way, and a shift to a true customer-based relationship management strategy. To help you see how these advanced strategies might help your business, let's look at each in detail.

Enhanced Training and Competency Building

Mercedes-Benz USA has invested heavily in the Brand Immersion Center and the Leadership Academy. The learning and performance team has spearheaded efforts to develop each of those breakthrough programs. In the future, the company's offerings will heavily emphasize a full career development curriculum or a CDA (career development academy), and the team will evolve into what will be called the "Mercedes-Benz Academy."

Since tremendous customer experiences are fueled by engaged, knowledgeable, and skilled work teams, the staff at the Mercedes-Benz Academy will be rewriting the job paths for all major roles in the dealer network. Every employee will be given a learning pathway to achieve a base certification, a star certification, and ultimately a master certification for his job category. Each quarter, staff members at dealerships will have recertification requirements to help them stay current on product knowledge and grow the skills they need if they are to deliver world-class customer experiences. Mercedes-Benz is banking on even greater success as it moves from being a training organization, where a lot of information is pushed out to the dealer body, toward being a certifiable, skills-based learning organization where competencies are defined and individuals grow in the direction of certified skill attainment. This learning and development shift should ultimately maximize the engagement of dealership employees by helping individuals go beyond simply performing jobs to empowering them to master a profession and embrace a meaningful career, well equipped with product knowledge and customer experience delivery skills.

In addition to continuing the brand's emphasis on training, MBUSA is fully committed to product experts. Since many studies have shown that customers' most salient desire is to work with a service provider who is highly knowledgeable, Mercedes-Benz USA has invested in "product concierges." Specifically, the product concierge program, which was announced by Steve Cannon at the 2014 National Dealer Meeting, involves multiday training of select dealership employees. The approximately 1,600 product concierges who are trained during the first year of the program will provide robust and personalized product demonstrations prior to purchase and at delivery (at the dealership, at home, or even at the customer's place of business), walk the service drives at dealerships answering customer questions, conduct product clinics, and train other staff members at the dealership—delivering much of their product information using iPad apps.

Steve Cannon notes, "The product concierge started with Mercedes-Benz USA and has become a global initiative for Daimler. One of our competitors has created a similar position and calls their people 'product geniuses.' To me, a product genius is a statement about the individual, not the customer. It in essence says, 'Look at me. I'm smarter than you. I'm a genius.' The name *product concierge* says something completely different. *Concierge* says, 'I'm at your service. How can I help?' To me, that little distinction in how we view our product concierges is indicative of the mentality and the culture we're trying to drive throughout the organization."

In the future, relevant training will need to assist team members in identifying opportunities to help customers make smooth transitions back and forth from the digital world to an in-store environment. In some cases, this journey will involve transitions for a customer who shops online but purchases in a physical store. In other cases, the flow will go in the opposite direction, with online purchases being serviced in a brick-and-mortar setting after the sale. As you look at your business, how well are your staff members being trained to provide a seamless experience as your customers move from online to the in-store experiences? How much of your future customer experience success will be linked to maximizing the product knowledge of your people and giving them pathways to develop core customer-facing competencies? Are you a training organization that pushes knowledge out or a learning organization that builds certifiable competencies?

The Return of the Mercedes-Benz Way

As you will recall from Chapter 7, in 2013, the leaders at Mercedes-Benz USA wanted to do more than be great at delivering experiences. They wanted to define a branded Mercedes-Benz Way of delivering sales and service experiences. In pursuit of the Mercedes-Benz Way, the leaders went to brands that were renowned for unique customer experiences (including Mandarin Oriental Hotel Group and Nordstrom) and produced a video about the experiences those brands were delivering. That benchmarking video was the beginning of an effort by Mercedes-Benz USA leaders to define a unique Mercedes-Benz style of customer experience execution. In short order, it became clear that it was too early in the transformation process to define the Mercedes-Benz Way. As a result, the leaders redirected their energy toward improving fundamental service delivery.

Given the progress in improving the customer experience that has taken place in the ensuing years, Mercedes-Benz leaders are once again exploring a uniquely Mercedes-Benz brand of customer experience. One of the first steps in this process has involved going through all the stories of customer delight that the leaders have received in the recent past. The best-of-the-best stories are then translated into video format to demonstrate what it means to deliver extraordinary sales and service the Mercedes-Benz Way. Those videos include not only what happened from the customer's perspective but also how leaders at the dealership are driving the Mercedes-Benz Way of delighting customers.

One representative example of the Mercedes-Benz Way involved a couple from California. The wife brought a car in for service and mentioned to the service advisor, "If, in the process of servicing the car, you find an earring on the floor, please let me know." In addition to performing the requested mechanical tune-up, the service advisor and a Mercedes-Benz technician took the seats out of the car to look for the earring. The astonished customer, upon being presented with the earring, burst into tears. As it turned out, the earrings had been a special gift from her husband and had significant sentimental value. The video will allow MBUSA to share this type of story in various settings to inspire *everyone* who represents the brand to try to create that type of customer experience every time and everywhere.

Gareth views the ability to define the Mercedes-Benz Way of customer experience excellence as a sign of transformational success. "A couple of years ago, we sat down with our dealers and we said, 'Let's script what we believe is the Mercedes-Benz Way.' After a two-day workshop with a number of dealers, we came out with a work product that we viewed as not good enough for us to call the Mercedes-Benz Way." Gareth adds, "You have to have processes and technology that give your customers a consistent experience, and you have to have the hearts of your people engaged behind a purpose before you can talk about your unique experience. That's what we were missing. But we went all-in for the best customer experience; we tactically generated the Leadership Academy, the Brand Immersion Experience, the employee engagement survey, consulting for employee engagement, the Drive a Star Home program, and so much more. All of these things were targeted to support our vision—to be Driven to Delight. As I recently started looking at the stories our customers have been telling us about their experiences, I realized those stories are the Mercedes-Benz Way. That was the moment when I knew we'd made a difference."

Given that the first enterprisewide training program, Driven to LEAD, occurred in the earliest phases of the Driven to Delight transformation, leaders at Mercedes-Benz USA are looking to develop a future round of training exclusively focused on what it means to deliver customer experiences the Mercedes-Benz Way. That training will likely address what the Mercedes-Benz Way looks like in terms of the behaviors that customers will experience. It will provide learning opportunities to help enhance staff members' understanding of customers' wants, needs, and lifestyles. In addition, it will likely include a focus on heightening dealer employees' awareness of the impact each individual has when interacting with customers. It will highlight, for all team members, the power and resources they have to personally deliver delight in both small and large ways.

Have you defined the unique customer experience that your business provides? Have you invested in the operational and cultural tools needed to make that experience come to life? What are the stories your customers are telling about your sales and service excellence? Do those stories offer insights into what makes your experience unique?

Developing a "True" Customer Relationship Management System, Digital Service, and the "Golden Record"

I have had many conversations with senior leaders about the future of customer experience excellence at Mercedes-Benz USA, and I view "Digital Service" and the "Golden Record" (a phrase used at MBUSA to describe the evolution to a true customer relationship management system) as the most exciting and inspiring vision of what will be possible for the brand. Before I share that vision, it is important to note that all of the people, process, and technology successes to date have been critical building blocks in making this digital/humanized/futuristic vision possible.

Let's start by understanding the basic vehicle/customer-tracking shift that will be necessary to position the Mercedes-Benz customer experience of the future. At present, Mercedes-Benz USA has most of its data processes linked to a vehicle identification number (VIN). That VIN tracks a product, not a customer. In the near future, the company will shift to a model similar to that of Apple, where the Apple ID tracks an individual customer and creates a record of all the products and services associated with that customer.

Once the customer identifier is joined to VINs, Mercedes-Benz USA will be better positioned to take advantage of the new telematics features onboard soon-to-be-released Mercedes-Benz vehicles. This technology will produce powerful communications between the customer, the dealership, MBUSA, and the brand.

Steve Cannon shares how this dynamic communication link will be a game changer for the brand experience. "Our transformation ambitions are not just for our culture, but for a combination of culture, processes, and technology. All of these components will be working perfectly and in concert for our customers. So in the future, you will see a more meaningful intersection of the car and the lifestyle of each individual customer. With telematics, the connected car, and the ability to customize, remotely update, and transport services into a car, our relationships with our customers will become much more robust." Specifically, Steve notes, "We're going to know how customers are using their vehicles, how quickly they accumulate miles or burn through their brake pads. That knowledge will allow us to be proactive in taking care of them and their cars. The future is going to allow a much tighter connection between the customer's single ID and how a dealer engages with that customer."

This close connection will also allow the dealer to package customized in-car services to make each customer's life easier. From Steve's perspective, "Great customer brands are focused obsessively on the customer. It's easier to demonstrate that obsession when you have regular contact with your customer. For example, the Starbucks barista sees you each morning and can engage you with a smile or delight you by knowing your name, remembering your drink, or customizing your beverage. The brand builds customer engagement, in part, through its frequency of contact with you. At Mercedes-Benz, we haven't had that kind of frequency. We'd sell a car and service it infrequently. Going forward, we'll have a linkage that will directly connect us to our customers and even be able to anticipate their needs in ways that we've never done before. Your car will communicate its status to your dealer, and your dealer can reach out to you and invite you into the dealership to address your maintenance and repair needs. For easier fixes, we will be able to remotely update the software in your car, just like receiving the latest update for your iPhone. All these technological possibilities are coming. But if you don't have a culture that obsesses about how to take care of the customer, you're not going to maximize the return on those technological investments."

Gareth Joyce picks up the future vision of the customer-obsessed/technology digital service experience at Mercedes-Benz. "Every dealer will have big data available to help them appreciate and drive loyalty. Dealers will quickly know how many cars you've owned in the past, your service history, and which dealerships you've visited. Added to that, we will know the experience you are having with your cars and with your dealership, as your internal metric surveys will be attached to your record. Additionally, we will know when you are running low on fuel and be able to send you information on the location of the nearest gas station. If we detect your tire is going flat, we would be able to send Roadside Assistance out to help you before you even knew you had a problem."

Gareth enriches his example by asking us to imagine a situation in the future in which "diagnostic data comes from the car to the dealership, alerting it to your need for service, and you are invited—through the car—to book your service appointment. Based on the diagnostics we receive from your car, we have an understanding of what it will take to resolve your need, so we can prepick the parts and know that we will be able to complete the job at the time you schedule your service visit. You come into the service drive. We don't need to do diagnostics because we already have that data. You are in and out quickly, with your courtesy vehicle ready and waiting, if needed. At that point, we will have created more than a Digital Service Drive. We will have created a digital channel that integrates perfectly with the physical delivery of service available at your dealership."

While the image of a future in which Mercedes-Benz automobiles communicate our service needs, preferences, and use patterns has a lot of appeal, it isn't without challenges or concerns. How will privacy issues be managed? Do I want Mercedes-Benz to know where I travel? Will I want the company to market products to me based on my interests? Mercedes-Benz is poised to handle these questions the way it is addressing all of its current business considerations—with a respect that is centered on the customers' desires and comfort. Customers will "opt in" to the technologies of the future, much the way smartphone users give permission for the location services requested by many apps today. Gareth notes, "Information is requested through the app so that the provider can serve you relative to your location. The apps scan your whereabouts in the background; customers are used to that today. In our case, we will evolve at a pace that customers will accept. We must first create a compelling vision for a product and service that we believe will add further value to our customers' lives, and then we can figure out the obstacles and the pace. All of that will result in a true customer relationship management (CRM) system. I say that with purpose because so many companies talk about CRM, but frankly, it's not CRM. In its truest form, CRM is an ongoing activity that runs all day, every day in a meaningful way for a customer. It adds value in their lives. We haven't gotten there yet, but we are journeying to that destination in the future."

How compelling does a digital sales and service experience sound to you as a consumer of automobile goods and services? More important, do you have an equally compelling vision of your future customer experience delivery? Are you willing to build that experience in a way and at a pace that matches the desires of your evolving customer base?

On the Move with HQ

Mercedes-Benz USA corporate staff will be challenged to continue to drive the brand toward even greater customer delight while undergoing a relocation of its corporate headquarters from Montvale, New Jersey, to Sandy Springs, Georgia. In announcing the new state-of-the-art facility being built on a 12-acre lot with easy access to Atlanta's Hartsfield-Jackson Airport, Steve Cannon noted, "Mercedes-Benz is a marquis brand that requires a marquis setting. Our ambition is to be more than just a great car company. We want to be among the best companies in the world, and Atlanta will serve as the perfect foundation to foster that ambition for the future."

As is always the case with major relocations, many Mercedes-Benz USA corporate staff members did not make the move from New Jersey. As such, MBUSA leadership selected new staff members based on likely cultural fit and oriented them to the importance of delivering excellent customer experiences. All the while, leaders sought to maintain momentum on the progress that had been achieved to date. Harald Henn, vice president finance & controlling, Mercedes-Benz USA, notes, "A relocation like ours can seriously disrupt a company, but I am seeing how our investments in people and culture are paying dividends. The engagement level of our people and their customer-focused mindset is resulting in a smoother transition."

Initially, Mercedes-Benz USA employees are working in temporary offices as the company's permanent campus is completed. That permanent headquarters facility, in and of itself, is in keeping with the brand's commitment to experiential excellence. Just as dealers have been expected to upgrade their physical environment in accordance with the Autohaus design, grow and develop their people, and upgrade their technology infrastructure to stay relevant to customers, so too is Mercedes-Benz USA upgrading the look, feel, technology infrastructure, and inspirational nature of the corporate office setting. Underneath the aesthetics, the new Mercedes-Benz USA headquarters will be fully equipped to handle the brand's future technological needs and serve as the place to assure that Driven to Delight has lasting impact.

➤ When attempting to move an entire organization in the direction of desired change, it is often a matter of "inspiring the best" and "requiring the rest."

➤ The core competencies needed for future success in any industry include speed of program design and deployment along with the ability of those programs to meet the relevant needs of your customers and the profitability needs of your stakeholders.

➤ Customer-centric brands are constantly refining the internal metrics that they use to measure and reward customer experience excellence. These refinements include increasing the weighting of more important target behaviors, investing money in performance rewards, improving the timing and methods of customer feedback, and expanding the number of products for which customer input is solicited.

➤ Customers want to interact with highly knowledgeable service providers. Future-thinking, customer-obsessed organizations will tirelessly drive both product knowledge and customer experience skills.

➤ Companies are shifting from a training mindset to a learning mindset. This transition involves offering certifiable skills and knowledge that will enhance the lives of employees and customers.

➤ To differentiate your business, you should define your unique customer experience. Your customers' stories will offer insights into the way your brand differs in its experience delivery.

➤ Collecting and sharing stories of customer experience excellence involving your brand helps to inspire your team to deliver that level of care to every customer, every time.

➤ To truly manage customer relationships, you must be able to track your business from the perspective of each unique customer, not just from the perspective of unique product identifiers, stock-keeping units, or universal product codes.

➤ In the words of Steve Cannon, "Great customer brands are focused obsessively on the customer," and, "It's easier to demonstrate that obsession when you have regular contact with your customer."

➤ Future-proofing your business will involve creating a compelling picture of the benefits of a customer experience that integrates technology and human service delivery. It will also require you to advance your use of technology at a pace that is in keeping with the comfort and desires of your customers.

Action is the foundational key to all success.

—Pablo Picasso

Conclusion:
Driving Your Road to
Customer Delight

◇◇

T he foundational premise of this book is that many companies weren't developed on a customer-centric platform.
Many great businesses have achieved success with a product-based
strategy—by creating innovative products, establishing effective
distribution channels, maintaining highly competitive pricing,
and executing against high-quality standards. Other companies
have taken a service approach and tried to add value to their product offerings by delivering them consistently and accurately. In our
current marketplace, however, traditional product- and service-
based strategies are often insufficient.

We live in a time when consumers have unprecedented levels of choice and customer opinions about products and brands have a wide reach. As a result, the age of the empowered customer has probably led your brand (and certainly has prompted Mercedes-Benz USA) to aggressively seek a truly customer-obsessed aproach to business. So how are you doing?

Hopefully, the breadth of information presented in this book will help you with various components of your customer-centric evolution. Some readers may find value in processes for mapping the customer journey, while others may benefit from understanding how Mercedes-Benz created its Brand Immersion Experience. In any case, I have taken the liberty of culling 20 key questions that you can use to diagnostically assess your progress in driving delight for your customers. I hope you will take the time to think about each of these questions and use them as discussion starters with your team:

1. What have you learned about your strengths, weaknesses, opportunities, and threats with regard to delivering customer experience excellence?

2. What is your compelling vision for elevating your customer experience delivery, and how is the buy-in for that vision across all key stakeholders?

3. How is customer experience excellence a driver for profitability and sustainability? What promises have you made to individuals in your organization regarding ways in which you will help them make that excellence a reality?

4. What resources have you deployed to build trust and drive customer experience improvement across every interaction point with your brand?

5. How are you streamlining and elevating your customers' journey across channels?

6. What are your real-time customer feedback tools? How are you using those tools to respond to individual customer issues and improve customer-facing processes?

7. How have you linked customer-centric performance metrics to the accountability and growth of your team members?

8. What have you done to align customer-centric performance metrics with your business's key performance indicators?

9. What programs have you developed to win the hearts and minds of your people in pursuit of customer experience greatness?

10. How are you actively measuring employee engagement and providing leaders with the tools they need if they are to improve the work environment for those they supervise?

11. What process improvements have you made to remove pain points for customers and enhance customer delight?

12. How is technology being deployed to streamline the customer experience that you deliver?

13. What steps have you taken to contemporize your customer experience to make it relevant to both existing and future customer segments?

14. How effectively are you integrating high-tech customer solutions with compassionate human care?

15. What measures are you relying upon to assess the success of your customer-facing efforts?

16. How do your customer metrics blend internal and external data points? What relationship-based and transactional assessments are you using?

17. How do you routinely enhance your processes for listening to your customers?

18. In what ways are you adjusting the behavioral targets of customer experience excellence to reflect the needs of your customers?

19. How have you communicated your compelling vision of the optimal future customer experience?

And finally,

20. What will the lasting impact of your customer experience leadership be?

While the information covered in this book should help you address the first 19 questions, the last query—about "lasting impact"—has yet to be answered by the leaders at Mercedes-Benz USA. In part, the answer is missing because of the relative newness of the shift. However, the way MBUSA leaders think and talk about their desired impact is likely to prove helpful as you seriously contemplate the lasting effects you want to achieve from your customer experience efforts.

Dynasty, Sustainability, and Legacy

When asked about how he assesses Mercedes-Benz USA's success in its customer-centric transformation, Steve Cannon is quick to point to direct observations of the way his staff members behave during interactions with dealers. "Driven to Delight is starting to reset the expectation bar for just about everything that we do. If it's a National Parts & Service Managers Meeting, a Mercedes-Benz National Dealer Meeting, or just an executive management event, our people are taking Driven to Delight seriously. I see the thousands of people across our organization committed to raising their game when it comes to delivering extraordinary experiences to everyone they serve. That commitment isn't limited to just the programs we launch, like Digital Service Drive or the Leadership Academy. When I compare how we execute and how we approached dealer events in the pre-Driven to Delight versus the post-Driven to Delight era I see an amazing increase in our attention to detail. Our staff members are obsessing on how to make things the best they can possibly be for our participants. Mercedes-Benz USA team members are asking how we can make events even more customer-friendly. They are looking at little things, like the appropriateness and quality of the coffee service at an event. Now, everything we do is seen as setting an example for our dealers, where we must give them living proof of what we are aspiring to as a brand. People are holding themselves accountable to be Driven to Delight, and that accountability is leading to runaway impact accumulating across the enterprise."

In addition to his observations of his people's collective efforts and actions, Steve Cannon looks for how those customer-obsessed actions are traveling out to the customer. "We have a number of departments here at corporate that have direct interactions with customers. Obviously, this includes departments such as our Customer Assistance Center and marketing activities like the US Open and the Masters. But most of what we do at corporate is dealer-facing. It is our dealers who ultimately have the most direct impact on our customers. Our dealer partners and MBUSA are in this together, and we see the success of our efforts in our customer feedback data as well as in the surveys of others. For me, however, I am most affected when I hear stories directly from our customers." One story that resonated with Steve follows:

I took my high-mileage Mercedes SUV in for much-needed repairs. I expected to see a newer version of the same old Mercedes repair center. Boy, was I in for a surprise. The service bay garage door opened in a flash. I pulled in and was immediately greeted by a service advisor. Within minutes, I described issues with my vehicle that had accumulated over the past 18 months. In the meantime, they'd done an electronic diagnostic on my car, checking for codes and other things. Wow. At every other dealer, I'd still be standing around hoping someone would greet me. My car disappeared as a loaner vehicle pulled in. And I was off on my way in a grand total of six or seven minutes. That was a great start, but would the new guys keep it up? A few hours later, they texted me and told me they'd call shortly. After a few conversations, we agreed on the necessary repairs and costs. They even talked me out of one repair, saying that it wasn't necessary. Hmmm. That put $200 extra in my pocket. Two days later, I receive a text and a call that my car is ready. They gave me the option to pay the invoice online and have my vehicle driven right to my office by the valet, which I declined. I wanted to go back to the dealership. The final invoice was slightly under their estimate. That's never happened before. Everything checked out perfectly, and I was on my way after thanking my service advisor. The whole experience made me a customer for life.

Steve adds, "With all the objective data telling me we are on the right track, I still like to hear customers say that the way we treated them made them customers for life. It is through increasing and consistent testimonials that I ultimately know we are doing what we set out to do—to be the best customer experience provider irrespective of industry."

Steve Cannon also measures the impact of Driven to Delight by looking beyond the United States. Since customer experience excellence is a top priority for MBUSA's parent company, Daimler AG, the global deployment of ideas rolled out in the United States (like product concierges) is evidence of the broad influence of MBUSA's customer experience leaders. Steve's scope of impact has also expanded to regional leadership, as he is now responsible for operations in the North American Region, which includes Canada and Mexico.

Steve notes that when it comes to moving the needle on customer experience for Mercedes-Benz globally, "MBUSA has had the role of being a fast mover. We have sought to put together an impressive body of work that encompasses technology, people, training, leadership, culture, and systems so that Mercedes-Benz leaders around the globe can borrow ideas from us as they elevate the customer experience in their markets." Tim Reuss, president and CEO of Mercedes-Benz Canada, agrees, noting that Steve Cannon and his team at MBUSA "have created the customer experience template for other countries to follow. While every country has unique customer needs to address, MBUSA is leading the way by providing the most integrated, forward-thinking approach to customer experience excellence."

When communicating with dealers about the progress Mercedes-Benz USA has made toward customer experience transformation, Steve Cannon shares, "We're proud that we continue to make progress. We will not take our foot off the accelerator. As we gain momentum, our competitors will continue to work harder to catch us and, more important, our customers continue to deserve the best. Together we will remain steadfast and determined to build a sustainable competitive advantage and a dynasty."

Coming off of the victories noted in Chapter 11, including domestic sales, J.D. Power SSI results, ACSI findings, Pied Piper rankings, and Polk loyalty achievements, the theme of a "dynasty" is one that Steve has maintained in meetings with various leaders. In fact, during the 2014 National Dealer Meeting, Steve reflected on recent customer-centric successes. "There are lots of ways to interpret our joint achievement. For some, it could mean 'mission accomplished.' Some might say, 'It's about time.' I like to think of it as a preview of coming attractions. Now that we know what we can do when we work together, it's time for us to build a dynasty! Who comes to mind when you talk about building a dynasty? Maybe the Yankees or the Celtics. How about the Crimson Tide, with three national titles in five years? For me, you can use the word *dynasty* only when you can demonstrate sustained excellence. When winning becomes a habit. When you're able to beat your opponents even when they know what plays you're going to run! I think the time has never been better for us to build a dynasty here in the United States. That should be our goal."

The rallying cry for a dynasty may sound somewhat audacious, but so did the idea that a product-centric brand like Mercedes-Benz could become so customer-obsessed that it would be a global leader in customer experience delivery. Behind the concept of a dynasty lives leadership skill and an acute understanding of human nature.

As difficult as it is to achieve a successful culture shift in a highly competitive marketplace like luxury automotive, it may be even more difficult to sustain it. People can be inspired to win a short-term victory like a number one sales ranking or struggle for an achievement like being first on the J.D. Power Sales Satisfaction Index study, but suggesting that they do the hard work that it takes to achieve that victory again (and again and again) often isn't as inspiring as securing that first victory. There is something special and different about musical bands like the Rolling Stones, who produce decades of hits, compared to "one-hit wonders." Steve's call to action is an inspirational exhortation for the sustained success reserved for elite "dynasties of victory."

In my conversations with Steve, it is clear that he expects Mercedes-Benz USA to be a dynasty of victory when it comes to customer experience. But will his desired legacy of customer experience excellence continue beyond his time as the leader of the organization? Steve notes, "I believe that we have now successfully pushed Driven to Delight into the organization to the point where its momentum is going to outlive me. The reality, of course, is that if any organization loses track of conversations centered around its customers, it will start moving backward."

Dietmar Exler, vice president sales, also emphasizes the importance of helping staff members stay centered on the customer. "I'm proud of what we've achieved, and I realize many of our process improvements were the easiest part of the journey. Making processes better is intuitive. We needed to offer a hassle-free sales experience and provide an express service lane. It is much harder to manage human capital and sustain the focus of our people. Success on those fronts is at the foundation of a dynasty."

Gareth Joyce, vice president customer services, has a similar perspective on the legacy of Mercedes-Benz leadership and a sustained culture of customer obsession. "We've made an inordinate amount of progress, and we also know that there is much work ahead for us. We are very pleased that we have begun a new conversation about our brand, one not just linked to product excellence but that looks at how we seek to be a leader in customer experience."

Gareth reminded his team that there had never been a book written about Mercedes-Benz being a leader in customer experience excellence until now. Therefore, he asked me to engage his management team in discussions on how such a book, in part, will shape their respective legacies. At the end of my time with his team, Gareth noted, "When you go into a bookstore and see this book on the shelves, you will know your efforts are influencing the experiences of customers well beyond the automobile industry.

Those readers, many of whom are corporate leaders, and our own customers will be looking to see if we sustain our passion and commitment to our vision or if this is but a brief season of customer experience excellence for the Mercedes-Benz brand." From my vantage point, Mercedes-Benz USA is positioned to build a dynasty of customer experience excellence.

Steve, Dietmar, and Gareth provide critical lessons about leaving a legacy. In essence, they help us realize that leaders must not just state their vision of customer experience excellence but also take action to manifest that vision on behalf of those they serve. Leaders should look to their people and see them demonstrate an obsession with details that make the difference between "good" and "the best" customer experiences. Ultimately, the impact of extraordinary customer care should be heard in the stories our customers share and seen in the data garnered from customer surveys.

The great business author Stephen Covey suggested, "There are certain things that are fundamental to human fulfillment. The essence of these is captured in the phrase 'to live, to love, to learn, to leave a legacy' . . . the need to leave a legacy is our spiritual need to have a sense of meaning, purpose, personal convergence, and contribution."

May you hit the gas pedal hard and accelerate in ways that help you live, love, learn, and drive a legacy of delighting your customers, your people, and all those you influence!

Glossary

American Customer Satisfaction Index (ACSI) The only national, cross-industry measure of customer satisfaction in the United States. This strategic economic indicator is based on customer evaluations of the quality of goods and services purchased in the United States that have been produced by domestic and foreign firms with substantial U.S. market share. The ACSI measures the quality of economic output as a complement to traditional measures of the quantity of economic output by surveying roughly 70,000 customers about the products and services they use the most. The survey data serves as inputs to an econometric model that benchmarks customer satisfaction at more than 300 companies in 43 industries and 10 economic sectors, as well as a multitude of federal agencies and departments and two high-usage local government services.

Autohaus The name of the global design, corporate identity, and facilities standard for Mercedes-Benz dealerships. It is defined by a modern aesthetic that makes use of steel and glass construction to provide maximum transparency, openness, and functionality. These attributes are reflected in the seamless flow of all customer contact functions within the dealership, which enhances the overall efficiency of the dealership's staff and creates an inviting and professional environment. Autohaus design elements also showcase products in a brand-commensurate setting and optimize customer convenience. The application of the Autohaus standard to Mercedes-Benz facilities in the United States has produced a uniform "look" that is consistent with the Mercedes-Benz brand DNA.

Best Practice Guides (also referred to as Sales Experience Best Practice Guide and Service Experience Best Practice Guide) A tool created by MBUSA to assist dealers in improving sales and service experiences. The guides were developed to align with the processes that affect MBUSA's Customer Experience Index (CEI), which, in turn, is correlated with the touchpoints and best practices that have the most impact on overall customer satisfaction.

The Brand Immersion Experience Inspired by the Mercedes-Benz Museum and Brand Centers worldwide, a program that aims to connect the hearts and minds of both dealership and corporate employees with the Mercedes-Benz brand. Brand Immersion is built on three tenets: (1) the standards of the brand, (2) the legacy of the brand, and (3) delivering the best customer experience. Participants travel to the Brand Immersion Center near the Mercedes-Benz U.S. International factory in Vance, Alabama, and participate in a variety of classes, offsite tours, and driving events over two full days.

Customer Assistance Center (CAC) The MBUSA area responsible for both inbound and outbound customer interactions. The CAC staff serves as the lifeline for all Mercedes-Benz customers, providing services ranging from roadside assistance deployment to inbound product inquiries and resolution of customer complaints. The CAC is also home to the customer advocacy team, which specializes in assisting both owners and dealers with obscure and/or difficult service issues.

Customer Experience Index (CEI) (also referred to as Service CEI and Sales CEI) Cumulative customer satisfaction scores as measured by the Customer Experience Program (CEP) surveys completed by customers following sales and service interactions at Mercedes-Benz dealerships. The surveys pose questions about specific aspects of the in-dealership experience through a combination of yes/no and 10-point scale questions.

Customer Experience Program (CEP) One of the key pillars of MBUSA's approach to customer experience management. The Customer Experience Program, or CEP, was developed in 2013 to gain insights into the sales and service experiences of Mercedes-Benz customers at the dealership level. At the heart of the program is a survey that measures the customer's experience (both quantitatively and qualitatively) with dealership transactions. Insights gleaned from the surveys ultimately drive retail performance improvement, and CEP scores affect dealers' performance bonuses.

Customer Relationship Management (CRM) A system or process for managing a company's interactions with prospective, current, and future customers. It often involves using technology to organize, automate, and synchronize sales, marketing, customer service, and technical communication and support.

Customer Satisfaction Program (CSP) Until 2013, MBUSA's proprietary customer satisfaction surveying program. It was the precursor to the Customer Experience Program (CEP).

Dealer Engagement Surveys An annual survey of all dealership employees, conducted by MBUSA with the goal of understanding retail employee sentiment. The results are used to identify opportunities for improvement and drive change, as well as to track the leadership's impact and progress over time. This survey is critical in measuring a dealership's ability to retain motivated, engaged staff.

Dealer Margin The difference between manufacturer's suggested retail price (MSRP) and true dealer cost. The margin is divided into fixed and variable components according to an agreement negotiated between the dealer body and MBUSA. The fixed portion is the difference between the MSRP and what most consumers would consider the "dealer cost" or "invoice." The variable component is held in reserve by MBUSA and paid to the dealer as a quarterly bonus based on the dealer's performance against specific financial, experiential, and operational goals.

Digital Dealer Network One of MBUSA's first customer experience–focused initiatives. Launched in 2010, the network allowed MBUSA to seamlessly upload fresh content to high-definition monitors in dealership showrooms, allowing customers to "virtually" browse features and configure vehicles. The up-to-date, interactive aspect of the monitor facilitated a more technologically engaging customer-to-salesperson connection by allowing the customer and the salesperson to "co-create" vehicles based on the customer's preferred specifications, features, and options.

Digital Service Drive (DSD) A service initiative that represents the ultimate integration of people, processes, and technology. It utilizes cutting-edge technology to provide customers with a seamless experience across all service touchpoints. It sets best-in-class standards for convenient online scheduling, efficient tablet-enabled vehicle check-in/check-out, a seamless transition to and from courtesy loaner vehicles, maintenance and/or repair status updates, and flexible postservice payment options.

Drive a Star Home (DaSH) An extended-drive product familiarization program. Launched in 2013 and designed for MBUSA and dealership staff members who wouldn't ordinarily have had the opportunity to drive Mercedes-Benz automobiles, Drive a Star Home was created to familiarize employees with both the brand and the vehicles on a deeper, more experiential level. The program combines two days of in-vehicle "seat time" with e-learning courses on topics ranging from Mercedes-Benz heritage to the brand's unique technological, safety, and luxury features.

Driven to Delight (D2D) The title given to MBUSA's customer-centric ethos. The phrase was originally coined by MBUSA president & CEO Steve Cannon as a way to connect every associate to the vision of delivering the very best for every customer (both internal and external), every time, everywhere, no exceptions. At Mercedes-Benz, "Driven to Delight" (D2D) expresses—in the simplest possible terms—the organization's responsibility for always delivering the best possible customer experience.

Driven to LEAD (D2L) MBUSA's customer experience training program, launched in 2011. Designed to enhance customer-centric thinking and focus at both the dealership and corporate levels, the acronym LEAD (Listen, Empathize, Add value, Delight) helped highlight, and serve as a daily reminder of, the essential tenets for delivering the very best customer experience. By focusing not only on leadership and employee engagement, but also on supporting policies, processes, and tools, the program served to advance sustainable customer experience solutions by driving cultural change.

J.D. Power Customer Service Index (CSI) A syndicated industry-wide study that measures the satisfaction of vehicle owners who visited the dealership service department for maintenance or repair work during the first three years of vehicle ownership. The study provides an overall customer service index (CSI) score based on five measures: service quality, service initiation, service advisor, service facility, and vehicle pickup. CSI is a nameplate study, which means that performance is reported at the nameplate level (i.e., Ford, Mitsubishi, etc.) rather than at the model level (i.e., Mustang, Eclipse, etc.). Many manufacturers, including MBUSA, closely monitor year-to-year performance and use the data from this survey to drive process improvement.

J.D. Power Sales Satisfaction Index (SSI) A syndicated industrywide study that examines the dealership's ability to manage the sales process from product presentation, price negotiation, and vehicle purchase to delivery and the finance and insurance process. SSI is a nameplate study, which means that performance is reported at the nameplate level (i.e., Mercedes-Benz, Ford, etc.) rather than at the model level (i.e., Mustang, S-Class, etc.). Many manufacturers, including MBUSA, closely monitor year-to-year performance and use the data from this survey to drive process improvement.

Leadership Bonus Part of the variable portion of the dealer margin, paid quarterly to the top-performing 70 percent of dealers who meet preset customer experience–related performance objectives. The leadership bonus is funded by the margin "breakage," which is the money that was accrued for the lowest-performing dealers but was not paid when they failed to reach the objective. The leadership bonus formula was a key factor in persuading the dealer body to adopt changes to the dealer margin for 2013–2015.

The Mantra A clarification of what the phrase "Driven to Delight" means at MBUSA; an explanation of why "customer satisfaction" isn't an acceptable phrase at a company whose brand promise is "The Best or Nothing." Quickly embraced by everyone associated with the three-pointed star, the mantra has become MBUSA's one and only true "north star," the guiding principle behind the company's customer experience strategies and overall business direction:

> driven to delight. it is not just a phrase. it is a path, a promise, a belief. it is a commitment to creating positive relationships. to making people smile. and to leaving them with a sense of complete trust. driven to delight means exceptional personal treatment. it is a reminder that the journey is never done. that there is always a more thoughtful way. and throughout each interaction

we must remember that *the best or nothing* cannot just be a description of our vehicles. but it must also represent the people behind them.

mbrace The brand name of the Mercedes-Benz "connected car" services platform and in-vehicle suite of services, which includes advanced safety and security, convenience, travel assistance, and Internet-based infotainment features such as remote access, remote lock/unlock, remote start, remote diagnostics, vehicle tracking, collision notification, parental controls, in-vehicle infotainment, personal assistance, and Wi-Fi, among many other features. Launched in select model year 2010 vehicles and standard in all 2016 model Mercedes-Benz vehicles, basic service is free for five years, with additional services/features available as add-on packages by subscription. mbrace maintains connections among the driver, the vehicle, and the world beyond by giving owners access to their vehicle when they are not at the wheel—and access to the world when they are.

MB SELECT The benchmark for customer care in the automotive industry. This program was developed to ensure that a suite of creative solutions is available should a customer experience any inconveniences in the first six months after purchase. MB SELECT provides both funds for customer goodwill gestures and an internal MBUSA rapid response team to ensure that larger issues are resolved quickly and personally.

Mercedes-Benz Courtesy Vehicle Program (CVP) A program that provides incentives to dealers to provide Mercedes-Benz "courtesy cars" for customers who are having their vehicles serviced or repaired at Mercedes-Benz dealerships. Dealers cycle new vehicles through the Courtesy Vehicle Program for a specific period of time and then sell the low-mileage "loaners" through the pre-owned vehicle program.

Mercedes-Benz Customer Experience Champions Program An enterprisewide, high-profile, action-oriented community of change agents empowered to make a difference every day. Each department within MBUSA nominates one individual (the Champion) to act as the voice of the customer and lead change. The Champions are given the task of ensuring that their respective departments demonstrate that they are Driven to Delight in everything they do while also influencing a customer focus mindset within the company.

Mercedes-Benz Dealer Board (MBDB) A team of 12 dealers who serve as high-level advisors and liaisons between MBUSA and the dealer body, conveying to MBUSA executive management their expert views, recommendations, and suggestions on important business matters that affect the mutual interests of MBUSA and Mercedes-Benz dealers in general. The MBDB meets quarterly (at a minimum), and its members serve three-year terms, participating in one or more of six committees: Sales, Customer Experience, Commercial Vehicles, Fixed Operations, Marketing and Technology, and Financial Services.

Mercedes-Benz Leadership Academy A development program for management-level employees at MBUSA and MBFS corporate offices and Mercedes-Benz dealerships. The program is designed to build a series of engagements, beginning with the foundations of leadership and building to leadership mastery. The Leadership Academy prepares Mercedes-Benz leaders to direct and manage growth and business opportunities through the development of a high-performance culture. It teaches the importance of culture in promoting employee engagement, teamwork, and a work environment that attracts and retains the best and the brightest.

Mercedes-Benz Loyalty Index (MBLI) A facet of the Customer Satisfaction Program (CSP). The Loyalty Index was a measure of customers' satisfaction with their recent sales or service experiences and their likelihood of returning and referring others to the dealership. The CSP and MBLI were replaced with the more robust Customer Experience Program (CEP) in 2013.

Mercedes-Benz Way (MB Way) An integral piece of MBUSA's customer experience awareness transition in which the MBUSA leaders sought to create a cultural touchstone through inspirational stories from both MBUSA and its dealership network and companies known for customer experience excellence. The collected examples formed the basis for an expected set of behaviors at both the corporate and retail levels: the Mercedes-Benz Way of delivering the best customer experience.

Pied Piper Prospect Satisfaction Index (PSI) A study in which "mystery shoppers" rate the effectiveness of a dealership's in-person, Internet, and telephone sales processes. Pied Piper conducts studies at the national/syndicated level as well as the regional, market, and individual dealership levels, where it benchmarks results against same-brand national and industry-level averages.

Polk Automotive Loyalty Awards IHS Automotive Loyalty Awards that recognize manufacturers for their ability to retain owners over repeat buying cycles. This occurs when a household returns to market and purchases or leases a new vehicle of the same make, model, or manufacturer as its previous vehicle. The awards are based on an analysis of personal new vehicle registrations over a given model year, which runs from October 1 to September 30.

Premier Express A program that provides customers with the option of expedited (about an hour) vehicle maintenance service. Premier Express doesn't require an appointment and provides owners with a menu of basic maintenance options guaranteed to be completed in 30 to 70 minutes (depending on the vehicle model and the service interval) while they wait in the customer lounge. Since the program was launched in 2014, dealership customer retention and service satisfaction have steadily improved across the dealership network.

The Standard President & CEO Steve Cannon's leadership vision, focusing on the core competencies required to deliver a best-in-class customer experience and designed to rally all MBUSA associates—both corporate and dealership—to the unifying common goal of providing a benchmark experience for all customers:

> The Mercedes-Benz automobile brings with it the expectation that every encounter with the brand will be as extraordinary as the machine itself—as thoughtful, innovative, and breathtaking, as confidence-inspiring and worthy of trust. When our customers enter our dealerships, their standards are predetermined. They rightfully anticipate and deserve the best or nothing. They will not be disappointed. 2012 will see the introduction of the most comprehensive pledge to provide an extraordinary customer experience in the history of Mercedes-Benz. Every department will be mobilized. Every touchpoint in the brand will be examined and refined. Every employee at every dealership will be trained and equipped. We will begin immediately and we will not rest until we are regarded as the global benchmark—until expectations are exceeded with such frequency that the Mercedes-Benz name will be as famous for our total customer experience as it is for our legendary engineering. Mercedes-Benz. The best or nothing.

Bibliography

Chapter 1

"In fact, Karl Benz invented the automobile itself (Benz "Patent Motorwagen") and invented the first commercial vehicle. Since then, Daimler vehicles have contributed to breakthroughs well beyond the internal combustion engine. A few of the areas in which Daimler has either introduced or advanced technological innovation include the first drop chassis, the original passenger car powered by a diesel engine, the creation of direct fuel injection, introduction of the first generation of antilock brakes": "Leading Through Innovation," MBUSA website, www.mbusa.com/mercedes/benz/innovation.

"When Lexus entered the luxury automotive marketplace in the United States in the late 1980s, the Lexus USA newsroom website signaled how that brand was going to differentiate itself based on the desired experience of customers": "The History of Lexus," Lexus USA Newsroom, http://pressroom.lexus.com /releases/history+lexus.htm.

"Fran O'Hagan . . . 'In 2007, visiting a Mercedes dealership was like visiting a museum. Salespeople were friendly and answered questions, but they did not take the next step of actually selling the car. They stopped short of saying, "I know you want to buy a car, and I want to work with you on figuring out how to make that happen"'": Steve Finlay, "What Do Customers Know?" *WardsAuto*, August 1, 2013, http://www.piedpiperpsi.com/download/documents /210.htm.

"For example, the research group Pied Piper (which utilizes a mystery shopper strategy) placed Mercedes-Benz at the top of the luxury automobile category for the experiences it provided in 2010": Ron Montoya, "Luxury Automakers Top Mystery Shopping Study," *EdmundsDaily*, July 13, 2010, http://www .piedpiperpsi.com/download/documents/111.htm.

"and 2011": Pied Piper Management Company LLC, "Mercedes-Benz Dealers Achieve Highest Pied Piper Prospect Satisfaction Index Ranking for Third Consecutive Year," http://www.piedpiperpsi.com/download/documents/144.htm.

"while J.D. Power (which measures the satisfaction of customers with the sales and service functions at dealerships) placed Mercedes-Benz in the middle to lower segment of luxury automakers": J.D. Power, "J.D. Power and Associates Reports: Low Vehicle Sales Likely to Cause Precipitous Drop in Auto Dealer Service Visits During the Next Several Years, Reaching Low Point in 2013," February 24, 2010, http://businesscenter.jdpower.com/news/pressrelease .aspx?ID=2010021.

"For example, in 2014, Interbrand (the world's largest brand consultancy group) placed Mercedes-Benz tenth among the top 100 of 'the world's most valuable brands' based on the company's longstanding excellence in performance, styling, and engineering": "Rankings," Interbrand website, http://www .bestglobalbrands.com/2014/ranking/.

"Interbrand has also noted that Mercedes-Benz has achieved the number one luxury manufacturer position in the United States and Germany, as well as cultivating strong popularity in Russia and China through a balance of traditional and forward-looking styling. Interbrand suggests that the future brand strength of Mercedes-Benz hinges on 'its 2020 growth initiative focused on building the best customer experience,' along with a new product lineup geared toward future generations of Mercedes-Benz buyers": "Best Global Brands 2013," Interbrand website, http://interbrand.com/assets/uploads /Interbrand-Best-Global-Brands-2013.pdf.

"Similarly, Harris's 2014 EquiTrend Automotive Scorecard of consumer sentiment placed Mercedes-Benz as the lead luxury auto brand. Reflecting on the EquiTrend Scorecard, Nielsen's automotive solutions consultant Mike Chadsey suggests that in the 'brutal' competition of the sector, 'As the luxury category reaches feature, performance and style parity, brands that fail to create connections and affinity with target customers will be left behind'": "Brand Equity for Many Luxury and Full Line Automotive Brands at 10-Year High, Finds 2014 Harris Poll EquiTrend Study," Harris website, http://www .harrisinteractive.com/NewsRoom/PressReleases/tabid/446/mid/1506 /articleId/1449/ctl/ReadCustom%20Default/Default.aspx.

"In 2013, the editors of *Forbes* magazine ranked Mercedes-Benz as the World's 16th Most Powerful Brand": "The World's Most Valuable Brands," *Forbes* website, http://www.forbes.com/pictures/mli45egehl/13153/.

"In a 2013 study conducted by research firms Brand Equity and Nielsen, Mercedes was viewed as India's ninth 'most exciting brand' across all industries and the number one automotive brand in India": "India's Youth Rank Mercedes-Benz as the #1 Auto Brand in Economic Times Brand Equity 'Most Exciting Brands' Annual Study," GermanCar4um, http://www .germancarforum.com/threads/indias-youth-rank-mercedes-benz-as-the-1 -auto-brand.47956/.

"In November 2013 the Mercedes-Benz S-Class was named the car of the year in China": "Mercedes S-Class Wins First Ever China Car of the Year," AutoGuide.com, December 2, 2013, http://www.autoguide.com/auto -news/2013/12/mercedes-s-class-wins-first-ever-china-car-of-the-year.html.

"Additionally, Russian prime minister Dmitry Medvedev gave Mercedes-Benz vehicles to each of his country's Olympic medalists during the 2014 games": Jay Busbee, "Russia Gives All Its Gold Medalists $120,000, a New Mercedes," *Fourth-Place Medal*, February 27, 2014, http://sports.yahoo.com /blogs/fourth-place-medal/russia-gives-all-its-gold-medalists--120-000--a -new-mercedes-174223357.html.

"For example, in 2015, Daimler CEO Dieter Zetsche told the *Wall Street Journal* that in China, sales growth was a primary focus, 'So the more we catch up in China, the faster we will be No. 1 [globally].' To that end, Dieter notes that in China, 'We have increased our dealer body. We've added 100 dealer[s…] last year': Christina Rogers, "Daimler CEO Revs Up Mercedes to Challenge BMW," *Wall Street Journal*, January 6, 2015, http://www.wsj.com/articles /daimler-ceo-revs-up-mercedes-to-challenge-bmw-1420592274.

"In 1998, Mercedes-Benz's parent company Daimler-Benz AG merged with the Chrysler Corporation. In an article for *CNN Money* around the time of the merger, Jürgen Schrempp, then chairman of Daimler-Benz, noted, "Today we are creating the world's leading automotive company for the 21st century. We are combining the two most innovative car companies in the world.'": "DaimlerChrysler Dawns," *CNN Money* website, May 7, 1998, http://money.cnn.com/1998/05/07/deals/benz/.

"Despite these aspirations, the merger of Daimler and Chrysler was undone nine years later. In a 2008 *Automotive News* article, Dieter Zetsche, the Daimler-Benz CEO who replaced Jürgen Schrempp, noted, 'We couldn't actually achieve global integration because it was at odds with the image of our brands, the preferences of our customers, and many other success factors—all of which were far more diverse and fragmented'": James Franey, "Zetsche: Daimler Learned Lesson from Chrysler Deal," *Automotive News*, May 16, 2008, http://www.autonews.com/article/20080516/COPY01/170077317 /zetsche:-daimler-learned-lesson-from-chrysler-deal.

"Writing in 2011 for the *Los Angeles Daily Journal*, Jonathan Michaels, a lawyer who specializes in the automotive industry, explains the rationale and substantial investment involved in transforming Mercedes-Benz dealerships to a new Autohaus design: 'The point of all of this is to create a uniform look among a sprawling dealer base and give their product brand identity. In years past, manufacturers only required dealers to use conforming trademarks and proper signage, but those days are long gone. Automakers now have complete design plans, and regulate which architects and vendors must be used and what type of furniture may be bought.' According to Jonathan, 'The cost of construction is borne almost entirely by the dealers and the costs are staggering. . . . To be fair, manufacturers do contribute to the cost of construction by providing incentives to dealers who participate in the programs. Mercedes pays its Autohaus dealers $400 per car sold over a three year period": Jonathan Michaels, "Spend It Like You Got It: Dealers Suffer Under Facility Design Programs," *Los Angeles Daily Journal*, December 6, 2011, http:// mlgautomotivelaw.com/press/2011-12-6-Daily-Journal-Spend-it-like-you -got-it.pdf.

Chapter 2

"In fact, Steve publicly and repeatedly declared the significance and importance of living the mantra and pursuing a customer-centric path. For example, in an interview with Diane Kurylko for *Automotive News*, where he suggested that in the future, luxury manufactures will battle over customer experience delivery. Steve went on to add, 'That is going to be my legacy. I am taking on what seems to be our biggest challenge and finding a way to collaborate with our dealers and leverage our resources to propel this brand where it belongs—to create a customer experience that fits with our tagline "The Best or Nothing."'

"In the same article, Steve emphasized that MBUSA would need time to change the Mercedes-Benz culture in a way that would place the brand in the upper tier of experience providers. In follow-up conversations with me, Steve added that prudent change had to occur without an influx of dollars into departmental budgets at Mercedes-Benz USA. The customer experience transformation needed to be achieved through efficiencies and a willingness to reprioritize resources": Diana T. Kurylko, "Mercedes CEO: Customer Service Will Be 'My Legacy,'" *Automotive News*, May 6, 2013, http://www.autonews.com/article/20130506/OEM02/305069979/mercedes-ceo:-customer-service-will-be-my-legacy.

"John Kotter, a thought leader and author on organizational change, characterizes the early phases of a successful change initiative as stages such as establishing a sense of urgency, creating the guiding coalition, developing a change vision, and communicating the vision for buy-in": Kotter International, "The 8-Step Process for Leading Change," http://www.kotterinternational.com/the-8-step-process-for-leading-change/.

Chapter 4

"In the mid-1980s, G. Lynn Shostack, then a senior vice president in charge of the Private Clients Group at Bankers Trust Company, was among the first to champion the concept of touchpoint assessment. In a 1984 article in the *Harvard Business Review* titled 'Designing Services That Deliver,' Lynn referred to the mapping process as a service blueprint in which processes, fail points, time frames, and profitability are all outlined in a single document. In her argument for the importance of dedicating time and resources to developing a 'blueprint' for the customer journey, Lynn noted that such a process 'helps cut down the time and inefficiency of random service development and gives a higher level view of service management prerogatives. The alternative—leaving services to individual talent and managing the pieces rather than the whole—makes a company more vulnerable and creates a service that reacts slowly to market needs and opportunities'": G. Lynn Shostack, "Designing Services That Deliver," *Harvard Business Review*, January 1984, https://hbr.org/1984/01/designing-services-that-deliver.

Chapter 5

"From the standpoint of conflicting results for Mercedes-Benz, in the 2012 time frame during which the Customer Experience team was mapping the customer journey, Pied Piper ranked Mercedes-Benz number one on its Prospect Satisfaction Index (PSI). The PSI links results from mystery shopping data conducted during the sales process to metrics of sales success": "Mercedes-Benz Dealers Top Ranked by 2012 Pied Piper Prospect Satisfaction Index," *PR Newswire*, July 9, 2012, http://www.prnewswire.com/news

-releases/mercedes-benz-dealers-top-ranked-by-2012-pied-piper-prospect
-satisfaction-index-161766325.html.

"On another national measure of customer experience, the American Customer
Satisfaction Index, which is also the only study that standardizes methods
and assesses satisfaction across industries, Mercedes-Benz ranked seventh in
the automobile category": "Quality Improvement Boosts Customer Satisfaction for Automakers," press release, August 2012, ACSI website, https://www
.theacsi.org/news-and-resources/press-releases/press-archive/press-release
-august-2012.

"When compared to other luxury manufacturers on the well-known J.D. Power
surveys, Mercedes-Benz ranked seventh in service": "Customer Satisfaction
with Dealer Service Facilities Outpaces Satisfaction with Independent Service Centers," J.D. Power website, March 13, 2012, http://www.jdpower.com
/press-releases/2012-us-customer-service-index-csi-study.

"and sixth in sales experience": "Online Ratings/Review Sites and Social
Networking Sites Impact New-Vehicle Buyers' Selection of Dealership,"
J.D. Power website, November 28, 2012, http://www.jdpower.com/es
/node/3055.

"In essence, it is in keeping with American composer Leonard Bernstein's observation that, 'To achieve great things, two things are needed; a plan, and not
quite enough time.' The Customer Experience team forged its plan and delivered the tool on time": BrainyQuote website, http://www.brainyquote.com
/quotes/quotes/l/leonardber140536.html.

Chapter 6

"Commercial vans are becoming increasingly important to MBUSA's parent
company, Daimler AG. According to *Forbes* magazine, vans were responsible
for approximately 9 percent of Daimler's net revenues in 2014": Trefis Team,
"Daimler Earnings Review: Robust Volume Growth and Rich Product Mix
Boost Profitability at Mercedes," *Forbes*, February 6, 2015, http://www.forbes
.com/sites/greatspeculations/2015/02/06/daimler-earnings-review-robust
-volume-growth-and-rich-product-mix-boost-profitability-at-mercedes/.

"Through 2015, Mercedes-Benz has offered only a large-sized van in the United
States: the Sprinter. The United States is second only to Germany in Sprinter
van sales. It is estimated that in 2014, Mercedes-Benz van sales in the United
States increased 20 percent year over year. End-of-year U.S. sales for the
Sprinter approached 26,000 units in 2014, with sales of 50,000 units expected
in 2016. This sizable increase will probably come from economic conditions
that favor small business owners as well as the introduction of a midsize
cargo/passenger van called the Metris. If there were any doubt about Daimler's commitment to the U.S. commercial van market, it was erased by the
company's $500 million investment in Sprinter van production in South Car-
olina": Trefis Team, "Daimler to Start Production of Sprinter Vans in North
America," *Forbes*, December 23, 2014, http://www.forbes.com/sites/great
speculations/2014/12/23/daimler-to-start-production-of-sprinter-vans-in
-north-america/.

Chapter 8

"Bestselling leadership author John Maxwell wrote about the importance of leveraging constructive energy by noting, 'While a good leader sustains momentum,
a great leader increases it': Alex McClafferty, "The Ultimate List of Inspirational Quotes for Entrepreneurs," *Inc.*, http://www.inc.com/alex-mcclafferty
/the-ultimate-list-of-inspirational-quotes-for-entrepreneurs.html.

"Psychologist Martin Seligman, Ph.D., has theorized, and much scientific research has affirmed, that authentic happiness emerges, in part, from 'attachment to and service of' something larger than oneself. Whether it is a Brand
Immersion Experience or some other ongoing effort that you create, driving
happiness for your employees is a noble goal. If you help your people foster an
attachment to your brand and inspire them to be of service to others in a way
that is consistent with the aspirations of your brand, you are serving both your
people and your customers": Martin Seligman, *Authentic Happiness: Using
the New Positive Psychology to Realize Your Potential for Lasting Fulfillment*
(New York: Atria Paperback, 2004).

"In keeping with management consultant Peter Drucker's words (and one of
Steve Cannon's leadership beliefs) that 'Culture eats strategy for breakfast'":
Quora, "Did Peter Drucker Actually Say "Culture Eats Strategy for Breakfast"—and If So, Where/When?" http://www.quora.com/Did-Peter-Drucker
-actually-say-culture-eats-strategy-for-breakfast-and-if-so-where-when.

Chapter 9

"In fact, David Barkholz, writing for *Automotive News*, notes that millennials
'are coming of age. And they demand a level of transparency, tech savvy and
barter-free buying unseen in previous generations'": David Barkholz, "Marketing to Millennials: Make It Online, Fast, Easy," *Automotive News*, August
6, 2012, http://www.autonews.com/apps/pbcs.dll/article?AID=/20120806
/RETAIL07/308069962/1422/marketing-to-millennials-make-it-online
-fast-easy.

"While small in scale, Tesla Motors created a disruption in the automobile
showroom experience by moving its dealerships from the periphery of town
into shopping malls. Tesla's store designs are in keeping with Apple's retail
approach, complete with interactive touchscreens and a direct-to-consumer
model. The resistance of the automobile industry to these types of changes
can be seen in the lawsuits brought against Tesla from groups like the Massachusetts State Automobile Dealers Association. While much of the litigation centers around a car manufacturer circumventing traditional franchised
dealership-based distribution, it also highlights the tension created as brands
look to lure customers away from a showroom experience that is sometimes
ranked below 'going to the dentist'": Michael Graham Richard, "Tesla Wins
Lawsuit to Protect Its Apple-Like Distribution Model," TreeHugger website,
January 7, 2013, http://www.treehugger.com/cars/tesla-wins-lawsuit-protect
-its-apple-distribution-model-traditional-auto-dealerships.html.

"From my perspective, the mindset and processes involved in developing the
Mercedes-Benz prepaid maintenance program are very consistent with

innovations in other industries, such as the Amazon Prime program. At Amazon, customers had traditionally experienced a recurring annoyance at the end of each purchase—the payment of shipping costs. Thus, a 'prepaid' shipping value program reduced that recurring irritant and gave economic price advantages to those who committed to prepayment. Research conducted by Consumer Intelligence Research Partners on the Amazon Prime program has shown that Prime not only improved customer loyalty but resulted in Prime customers spending on average $1,500 with Amazon as of December 2014. That is $625 more than their non-Prime cohorts": Tricia Duryee, "The Number of People Who Ultimately Pay for That 'Free' Amazon Prime Trial: 70 Percent," *GeekWire*, December 30, 2014, http://www.geekwire.com/2014/number-people-ultimately-pay-free-amazon-prime-trial-70-percent/; Don Reisinger, "Amazon Prime Members Spend Hundreds More than Nonmembers," cnet website, January 27, 2015, http://www.cnet.com/news/amazon-prime-members-spend-hundreds-more-than-non-members/#!.

"Wisely, leaders at Mercedes-Benz leverage process innovation and technology consistent with the guidance given by Tim O'Reilly, the computer expert who popularized the term *open source*. Tim suggests, 'What new technology does is create new opportunities to do a job that customers want done.' At Mercedes-Benz, customer experience technology is not there for technology's sake; it is present to drive delight for increasingly technology-savvy consumers": Richard MacManus, "Tim O'Reilly Interview, Part 2: Business Models & RSS," *ReadWrite*, November 17, 2004, http://readwrite.com/2004/11/17/tim_oreilly_int_1.

Chapter 10

"In a *PC Magazine* review of Mayday, Sascha Segan touted Amazon's rich integration of cutting-edge technology and human service components, 'Mayday is the new tablets' most flashy feature. By hitting a button on a pull-down menu, you can start a video chat with an Amazon support rep who has the ability to control your tablet.' Sascha goes on to describe how the Amazon support representative can press virtual buttons and draw on the customer's tablet. Additionally, these representatives do more than answer customers' questions. They frequently serve to fuel customer discovery by making suggestions on books to read and apps to loan on the Kindle Fire. According to Sascha, Amazon targeted 'no more than a 15-second wait time for anyone requesting Mayday assistance.' Mayday is in keeping with a type of human/technology integration developed by Mercedes-Benz called mbrace": Sascha Segan, "New Kindle Fire Tablets Feature Live Customer Support," *PC Magazine*, September 25, 2013, http://www.pcmag.com/article2/0,2817,2424814,00.asp.

Chapter 11

"Former NBA star and U.S. Senator Bill Bradley once said, 'Ambition is the path to success and persistence is the vehicle you arrive in'": BrainyQuote website, http://www.brainyquote.com/quotes/quotes/b/billbradle384430.html.

"Official figures for luxury new vehicle sales in 2012 show that both Mercedes-Benz USA (274,134 vehicles) and its significant competitor BMW North America (281,460 vehicles) posted double-digit increases and record sales when compared to 2011": Viknesh Vijayenthiran, "BMW Tops U.S. Luxury Auto Sales in 2012," Motor Authority website, January 4, 2013, http://www.motorauthority.com/news/1081451_bmw-tops-u-s-luxury-auto-sales-in-2012.

"In 2013, Mercedes-Benz overtook BMW for the U.S. luxury automotive sales title with an additional 14 percent sales growth over 2012, ending the year with a record-shattering 312,534 vehicles sold (compared to the 9 percent increase for BMW, to 309,280 vehicles)": Joseph B. White, "Mercedes Eked Out U.S. Win Vs. BMW Brand in 2013," *Wall Street Journal*, January 3, 2014, http://www.wsj.com/articles/SB10001424052702303370904579298700881945752.

"In 2014, the seesaw battle for the top sales spot went back to BMW, with both brands continuing to experience growth and set sales records (339,738 BMW vehicles and 330,391 Mercedes-Benz vehicles sold)": Anita Lienert, "BMW Snags Luxury Car Crown Back from Mercedes-Benz," Edmunds.com, January 7, 2015, http://www.edmunds.com/car-news/bmw-snags-luxury-car-crown-back-from-mercedes-benz.html.

"Throughout the customer experience transformation, MBUSA has received various awards for its workplace culture and its highly engaged employee base. In 2014, Mercedes-Benz enjoyed a fifth consecutive year on *Fortune* magazine's '100 Best Companies to Work For' list and has been acknowledged by other work environment evaluators as well": "Mercedes-Benz USA Named to FORTUNE's 100 Best Companies to Work For in 2014," *PR Newswire*, http://www.prnewswire.com/news-releases/mercedes-benz-usa-named-to-fortunes-100-best-companies-to-work-for-in-2014-240525211.html.

"In May of 2014, for example, Mercedes-Benz was ranked number four among large companies on the annual NJBIZ list of 'The Best Places to Work in NJ'": "NJBIZ Ranks the Best Places to Work in New Jersey," NJBIZ website, May 2, 2014, http://www.njbiz.com/article/20140502/NJBIZ01/140509963/njbiz-ranks-the-best-places-to-work-in-new-jersey.

"In his response to that selection, Steve Cannon alluded to synergies that occur when sales numbers, employee engagement, and customer experience are strategic priorities. 'We're four months into another record sales year at MBUSA, and that wouldn't be possible without the dedicated team of employees at our headquarters in Montvale and regional offices in Parsippany and Robbinsville. Their passion for the product and laser focus on delighting our customers is central to our business, and a great workplace culture is paramount to continued success'": "Mercedes-Benz USA Ranks Among Top 10 'Best Places to Work in New Jersey,'" *PR Newswire*, May 5, 2014, http://www.prnewswire.com/news-releases/mercedes-benz-usa-ranks-among-top-10-best-places-to-work-in-new-jersey-257938041.html.

"The 2014 J.D. Power Sales Satisfaction Index victory was not the only independent verification of the customer experience transformation that was occurring in Mercedes-Benz dealerships across America": "Product Specialist Role in Sales Process Grows as Vehicle Technology and Complexity Increase," J.D. Power, November 13, 2014, http://www.jdpower.com/press-releases/2014-us -sales-satisfaction-index-ssi-study.

"In fact, Mercedes-Benz finished first in the 2014 American Customer Satisfaction Index (ACSI) automotive study for the second consecutive year": Paul Ausick, "Mercedes Ranks Number 1 in Customer Satisfaction," 24/7 Wall St website, August 26, 2014, http://247wallst.com/autos/2014/08/26/mercedes -ranks-number-1-in-customer-satisfaction/.

"Looking across industries, in 2014 Mercedes-Benz also tied on the ACSI study with The Ritz-Carlton Hotel Company (the top performer in the highly competitive hotel sector). Additionally, the performance of Mercedes-Benz on the ACSI surveys in both 2013 and 2014 was comparable to highly regarded service companies such as Amazon, Nordstrom, Apple, and Starbucks": Forrest Morgeson and A. J. Singh, "Ritz-Carlton, JW Marriott Tops in Satisfaction," Hotel News Now website, May 1, 2014, http://www.hotel newsnow.com/article/13615/ritz-carlton-jw-marriott-tops-in-satisfaction; Bob Fernandez, and https://www.theacsi.org/customer-satisfaction -benchmarks/benchmarks-by-company.

"Other consumer research results corroborate the ACSI findings concerning the loyalty of Mercedes-Benz customers. The Polk Automotive Loyalty Awards, presented by IHS Automotive, are based on the repurchase behavior of customers as reflected by state automobile registration and lease transaction data. In essence, brands that win the Polk Automotive Loyalty Awards have the highest percentage of households who remain brand-loyal when they return to market. In the luxury category, Mercedes-Benz has been a Polk Automotive Loyalty Award leader in various categories for nine consecutive years": IHS Inc., "Automotive Industry Celebrates Polk Automotive Loyalty Winners," January 14, 2014, http://press.ihs.com/press-release/automotive /automotive-industry-celebrates-polk-automotive-loyalty-winners; "Ford Earns Top Marks in Polk Automotive Loyalty Awards; Volkswagen Named Most Improved," *PR Newswire*, January 15, 2013, www.prnewswire.com /news-releases/ford-earns-top-marks-in-polk-automotive-loyalty-awards -volkswagen-named-most-improved-187047751.html.

"Many of the factors that lead Mercedes-Benz owners to stay loyal to the brand are clearly linked to the handling, style, quality, and safety of the vehicles, as well as the ownership experience. However, research from retention specialists like the Accenture group suggests that loyalty is often lost as a result of the way people are treated during sales and service interactions, not as a result of product issues. An Accenture report titled "Maximizing Customer Retention" notes, 'The root causes of customer churn can be hard to trace. They may lie buried in negative experiences associated with any one of multiple interactions. In order to improve and sustain customer retention rates over time, companies must improve the customer experience of all these interactions'": Accenture, "Maximizing Customer Retention," http://www.slideshare .net/amora3/accenture-maximizingcustomerretention-40022831.

"Improvements in sales and service excellence at Mercedes-Benz are further validated by recognition from many others involved in assessing the automotive industry. For example, Mercedes-Benz dealerships ranked highest in the United States on the 2015 Pied Piper Prospect Satisfaction Index (PSI) for the seventh straight year. Pied Piper differentiates the PSI from other studies through its use of 'mystery shoppers,' who report their experiences with the sales process": "Benz Dealerships Score With Mystery Shoppers,"Automative News First Shift, July 2015, www.piedpiperpsi.com/press-automotive-news -first-shift-241.htm.

"Similarly, Mercedes-Benz has been named the best automotive brand for service by Women-Drivers.com, while also showing steady improvements on the J.D. Power Customer Service Index (more on CSI in Chapter 12 as we look at the future of customer experience elevation at Mercedes-Benz)": "2014 Top Brands as Rated by Women When Servicing their Vehicle," Women-Drivers. com, April 28, 2014, http://www.women-drivers.com/media/press-releases /2014-Top-Brands-as-Rated-by-Women-when-Servicing-their-Vehicle.pdf.

"Plato once said, 'Human behavior flows from three main sources: desire, emotion, and knowledge'": GoodReads website, http://www.goodreads.com/quotes /28152-human-behavior-flows-from-three-main-sources-desire-emotion -and.

Chapter 12

"An article in the February 2015 issue of *Automotive News* began with, 'Mercedes-Benz USA CEO Steve Cannon says the brand plans to prod dealers to improve sales processes even though Mercedes scored the top luxury-brand ranking' on the 2014 J.D. Power Sales Satisfaction Index (SSI) study. The article goes on to quote Steve as saying that he would continue to provide inspiring programs to the top-performing dealers and require the lowest performers to invest their own money in 'process training to get better'": Dave Guilford, "M-B Pushes Dealers to Lift Customer Experience," *Automotive News*, February 2, 2015, http://www.autonews.com/article/20150202/RETAIL 06/302029970/m-b-pushes-dealers-to-lift-customer-experience.

Conclusion

"The great business author Stephen Covey suggested, 'There are certain things that are fundamental to human fulfillment. The essence of these needs is captured in the phrase "to live, to love, to learn, to leave a legacy" . . . the need to leave a legacy is our spiritual need to have a sense of meaning, purpose, personal congruence, and contribution'": Inspirational Stories website, http://www .inspirationalstories.com/quotes/stephen-r-covey-the-core-of-any-family-is -what-is/.

Much of the content of this book emerged from face-to-face meetings, telephone interviews, and other forms of support from Mercedes-Benz USA and

Mercedes-Benz Financial Services employees, customers, and other stakeholders. These include but are not limited to:

Alan Hill, Alexander Blastos, Andrea Conklin, Andrea Doukas, Andrew Noye, Anna Kleinebreil, Anthony D. Zepf, M. Bart Herring, Bernhard J. Glaser, Bill Faulk, Blair Creed, Brandon Newman, Brian Fulton, Cai Ramhorst, Carin Henderson, Carl Burba, Celso Rochez, Cesare De Novellis, Charles DeFelice, Christine Lohrfink-Diaz, Christopher Lantz, Cindy (Cid) Szegedy, Craig Hugelmeyer, Craig Iovino, Dara Davis, Darryl B. Dalton, David Lynn, David Thorne, Debra Eliopoulos, Dianne Quinn, Dianna du Preez, Dietmar Exler, Donna Boland, Donna Pompeo, Drew Slaven, Ellen M. Braaf, Erin Presti, Frank J. Diertl, Fred W. Newcomb, Gareth Joyce, George Levy, Gregory Forbes, Greg Gates, Greg Settle, Gus Corbella, Harald Henn, Harry Hynekamp, Heike Lauf, James Hall, James A. Krause, James Wiseman, Jane Gedeon, Jay Borden, Jay Wojcik, Jeff Kroener, Jenni Harmon, Jennifer Kircher, Jennifer A. Perez, Joe Haury, John D. Ely, John R. Modric, Joe Wankmuller, Jon Whittaker, Julian Soell, Katie Railey, Karen Matri, Kelly Tanis, Kerry Klepfer, Kimberly Sokolewicz, Kristi Steinberg, Kurt Grosman, Lawrence Jakobi, Len Barbato, Lin Nelson, Lisa Rosenfeld, Lourence du Preez, Margaret Negron, Margret Dieterle, Mark Aikman, Markus Bischof, Matt Bowerman, Maura Gallagher-Wilson, Michael T. Barrett, Michael J. Cantanucci, Michael Cronk, Michael Doherty, Michael Dougherty, Michael Kamen, Michael Nordberg, Michael J. Viator, Michele Ventola, Mike Figliuolo, Mike Slagter, Mindy Hatton, Mustafa Ramani, Nancy Rece, Niky Xilouris, Niles Barlow, Pat Evans, Patrick Osweiler, Paul David, Paul Nitsche, Peter Collins, Randy West, Rob Moran, Robert Policano, Robert Tomlin, Roger Loewenheim, Ronald D. Moore, Ronald D. Ross, Sandra Eliga, Scott Penza, Simon Huang, Sonja Bower, Stephen Quinones, Steve Cannon, Steve Frischer, Steve H., Steve Kempner, Steve Levine, Tim Gogal, Thomas Chen, Todd Mulvey, Tomas Hora, Tonia Palmieri, Tylden Dowell, Wanda Lubiak-Schneider, Wen Liu, and Wendell F. McBurney.

Please go to www.driventodelight.com/customerstories to read about more MBUSA customer experiences.

Index

About the Author

Dr. Joseph Michelli helps business leaders and frontline workers create high-performance cultures and "craveable" customer experiences. His consulting services, presentations, and publications show leaders how to engage their employees, elevate human experiences, master service skills, and innovate relevant customer solutions.

To achieve these measurable outcomes, Dr. Michelli provides:

Keynote speeches

Workshop presentations

Panel facilitation

Leadership retreats

Customer experience audits

Consulting services targeted at culture change and customer experience elevation

Dr. Michelli, the chief experience officer of The Michelli Experience, has been recognized globally for his thought leadership on customer experience design as well as his engaging speaking skills and influential impact on service brands. In addition to *Driven to Delight*, Dr. Michelli is the author of several *New York Times*, *Wall Street Journal*, *USA Today*, and *Bloomberg Businessweek* bestsellers.

For more information on how Dr. Michelli can present at your event, provide you with training resources, or help you elevate your culture and/or customer experience, visit www.josephmichelli .com.

Dr. Michelli is eager to assist you to drive delight for your people and your customers. He can be reached through his website, by e-mail at josephm@josephmichelli.com, or by calling either (734) 697-5078 or (888) 711-4900 (toll free within the United States).

Essential leadership guides from *New York Times* bestselling author Joseph Michelli!

0-07-180125-1

0-07-147784-5

0-07-174958-6

0-07-177354-1

0-07-154833-5

All titles are available as a print and eBook

PRAISE FOR JOSEPH MICHELLI

"Required reading for anyone who wants to learn how to create passionate employees and customers!"
—Ken Blanchard, coauthor of *The One Minute Manager* and *The One Minute Entrepreneur*

"If you're looking for an inspirational path for creating a likable, trustworthy, and wow! organization, you've hit the mother lode."
—Guy Kawasaki, former chief evangelist of Apple and author of *Enchantment*